THE EQUITY GAP

LATIN AMERICA, THE CARIBBEAN AND THE SOCIAL SUMMIT

UNITED NATIONS
Santiago, Chile, 1997

LC/G.1954/Rev.1-P
December 1997

UNITED NATIONS PUBLICATION

Sales No.: E.97.II.G.11

ISBN 92-1-121222-7

Applications for the right to reproduce this work or parts thereof are welcomed and should be sent to the Secretary of the Publication Board, United Nations Headquarters, New York, N.Y. 10017, U.S.A. Member States and their governmental institutions may reproduce this work without application, but are requested to mention the source and inform the United Nations of such reproduction.

Copyright © United Nations 1997
All rights reserved
Printed in Santiago, Chile

CONTENTS

	Page
FOREWORD	11
SUMMARY AND CONCLUSIONS	13
PART ONE: SUMMIT ISSUES	21
I. POVERTY AND DISTRIBUTION	23
1. Extent and trends	23
2. Urban poverty	33
3. Rural poverty	38
4. Household income distribution trends	44
II. PRODUCTIVE JOB CREATION	55
1. Moderate, unstable growth	55
2. Employment: growth and trends	60
3. Job creation	65
4. Remunerations	66
5. Labour income disparities	70
III. SOCIAL INTEGRATION	73
1. Social integration and diversity	73
2. Situations that undermine social integration	75
PART TWO: REFORMS NOW UNDER WAY	81
IV. ECONOMIC REFORMS	83
1. An overview	83
2. Employment and labour reforms	86

Page

V. SOCIAL REFORMS 95

    1. Social expenditure 95
    2. Educational reforms 111
    3. Health system reforms 125
    4. Housing 142
    5. Social security reform 150

PART THREE: GUIDELINES FOR AN INTEGRATED APPROACH 159

VI. ECONOMIC POLICIES 161

    1. The challenge of changing production patterns with social equity . 161
    2. Public policies and the quality of growth 163
    3. Promotion of micro-enterprises 172
    4. Policies against rural poverty 174
    5. Agricultural modernization policies 180

VII. SOCIAL POLICIES 185

    1. Traditional features of social policies 185
    2. The role of social policies in achieving the objectives of the World Summit for Social Development 186
    3. Social integration: action guidelines 192
    4. Suggestions and recommendations on sectoral policies 193

BIBLIOGRAPHY 209

BOXES, TABLES AND FIGURES

Box I.1	Poverty in Brazil	27
Box I.2	Caribbean Ministerial Meeting on Poverty Eradication	32
Box I.3	Indicators used to characterize urban poverty	35
Box III.1	Violence in Colombia	77
Box IV.1	Latin America: proposals concerning unemployment insurance	89
Box V.1	Trends in social expenditure in Latin America during the 1990s	98
Box V.2	Methodological note on social expenditure statistics	102
Box V.3	Public social expenditure in dollars per capita and as a percentage of GDP	103
Box V.4	The basic components of expenditure on human capital	106
Box V.5	Inequity in educational performance and attainment in Chile	113
Box V.6	National systems for measuring quality of education	119
Box V.7	Educational reform in Jamaica	123

Page

Box V.8	The population's health profile	126
Box V.9	Altruism and efficiency in health insurance	132
Box V.10	The challenges of public/private partnerships	133
Box V.11	Health system reform in the Caribbean	136
Box V.12	Housing: availability and needs	146
Box VI.1	Training policies	170
Box VI.2	Public-private association and cooperation in enterprise clusters in Peru	173
Box VI.3	El Salvador: integration of small producers of basic crops into international horticultural marketing chains	184
Box VII.1	What is impact?	189
Box VII.2	Influence of educational climate and income level of the home on educational performance	194
Box VII.3	Children and young people who neither study nor work: the low opportunity cost of achieving continuity of education	198
Table I.1	Level of urban poverty and changes in the 1990s	24
Table I.2	Poverty and indigence levels	25
Table I.3	Extent of poverty and indigence	28
Table I.4	Number of poor and indigent	31
Table I.5	Percentage breakdown of poor urban households by chief determining factors	34
Table I.6	Percentage of employed poor in each occupational category and percentage of total poor	36
Table I.7	Levels of rural poverty	39
Table I.8	Recent trends in rural poverty by area of predominance	39
Table I.9	Incidence of poverty in selected occupational categories	41
Table I.10	Breakdown of total employed rural population living in poverty, by occupational category	42
Table I.11	Changes in income distribution in urban areas, 1986, 1990, 1992 and 1994	46
Table I.12	Changes in household income levels and distribution	51
Table I.13	Urban income distribution	53
Table II.1	Economic growth in the 1990s	57
Table II.2	Rate and variability of growth in the 1990s	60
Table II.3	Growth and performance of the labour market	62
Table II.4	Urban unemployment	63
Table II.5	Average incomes and labour income disparities	72
Table IV.1	Issues addressed by labour reforms, by country, 1990-1995	87
Table IV.2	Latin America: applied job programme models	91
Table V.1	Social expenditure	96
Table V.2	Public expenditure on human capital	107
Table V.3	Social investment and emergency funds for the alleviation of poverty in Latin America up to 1997	108

		Page
Table V.4	Average educational performance by socio-economic stratum	113
Table V.5	Percentage distribution of students according to socio-economic stratum and overall performance quartile	114
Table V.6	Increase in per capita expenditure on education	115
Table V.7	Declining trend in expenditure on education between 1982 and 1991	116
Table V.8	Educational reform in selected countries of the region, 1996	120
Table V.9	Health access	127
Table V.10	Instruments of health sector reform, 1995	135
Table V.11	Trends in per capita expenditure on health	141
Table V.12	Households and available housing	144
Table V.13	Current housing stock deficit and housing needs of new households	145
Table V.14	Total population and economically active population with social security coverage 1970-1995	152
Table V.15	Trends in per capita social security expenditure	153
Table V.16	Pillars of pension reform in seven countries of Latin America	157
Table V.17	Classification of redistributive systems	158
Table VI.1	Strategies for the development of micro-enterprises (MEs) in the 1990s	175
Table VII.1a	Uruguay: results in mathematics, by socio-cultural context of schools	195
Table VII.1b	Uruguay: results in mother tongue, by socio-cultural context of schools	195
Table VII.2	Indicators of coverage and access to school system	197
Table VII.3	Present costs of compensatory programmes for adults (equivalent to secondary education), compared with the cost of four years of conventional secondary education	200
Figure I.1	Economic growth and decline in the percentage of households below the poverty line	29
Figure I.2	Income share of the poorest 40%	47
Figure I.3	Income share of the richest 10%	48
Figure I.4	Changes in income distribution: 1986, 1990 and 1994	49
Figure II.1	Per capita GDP, 1996	58
Figure II.2	Per capita GDP, 1996	59
Figure II.3	Real average remunerations	68
Figure II.4	Real urban minimum wage	69
Figure III.1	Chile: perception of increase in crime in 1996 over the past year	78
Figure III.2	Chile: perception of increase in violence of crimes in 1996 over the past year	78
Figure III.3	Crime over the last five years	78
Figure III.4	Most pressing problems	79

CONTENTS

Page

Figure III.5	Chile: habits adopted during the past year to avoid crime	80
Figure V.1	Trends in social expenditure	97
Figure V.2	Trends in real per capita social expenditure, 1980-1994 or 1980-1995	99
Figure V.3	Social expenditure as a percentage of GDP, 1994-1995	101
Figure V.4	Per capita social expenditure, 1994-1995	101
Figure V.5	Social expenditure compared with GDP 1990-1991 and 1994-1995	104
Figure V.6	Comparative trends in public expenditure/GDP and social expenditure/GDP	105
Figure V.7	Comparative trends in social expenditure/GDP and social expenditure/public expenditure 1990-1991/1994-1995	105
Figure V.8	The demographic transition in Latin America and the Caribbean	131
Figure VII.1	Chile: components of saving as a percentage of GDP	207

FOREWORD

The World Summit for Social Development, held in Copenhagen, Denmark, from 6 to 12 March 1995, brought together a large number of heads of State and Government and official representatives from States Members of the United Nations and culminated in the adoption of the Copenhagen Declaration on Social Development and the Programme of Action of the World Summit for Social Development. These two documents —the first containing policy statements, the other dealing with their practical application— imply commitments at the national, regional and international levels.

Barely two years have passed since this summit was held, too short a period to permit an evaluation of the impact of the actions that the Latin American and Caribbean Governments set out to undertake. On the other hand, most of the countries were already implementing a variety of official policies related to the great objectives of the World Summit for Social Development.

As States members of the Economic Commission for Latin America and the Caribbean (ECLAC) now gather for the first time to consider the progress achieved in implementing the outcomes of the Summit,[1] the ECLAC secretariat submits for their consideration a study that focuses on three aspects. First, it analyses existing conditions of poverty, employment and social integration, the chief issues examined at the Summit, from a Latin American and Caribbean perspective. Second, at the policy level, it reports on the developments that have proven most relevant to the fulfilment of the afore-mentioned commitments. Third, it proposes a few additional guidelines on the content and scope of policies designed to facilitate the full realization of these commitments. The hope is that the document may serve as a basis for discussion by Governments and civil society in Latin America and the Caribbean on how the commitments of the Summit are being implemented in the region.

---

[1] Paragraph 95(h) of the Programme of Action of the World Summit for Social Development.

SUMMARY AND CONCLUSIONS

Although the World Summit for Social Development took place only recently, the guidelines that emerged from the Summit proved to be broadly consistent with the general thrust of the actions Governments in the region were taking in the economic and social spheres during the 1990s. This document attempts to summarize the situation in Latin America and the Caribbean in relation to the three main issues addressed at the Summit —poverty, employment and social integration— within the wider context of economic change and social policy reform, and to formulate proposals on these issues that will help in fulfilling the commitments undertaken in Copenhagen.

The context of economic reform

1. Latin America and the Caribbean are presently undergoing a period of intensive change characterized by progress towards democratic pluralism and governability and by far-reaching economic reforms. Some of these reforms have brought significant advances in terms of macroeconomic stability, international linkages and regional integration. These advances have improved access to enhanced external financing, which, if administered appropriately, could provide an opportunity to boost growth in the next few years.

2. At the same time, however, recent economic trends have brought to light a number of major deficiencies. First, with very few exceptions, rates of growth have been only moderate (3% per year between 1990 and 1996), falling short of both past performance levels (5.5% per year between 1945 and 1980) and the levels ECLAC estimates are necessary (6% per year) in order for the region to be able to catch up in technological and social development. Second, the development of most economies in the region still rests on a shaky foundation; many countries have achieved macroeconomic stability by relying on large current-account

deficits, sometimes financed with volatile capital, and this situation has tended to produce short cycles of growth and contraction, reflecting the movements of short-term capital flows. On a number of occasions the situation has been compounded by the fragility of financial systems, at high cost to the public purse. Third, the 1990s have seen only slow recovery from the sudden drop in the savings ratio and, even more importantly, in the investment ratio that occurred during the crisis of the 1980s. The great majority of countries still have not regained pre-crisis levels of saving and investment.

3. Moreover, the depth of economic restructuring has produced new winners and losers. The structural disparities characteristic of the region's systems of production have been exacerbated by the increasing productivity gap between large companies in the vanguard of the modernization process and the wide assortment of activities that have failed to keep pace, where the bulk of employment is concentrated. Not only does this situation provide a material basis for greater social inequities by emphasizing domestic disparities in productivity and income; it also affects the capacity for growth by restricting linkages between different sectors of production, the dissemination of technical progress and the momentum that exports could provide.

4. The most significant deficiency, and one that is closely related to the phenomena described above, is to be found in precisely the areas addressed by the Summit in Copenhagen. The great accumulation of social deficits that built up during the economic crisis of the 1980s is diminishing only slowly, particularly in three interrelated areas: employment, poverty and social exclusion.

Poverty and social integration

5. Poverty trends in the region vary considerably from country to country in terms of both extent and direction. On average, the incidence of poverty declined from 41% to 39% of all households during the first half of the 1990s, not enough to offset the increase in the 1980s (from 35% to 41%). In absolute terms, the number of people living in poverty —210 million— in Latin America and the Caribbean is higher now than ever before.

6. Even so, a certain amount of progress has been made recently, particularly where there has been sustained economic recovery. Between 1990 and 1994 for example, out of 12 countries poverty declined in nine and increased in only one. This trend of gradual improvement was interrupted in 1995 —perhaps only temporarily— by the slowdown in growth in a number of countries (notably Mexico and Argentina). The trend was greatly reinforced, however, when the incidence of poverty in Brazil fell sharply as a result of the country's stabilization programme. Less headway was made in reducing indigence, which dropped only from 18% of families to 17%, still two percentage points higher than the 1980 figure.

7. The chief determining factors in the reduction of poverty have been the level of economic growth and inflation reduction; the next most important has been the continuing effort to increase social expenditure and, more recently, to find more efficient ways to allocate it. The countries that have made most progress in reducing poverty are those that have successfully combined relatively high growth rates over a period of years with a

reduction in unemployment rates and an increase in the number of persons employed among the poorest families. Cutting the inflation rate has also made it possible to improve earnings and in some cases pensions in real terms and ensured continuity of investment, with a favourable impact on the labour market.

8. It is not only macroeconomic equilibria *per se* that are critical for rapid and more equitable growth, but also the manner in which they are achieved. In addition to reducing the rate of inflation and strengthening fiscal equilibrium, it is also necessary to reduce the current account deficit to a sustainable level to maintain an appropriate real exchange rate and to achieve a domestic savings rate commensurate with the investment process and a level of domestic expenditure consistent with sustainable utilization of productive capacity. Moreover, growth does not in itself guarantee better income distribution. What is crucial is the quality of that growth, i.e., whether it can continue over time —which is a matter of macroeconomic management—, whether it translates into productive employment and wages and, lastly, how efficient social policy is and how social and economic policies interact.

Employment, wages and productivity

9. As mentioned above, the region's scant progress in combating poverty is associated with inadequate growth, the low impact of growth on the labour market and the almost total lack of improvement in average labour productivity, a problem that must be tackled to attain improved international competitiveness and higher sustainable growth rates.

10. Most of the employment created during the 1990s has been in the informal sector. According to International Labour Organization (ILO) estimates, out of every 100 new jobs created between 1990 and 1995, 84 were in the informal sector, and it is in this sector that 56% of all employed people in the region work. This explains the current sluggishness of average labour productivity levels (a figure which, nevertheless, conceals significant differences between countries).

11. The foregoing helps to explain why wage levels are below those of 1980 and also why wage differentials between occupational strata are widening. Real average wages, despite marked differences between countries, have increased almost across the board during the 1990s. Even so, wage levels are still lower than they were in 1980.

12. Except for a few countries where the upward trend continued, the wage recovery seemed to stall in 1996. This is explainable by the fact that the income effect of slowing inflation on real wages diminishes as the inflation rate falls, while lower inflation rates mean longer periods between wage adjustments. More generally, competitive retooling in modern enterprises favours productivity increases and labour flexibility, with a marked decline in job creation per unit of output.

13. The slow growth of real average wages reflects the counteracting tendencies of large wage increases among those employed in skilled work in more vigorous and modern sectors and moderate wage increases or declining pay in the remainder of the economy. The real minimum wage in 1995 in 13 out of 17 countries was lower than in 1980. Informal workers earn on average half what manual and non-manual workers in modern enterprises are paid.

Since they also work longer hours, this inequality increases when the factorial distribution of informal and formal earnings is corrected for hours worked.

14. The gap between earnings of professional and technical workers and those of workers in low-productivity sectors grew by 40%-60% between 1990 and 1994. Constant or widening differentials in earned income reflect marked disparities in productivity among companies and sectors and are good indicators of the inelasticity of income distribution that has characterized recent economic growth, even where growth has been most vigorous.

15. In order to boost productivity in lagging sectors, it seems essential to complement general policies with some specific measures, including credit, marketing and technical assistance programmes and heavy investment in education and training. The push towards technological modernization is crucial, not only to cope with the demands of international competition, but also to meet the need for better-quality employment and higher wages. This objective ranks rather low on the agendas of most of the countries, however, since they lack both the requisite resources and institutional networks capable of coping with a challenge of this magnitude.

16. The impact of economic reforms on labour markets has been uneven, owing in large part to significant national differences in their scope and timing. Other factors that have contributed to the unevenness of labour market response are the differences between countries in their productive and technological bases and labour institutions, and in demographic and social characteristics.

17. At present, growth in the region is closely tied to the dynamism of natural resource-based activities. In order to heighten the impact of growth on employment, then, stronger linkages should be fostered between these activities and those of the other productive sectors. Such linkages not only create an intermediate demand for goods, services and labour, but also provide a stimulus for improvements in quality and the spread of technical progress and business and management practices: they foster the establishment of quality standards; they lead to the creation of institutions providing technical training and modern support services to productive activity; and they give rise to training activities and technical, financial and organizational support for small, medium-sized and micro-enterprises.

18. During the 1990s, a number of countries have amended their labour legislation, especially with regard to employment contracts, dismissals and collective bargaining. The direction of these reforms has been mixed, so that it is difficult to discern a uniform trend, but most of the recent changes have introduced more flexibility into hiring and firing procedures. Other legislation has been aimed at improving working conditions and minimum wages; protecting particular labour sectors (seasonal workers, wage earners in small and medium-sized firms, domestic workers); preventing discrimination against women; abolishing child labour and regulating youth labour.

19. Another new concern is that labour legislation should also address the issue of unemployment insurance or income protection for the unemployed. Consideration has been given to a number of alternatives that would allow unemployed workers' needs to be covered for a certain period of time without creating major administrative snarls or incurring the same microeconomic and budgetary inefficiencies that unemployment insurance has generated in other parts of the world.

20. The concern is to reconcile increased labour flexibility with minimum levels of social safeguards for the worker by protecting income rather than job security, i.e., encouraging

labour mobility. For such measures to work properly, they need to be backed up by fuller training and redeployment programmes, and there should be a link between unemployment insurance and initiatives of that kind.

Social integration

21. In the space of a decade, the increase in poverty —already at high levels— and the deterioration or stagnation of income distribution in the region have coincided with an explosion of access to communications that has tended to produce a common set of consumer aspirations. Whole sectors of society see their expectations frustrated, particularly urban youth, whose educational levels are greater than that of their parents but whose unemployment rates are higher. These young people are exposed to information and stimuli about a wide range of novel goods and services that are symbols of social mobility, but inaccessible for the majority of them.

22. The intensification of "hard-core poverty", ethnic discrimination and residential segregation, the proliferation of private urban security services and the rise of violence in the cities all seriously affect levels of social integration and governability. Strengthening governability under democracy requires above all —and urgently— transparent, fair and effective judicial machinery that can restore citizens' confidence in their systems of justice, protection and security. It also demands perseverance in the search for pluralistic and participatory political systems capable of absorbing internal differences and mediating national agreements on broad lines of development.

23. Such national agreements might have greater appeal if they included more social safety-net mechanisms to reduce the social costs of economic transition and provide safeguards in the event of retooling or redeployment that could affect large segments of the population. Such mechanisms might include, for example, work training schemes for urban youth who have little formal education and are excluded from the social networks that furnish access to productive life. Other initiatives already under way to improve social integration are support programmes for female-headed low-income families, protection for children, young people and mothers exposed to domestic violence, and drug-abuse prevention programmes. There are also projects to support personal and community development, and public housing programmes designed to transform living spaces by providing communal equipment and areas for cultural and recreational activity.

Social reforms

24. In contrast to the 1980s, when social expenditure fell considerably as a result of financial constraints on Governments, during the 1990s the level of public spending allocated to social sectors has risen in most countries in the region. This is a clear indication of the political will of Governments to tackle the social deficit, and bodes well for social policy reform. In 7 out of the 11 countries that reported social spending increases, expenditure

levels exceeded those at the beginning of the 1980s. Public social expenditure as a proportion of GDP rose on average by 1.8%, even in countries where the public expenditure ratio fell.

25. The greatest increase in social expenditure between 1990 and 1995 occurred in the education and social security sectors. In education, real per capita spending went up in 12 out of 15 countries; in social security, in 10 out of 15 countries; and in health, in 10 out of 13 countries. Spending on education expanded as a reflection not only of increased coverage, but also of improvements in quality, relevance and social equity thanks to a series of educational reforms that were the focus of lively national debates. Increases in spending on social security were chiefly due to adjustments in retirement and other pensions, payment of retirement pension liabilities and extensions of coverage.

26. The educational reforms currently under way, with variations from country to country, seek to correct the deficiencies of the region's educational systems in terms of quality, social equity and the relevance of what is taught. A number of countries are trying to change outdated curricula and teaching methods, alter the social segmentation of access to education, improve the quality of education available and reverse the decline of teaching as a profession. Towards the same ends, countries are making changes to educational financing and resource-allocation systems and expanding the scope for private input; they are also trying to decentralize educational administration, train teachers and improve the quality of education, gradually bringing it into line with the requirements of the labour market.

27. Clearly, new relationships need to be established between education, society and production. This will require qualitative changes in educational systems, aided by an ongoing assessment of performance, and closer ties with companies and the labour market. This could be accomplished by setting up a system of appropriate incentives, such as national scholastic achievement tests, support for innovative initiatives in schools, competitions with prizes for contributions that result in improved quality and financial incentives for schools and teachers who succeed in improving their students' performances.

28. ECLAC has estimated that, for the region as a whole, the additional cost of implementing a strategy to improve the quality of school and pre-school education would amount to 3.9% of gross domestic product (GDP). Since this is more than budgets can support, Governments will have to concentrate their spending on areas of education where the social and economic impact are greatest, while at the same time encouraging any private initiatives that could make a positive contribution to educational equity.

29. The technological change in education implies changing both methods and materials. In terms of methods, the key will be to adapt teaching practices by applying new technologies effectively to learning. In terms of materials the key will be to encourage broad-based networks for industrial-scale production of educational aids, drawing on the state-of-the-art educational technologies and creating new institutions to promote the technologies and adapt them to suit local needs. All this will require changes in school infrastructure, individual and institutional investment in equipment and materials, and training and redeployment of teachers. Private initiative could play an important part in such developments.

30. Health service coverage in the region varies widely. Coverage, however, is only a rough measure, concealing significant differences in the quality, efficiency and cost of care. The regional health reform agenda —with variations from country to country— includes improving the equity of access to benefits and the efficiency and quality of care and raising sector productivity by reforming management, encouraging synergies between the public and

private health systems, bringing escalating costs under control and regulating private medicine. A number of reforms that aim at a more integrated approach focus on aspects of financing, intersectoral competition, regulation and administration. Despite differences, national programmes have several points in common: promoting health campaigns, strengthening primary care, supporting decentralization of local health services and systems and dealing with inequities of access through basic universal care or targeted interventions.

31. Reforms in the health sector must also extend to the institutional framework and aim at increasing the efficiency, coverage and quality of care, targeting subsidies more accurately and strengthening regulatory and supervisory capacity. The public health system could benefit from a greater separation between the different functions: the regulatory and institutional frameworks; financial operations and procurement; and service providers and producers. The greater effort of coordination this entails might then require contractual undertakings specifying the resources needed to supply a service, the quality and type of service to be supplied and indicators enabling the service to be evaluated. Experience has shown the need for all the parties involved in public health to reach agreement from the start on performance indicators and their interpretation; and for new remuneration systems that include flexible components and incentives related to performance and quality of service.

32. Private health care provision can raise the efficiency of the sector if there is an improvement in the regulatory system regarding contract transparency, access by the private sector to subsidies, cost control (encouraging greater integration between service providers and insurance companies), the treatment of some categories of catastrophic illnesses and illnesses of the elderly and, in relation to risk insurance, the inclusion of some altruistic mechanisms.

33. The need for housing construction has diminished only marginally despite the recent easing of demographic pressures. Construction has also had to adapt to a greater variety of family structures, which in turn has brought new demands in terms of standards. The regional housing deficit is estimated at roughly 50 million dwellings; the figure includes both new construction and renovation of older stock. Out of every 100 households in the region, 60 have adequate housing, 22 need housing repairs and 18 need either new housing or reconstruction of their present dwelling. In view of the rate at which new households are forming, the deficit will expand by 2.7 million per year.

34. Government policy is gradually coming to grips with the reality of this situation, and public expenditure on housing has risen again in the 1990s. To deal with the housing deficit, the countries are trying, on the one hand, to bring in private-sector resources and, on the other, to adjust their programmes to improve efficiency and to allocate available resources more precisely. A number of countries are moving from the traditional system of specialized home-loan banks —operating separately from the rest of the financial system— to open financing systems. Supply-side subsidies such as tax exemptions or preferential credits for the production of housing are being replaced by demand-side subsidies in the form of direct transfers to families. With adequate application and allocation procedures, this approach allows for more accurate targeting. Public housing policy makers are also trying to avoid increasing urban segregation despite the fact that they are forced to look for low-cost land.

35. Pension systems in the region are characterized in general by low coverage and a multiplicity of plans offering different benefits. This situation is not conducive to equity, either between members of different plans or between those who have a plan and those who

do not. Costs are often excessive and funds poorly administered, so that they incur large actuarial or cash deficits. The challenge for reformers under these circumstances is to broaden coverage, improve benefits through more efficient fund management and establish an altruistic mechanism (with appropriate financing) for those who are unable to save for their old age. Hence, the reforms currently under way aim to administer fund finances efficiently without threatening macroeconomic stability, by separating risks and adjusting fund management to the likelihood of occurrence of given events and by increasing private-sector participation in fund management and service provision.

36. With current trends leaning towards fully funded (capitalization) schemes and private administration of social security contributions, it is essential to look closely at the fiscal cost such changes would entail, at ways of covering that cost and at how the funds accumulated through financial intermediation are to be used. By way of illustration, mention may be made of two policies that could be conducive to social equity: making social insurance contributions and taxes progressive; and using pension funds in such a way as to stimulate productive investment and help eliminate the obstacles in the way of achieving high, stable growth rates. Analysis of the pension system reforms being carried out in the region shows that they vary in two respects: i) in the design of the altruistic component and ii) in the institutional framework that is set up in order to ensure that workers' savings contribute to the vigour and efficiency of the economy.

37. Social policy reform puts special emphasis on more efficient resource management. It is therefore essential that such reforms should go hand in hand with institutional changes aimed at better service to the user, better targeting and greater decentralization and linking resources to performance and quality of service. The current fragmented institutional structure of State social services tends to scatter resources and duplicate functions. This situation needs to be changed in order to improve programme supervision and enable a standard set of criteria to be used in programme evaluation. Superfluous programmes could be discontinued and others updated in order to deal with enclaves of "hard-core poverty". On the other hand, links could be forged or strengthened between social programmes and productive development initiatives, i.e., training, dissemination of technology and support for small and medium-sized enterprises and micro-enterprises.

A vision of the whole

38. More effective progress in fulfilling the commitments made at the World Summit for Social Development demands an approach that integrates economic and social policy in a mutually supportive relationship and permits complementarity between measures to encourage competitiveness and measures to promote social cohesion. Although they may seem to conflict in the short run, public policy can benefit from the many points of complementarity between economic and social measures, chiefly in the areas of macroeconomic management capable of stimulating high, stable growth rates; promotion of competitiveness; and public policies that enhance the contribution of growth to employment. Investment in human resources and an approach that integrates the concepts of territory, business linkages and productive development offer the most promise for progress in these tasks. In addition, agricultural modernization can assist in overcoming rural poverty, provided there are public policies to grant access to land and regularize land tenure and provided an effort is made to improve the infrastructure of production and establish closer links between agro-industry and small-scale producers.

PART ONE: SUMMIT ISSUES

I.   Poverty and distribution

II.   Productive job creation

III.   Social integration

I. POVERTY AND DISTRIBUTION[2]

1. Extent and trends

The extent and characteristics of poverty in Latin America and the Caribbean vary considerably from one country to another. Of the 12 countries analysed by ECLAC, only two (Argentina and Uruguay) have less than 15% of households below the poverty line. Three others (Chile, Costa Rica and Panama) are in a mid-range, with 15% to 30% of households living in poverty. A group of five (Brazil, Colombia, Mexico, Peru and Venezuela) are in a high poverty range with 31% to 50% of households affected. Lastly, Bolivia and Honduras have a very high level of poverty, with 50% or more households below the poverty line[3] (see tables I.1 and I.2).

a) Changes in poverty

Along with the economic upturn between 1990 and 1994, significant advances were made in alleviating poverty over that period. It diminished in 9 out of 12 countries and increased in only one. Since the end of 1994, however, results have been very uneven: only 3 out of 12 countries have achieved reductions, and the situation has deteriorated in four countries while remaining the same or varying slightly in another five (see table I.1).

---

[2] This chapter is based on information contained in the *Social Panorama of Latin America. 1996 Edition* (ECLAC, 1997).
[3] Almost all the other countries in the region are classified as having high or very high poverty ratios. These do not appear on table I.1, as the available information is not wholly comparable with information existing for the countries analysed.

In any event, the overall assessment for the first six years of the 1990s is positive, since 8 out of 12 countries have recorded lower levels of poverty than at the start of the decade. Compared with 1980, however, only four countries show a lower level of poverty (Brazil, Chile, Panama and Uruguay), while four others show higher levels.

Table I.1
LEVEL OF URBAN POVERTY AND CHANGES IN THE 1990s a/

Extent of poverty in 1994 b/	Variation from 1990 and 1994	Trend 1995-1996 f/	Current versus previous poverty levels:	
			1990	1980
Low (below 15%)				
Argentina	downward +	upward +	lower	higher
Uruguay	downward +	stable	lower	lower
Average (15% to 30%)				
Chile	downward +	downward	lower	lower
Costa Rica	downward	stable	lower	same
Panama	downward c/	stable	lower	lower
High (31% to 50%)				
Brazil	stable	downward	lower	lower
Colombia	stable	+	same	same
Mexico	downward e/	stable	higher	higher
Peru	downward + d/	upward +	lower	same
Venezuela	upward +	downward upward +	higher	higher
Extremely high (above 50%)				
Bolivia	downward + e/	stable	lower	...
Honduras	downward	upward	higher	higher

Source: ECLAC, *Social Panorama of Latin America. 1996 Edition* (LC/G.1946-P), Santiago, Chile, 1997, chapter I. United Nations publication, Sales No. E.97.II.G.4.
a/ The "+" sign indicates a variation in poverty level of over 4 percentage points.
b/ Percentage of households below the poverty line.
c/ 1991-1994.
d/ 1991-1994. Estimates based on results of surveys on living standards.
e/ 1989-1994.
f/ Estimated trend between late 1994 and early 1996, based on variations in macroeconomic indicators closely associated with variations in poverty levels.

Table I.2
POVERTY AND INDIGENCE LEVELS
(Percentages)

Country	Year	Households below the poverty line [a]					Households below the indigence line				
		Total	Urban			Rural	Total	Urban			Rural
			Total	Metropolitan area	Other urban areas			Total	Metropolitan area	Other urban areas	
Argentina	1980	9	7	5	9	16	2	2	1	2	4
	1986	13	12	9	15	17	4	3	3	4	6
	1990	-	-	16	-	-	-	-	4	-	-
	1992	-	-	10	-	-	-	-	1	-	-
	1994	-	12	10	16	-	-	2	2	3	-
Bolivia	1989	-	49	-	-	-	-	22	-	-	-
	1992	-	45	-	-	-	-	18	-	-	-
	1994	-	41	-	-	-	-	14	-	-	-
Brazil	1979	39	30	21 [b]	34	62	17	10	6 [b]	12	35
	1987	40	34	24 [b]	37	60	18	13	8 [b]	16	34
	1990	42	37	28 [b]	41	55	19	16	9 [b]	19	30
	1993	41	39	31 [b]	41	51	19	16	11 [b]	18	30
	1995 [c]	...	...	...	...	...	...	...	...	...	...
Chile [d]	1987	39	38	33	41	45	14	14	11	15	17
	1990	33	33	28	37	34	11	10	8	11	12
	1992	28	28	21	31	28	7	7	5	8	8
	1994	24	24	17	27	26	7	6	4	7	8
Colombia	1980	39	36	30	37	45	16	13	10	14	22
	1986	38	36	31	37	42	17	15	11	16	22
	1990	-	35	-	-	-	-	12	-	-	-
	1992	-	38	-	-	-	-	15	-	-	-
	1993 [e]	49	42	39	43	60	27	17	15	18	40
	1994 [e]	47	41	35	43	57	25	16	12	18	38
Costa Rica	1981	22	16	15	17	28	6	5	5	6	8
	1988	25	21	19	22	28	8	6	5	6	10
	1990	24	22	20	25	25	10	7	5	9	12
	1992	25	25	22	29	25	10	8	7	9	12
	1994	21	18	16	21	23	8	6	4	7	10
Guatemala	1980	65	41	26	52	79	33	13	5	19	44
	1986	68	54	45	59	75	43	28	20	31	53
	1990	-	-	-	-	72	-	-	-	-	45
Honduras	1986	71	53	-	-	81	51	28	-	-	64
	1990	75	65	-	-	84	54	38	-	-	66
	1992	73	66	-	-	79	50	38	-	-	59
	1994	73	70	-	-	76	49	41	-	-	55
Mexico	1984	34	28	... [f]	... [f]	45	11	7	... [f]	... [f]	20
	1989	39	34	-	-	49	14	9	-	-	23
	1992	36	30	-	-	46	12	7	-	-	20
	1994	36	29	-	-	47	12	6	-	-	20

Table I.2 (concl.)

Country	Year	Households below the poverty line [a]					Households below the indigence line				
		Total	Urban			Rural	Total	Urban			Rural
			Total	Metropolitan area	Other urban areas			Total	Metropolitan area	Other urban areas	
Panama	1979	36	31	27	42	45	19	14	12	19	27
	1986	34	30	27	41	43	16	13	11	19	22
	1989	38	34	32	42	48	18	15	14	20	25
	1991	36	34	32	40	43	16	14	14	15	21
	1994	30	25	23	35	41	12	9	8	13	20
Paraguay	1986	...	...	46	...	...	...	...	16	...	...
	1990	...	...	37	...	...	...	...	10	...	...
	1992	...	...	36	...	...	...	...	13	...	...
Peru	1979	46	35	29	41	65	21	12	9	15	37
	1986	52	45	37	53	64	25	16	11	22	39
Uruguay	1981	11	9	6	13	21	3	2	1	3	7
	1986	15	14	9	19	23	3	3	2	4	8
	1990	-	12	7	17	-	-	2	1	3	-
	1992	-	8	4	12	-	-	1	1	2	-
	1994	-	6	4	7	-	-	1	1	1	-
Venezuela	1981	22	18	12	20	35	7	5	3	6	15
	1986	27	25	16	28	34	9	8	4	9	14
	1990	34	33	25	36	38	12	11	7	12	17
	1992	33	32	21	35	36	11	10	6	12	16
	1994	42.1	41	21	46.2	47.7	15	14	4	16	23
Latin America [g]	1980	35	25	-	-	54	15	9	-	-	28
	1986	37	30	-	-	53	17	11	-	-	30
	1990	41	36	-	-	56	18	13	-	-	33
	1994	39	34	-	-	55	17	12	-	-	33

Source: ECLAC, *Social Panorama of Latin America. 1996 Edition* (LC/G.1946-P), Santiago, Chile, 1997, table 16 of the Statistical appendix. United Nations publications, Sales No. E.97.II.G.4.
[a] Includes households below the indigence line.
[b] Average of the figures for Rio de Janeiro and São Paulo.
[c] See box I.1.
[d] Calculations based on the 1987, 1990, 1992 and 1994 national socio-economic survey (CASEN) data. Estimates adjusted for the latest figures for the household income and expenditure account from the Ministry of Planning and Cooperation (MIDEPLAN).
[e] Beginning in 1993, the geographical coverage of the survey was extended to nearly the entire urban population of the country, plus the rural population. Until then, the survey covered approximately half the urban population.
[f] Estimates could not be made for the Federal District because the sample size is too small.
[g] Estimates for 19 countries in the region.

Chile and Uruguay stand out as countries that have achieved significant and sustained reductions in poverty levels since the mid-1980s. In Brazil, the improvement is more recent, having occurred chiefly over the last two years since inflation rates were slashed. In Panama, improvement began in 1991 and is related to the high rate of growth in gross domestic product (GDP) and strong job-generating capacity.

In Costa Rica and Peru, the situation is more or less unchanged, despite improvements in the early 1990s. In Colombia as well, the level of poverty is believed to have remained the same, as the net result of an increase between 1990 and 1992 and a subsequent decline.

The most recent comparable information from Brazil is for 1993; however, preliminary estimates from survey results still being compiled and analysed suggest that there was a significant reduction in poverty between 1993 and 1995 (see box I.1).

In Argentina, Honduras, Mexico and Venezuela poverty has worsened since 1980, although economic recovery in some of these countries may result in a significant drop in the percentage of poor households in the future.

Box I.1

POVERTY IN BRAZIL

The Brazilian Geographical and Statistical Institute (IBGE) introduced substantive changes beginning in 1992 in the subject areas covered by its annual national household surveys and also initiated a survey of household income and expenditure. The mass of information collected is now being compiled and analysed, and when that is done an estimate comparable to those that exist for other countries of the region will be available for the last few years. Nevertheless, some preliminary conclusions may be drawn from an analysis of statistical data available at the time of writing.

For over a decade, the country suffered from inflation at times exceeding 1,000% per year. The high growth rates of the 1960s and 1970s were followed by periods of zero growth, which exacerbated poverty. Renewed efforts to stabilize prices in the 1980s and early 1990s did cause sharp drops in inflation, increases in real income and consumption and appreciable declines in poverty rates, but these were short-lived. Stability soon gave way to inflation and poverty reductions were limited to brief spells.

However, the recent stabilization plan (*Real* Plan) and the steady increase in national income in the three-year period 1993-1995 gave rise to new conditions. This time, until mid-1995, falling prices combined with economic growth of close to 15% over three years had a major impact on the real income of the poorest, resulting in a significant reduction in poverty levels. Moreover, in early 1995, other factors reinforced this positive effect. First, wage indexation was maintained in many sectors of the economy in the first few months of the year, so that real wages continued to improve once inflation had been brought under control. Second, a decline in farm prices reduced the real price of staple foods, resulting in an appreciable increase in their consumption.

Consequently, although ECLAC does not have final figures on poverty levels in Brazil for the last few years, preliminary estimates suggest that between 1993 and 1995 the number of people living in poverty declined by at least eight million, or approximately 10%. Furthermore, the income of those still below the poverty line is thought to have improved somewhat.

At the regional level, the poverty rate declined from 41% to 39% in the first five years of the 1990s. This advance was not sufficient to make up for the sharp increase in poverty recorded during the 1980s, when it rose from 35% to 41%, or to make any headway in eradicating the long-standing structural poverty characteristic of the region (see table I.3).

Nevertheless, a review of the regional situation indicates that while it may be difficult to make progress and consolidate poverty alleviation, significant improvements can be —and have been— achieved within a reasonably short time. Chile and Uruguay differ with respect to how much the lower income strata have benefited from gains made by the society, but both countries have managed to reduce urban poverty by between six and nine percentage points. In Chile, this occurred as a result of more rapid growth without major changes in income distribution; in Uruguay substantial improvements were recorded in terms of social equity, despite a much lower growth rate.

Table I.3
EXTENT OF POVERTY AND INDIGENCE a/
(Percentages)
1980 - 1994

	Poor b/			Indigent c/		
	Total	Urban	Rural	Total	Urban	Rural
1980	35	25	54	15	9	28
1990	41	36	56	18	13	33
1994	39	34	55	17	12	33

Source: ECLAC, *Social Panorama of Latin America. 1996 Edition* (LC/G.1946-P), Santiago, Chile, 1997, chapter I. United Nations publication, Sales No. E.97.II.G.4.
a/ Estimates cover 19 countries of the region.
b/ Percentage of households with income below the poverty line. Includes indigent households.
c/ Percentage of households with income below the indigence line.

b) **Factors associated with poverty reduction**

i) **Economic growth**. The decline in poverty in the first five years of the 1990s was closely linked to the level of economic growth. Several countries had cumulative per capita GDP growth from 14% to 28%. Of these, the three where this variable increased the most (Argentina, Chile and Uruguay) achieved a greater proportional drop in the percentage of poor households (see figure I.1).

Figure I. 1
ECONOMIC GROWTH AND DECLINE IN THE PERCENTAGE OF HOUSEHOLDS BELOW THE POVERTY LINE, 1990-1994.

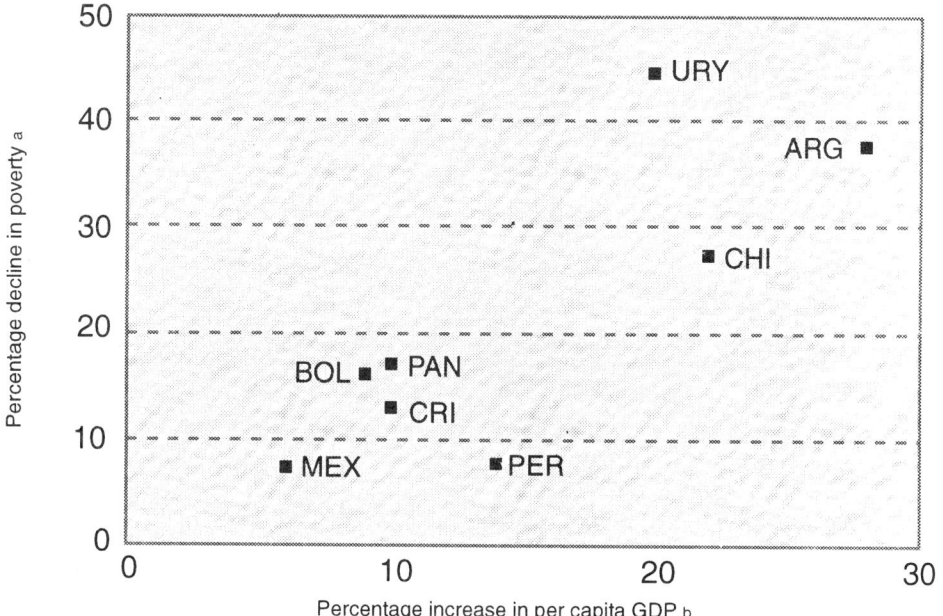

SOURCE: ECLAC, *Social Panorama of Latin America. 1996 Edition* (LC/G. 1946-P), Santiago, Chile, 1997, figure I.4. United Nations Publication, sales No. E.97.II.G.4.

a Percentage point decline in poverty from 1990 to 1994, as a percentage of the poverty level in the initial year.
b Refers to cumulative per capita GDP growth between 1990 and 1994.

ii) **Reduction in inflation.** The decline in poverty levels, especially in urban areas, was also related to falling inflation rates; the effect was particularly marked in the countries where inflation plummeted from extremely high levels, as occurred in Argentina and Peru and in Brazil towards the end of the period, and to a lesser extent in Chile, Mexico and Uruguay.

iii) **Open unemployment.** On the other hand, very little of the poverty reduction was due to changes in open unemployment because of problems in reducing urban unemployment, even in countries that achieved relatively high and sustained growth rates. In Bolivia, Chile and Costa Rica, a reduction in open unemployment contributed, somewhat more than in other countries, to a decline in urban poverty. All three countries saw an increase in the number of employed in low-income households and striking declines in open unemployment among the economically active population in the lowest quintile, especially in the urban areas of Bolivia and Costa Rica.

iv) **Low productivity.** There are various reasons for the preponderance of low-productivity jobs in the region. First, a large number of companies use outdated technologies and processes. Second, owing to inadequate savings, there is insufficient investment in equipment and machinery. Moreover, small and medium-sized firms (SMEs), which generate the bulk of jobs and are more backward technologically, have little access to savings. In addition, little is spent on training the workforce, as will be seen below. The existing system of industrial relations is another factor; it fosters confrontation rather than cooperation, underestimates workers' potential for innovation and limits their participation in areas of technology and training. Lastly, the current production base is not geared towards penetrating the most demanding, largest and most dynamic foreign markets.

c) **Changes in indigence levels**

Less progress was made in reducing indigence levels, which barely declined from 18% to 17%, still two percentage points above the 1980 level. In Latin America, one out of every six households is still not in a position to satisfy its basic nutritional needs, even if it were to spend its entire income on food.

d) **Differences between urban and rural areas**

The lower rate of poverty in the region is largely a reflection of its lower incidence in urban areas, where it declined from 36% to 34%. In rural areas, it diminished only marginally (from 56% to 55%), albeit from high initial levels. The proportion of the population living in urban areas rose from the already high level of 71% in 1990 to 74% in 1994, which means that 65% of all poor Latin Americans are concentrated in urban areas, although the poverty rate among rural populations is higher.

Changes in indigence levels followed a similar pattern in all areas. In the first half of the 1990s, the percentage of extremely poor urban households declined only from 13% to 12%, while the percentage for rural areas remained at around 33%. Here again, the sharp increase in the urban population meant that the urban indigent population exceeded the rural indigent population.

e) **Numbers of poor and indigent**

Notwithstanding the percentage decline in poor and indigent households, the numbers of persons affected increased by 12 million, from 197 million in 1990 to 209 million in 1994. The indigent population grew by 6.4 million, concentrated almost exclusively in urban areas (see table I.4).

f) **Poverty in the Caribbean**

Poverty has been on the rise in the Caribbean over the past two decades, despite the considerable growth experienced throughout the region in the 1980s, except in Guyana and Trinidad and Tobago, which suffered an economic downturn. The spread of poverty, which according to estimates affects around 38% of the population of the Caribbean, is attributable chiefly to inadequate poverty alleviation policies. At the country level, the rate varies between 12% and 42%, a spread that shows the striking differences between countries of the subregion.

General living conditions have been deteriorating along with the spread of poverty. This is due essentially to the worsening economic situation and to the Caribbean economies' low level of competitiveness. It also stems from the adoption of government policies that at times indirectly exacerbate the situation. Among other things, the public sector has cut back on staff, who then cannot be absorbed by the private sector.

Table I.4
NUMBER OF POOR AND INDIGENT a/
(Thousands)
1980 - 1994

	Poor b/			Indigent c/		
	Total	Urban	Rural	Total	Urban	Rural
1980	135 900	62 900	73 000	62 400	22 500	39 900
1990	197 200	120 800	76 400	91 900	45 400	46 500
1994	209 300	135 400	73 900	98 300	51 900	46 400

Source: ECLAC, *Social Panorama of Latin America. 1996 Edition* (LC/G.1946-P), Santiago, Chile, 1997, chapter I. United Nations publication, Sales No. E.97.II.G.4.
a/ Estimates cover 19 countries of the region.
b/ Persons in households below the poverty line. Includes the indigent.
c/ Persons in indigent households.

For Governments, it is increasingly difficult to maintain the level of public spending, especially the level of funds earmarked for human resource development and other basic social spending. Cutbacks have affected education, health services, systems of security and community facilities. The demographic transition and aging of the population could lead to an increase in the dependent population.

The informal sector has absorbed workers who have lost jobs in the public and private sectors, but is characterized by low productivity, limited access to credit, low income, poor working conditions and very few benefits. An increasing number of households have fewer resources with which to maintain adequate levels of nutrition, to pay for health care and education and to make contributions to the pension scheme and health insurance plans. According to some estimates, the informal sector represents up to 37% of the workforce, but since the role of women may be underestimated, the percentage could be even higher.

Box I.2

**CARIBBEAN MINISTERIAL MEETING ON POVERTY ERADICATION
GUIDELINES FOR POVERTY ERADICATION IN THE CARIBBEAN**

In October 1996, the United Nations convened a Caribbean Ministerial Meeting on Poverty Eradication in Port of Spain, Trinidad and Tobago, at which the Directional Plan of Action for Poverty Eradication in the Caribbean was drafted and approved. The Meeting was both a follow-up to the World Summit for Social Development in Copenhagen and an opportunity to assess the current situation in the Caribbean with respect to poverty and to discover what plans for combatting it were being implemented at the national and subregional levels. It was also an excellent opportunity for drafting a regional plan of action that could serve as a contribution to the first Regional Conference in Follow-up to the World Summit for Social Development, to be held in 1997 in São Paulo, Brazil.

The measures outlined in the Plan of Action are a necessary complement to strategies for sustainable economic growth. The long-term poverty eradication programme should be closely linked to the Caribbean countries' capacity to compete effectively in the world market. The plans formulated and activities envisaged by the countries represented at the meeting in Port of Spain accorded priority to the human factor, considered the key to development. They therefore called for effective participation by people in the processes of social change and development and in planning and implementing the projects that affect them.

The Directional Plan of Action was divided into the 10 main areas indicated below. For each area, existing problems were identified, an assessment was made of the current situation and a description was given of the constraints and opportunities, goals and targets, strategies and actions. Wherever possible, a time frame was established and responsibilities were assigned.

- Enhanced social protection and reduced vulnerability
- Productive employment and sustainable livelihoods
- Health
- Education
- Population and development
- Environmental realities
- Housing, settlement and infrastructure
- Management/financial resources for social development programmes
- Violence, drugs and crime
- Integrated social and economic strategies
- Institutional mechanisms
- Measurement and monitoring instruments and mechanisms for effective poverty eradication

Source: ECLAC Subregional Headquarters for the Caribbean, Directional Plan of Action for Poverty Eradication in the Caribbean (LC/CAR/G.490), Port of Spain, November 1996.

2. Urban poverty

a) Characteristics of urban poverty and policies for its alleviation

Out of every 10 poor households, seven are below the poverty line because of low earned income, two because at least one person in the household is unemployed and one chiefly because it comprises a large number of minors.[4]

The above suggests that policies geared to raising productivity and earnings (wage policies, training and retraining policies and support policies for micro-enterprises) would help considerably to relieve the situation of around 70% of poor urban households.

Job creation policies, on the other hand, would help approximately 16% of poor households, while for countries with high unemployment rates the percentage could reach 20% or more.

The 40% of poor urban households that have a high dependency ratio stand to benefit from policies geared to increasing the quantity and quality of education, which would have positive effects on future earnings and contribute indirectly to a reduction in fertility rates.

Regional statistics reveal marked similarities in these patterns, between countries despite widely varying poverty rates. Nevertheless, there are a few atypical cases that deserve mention. With respect to unemployment, Argentina stands out as an exception, since four out of every ten households living in poverty had at least one member out of work in contrast to the regional average of two out of every ten. This ratio reveals the high risk in that country of sinking into poverty as a result of unemployment. A similar situation, although less extreme, may be noted in Panama, Uruguay and Venezuela (see table I.5).

Since there is no guarantee that similar government policies will have the same degrees of effectiveness, policy instruments must be adapted to the specific characteristics of each country. For example, in countries with similar urban poverty rates attributable to low earned income, but with significant differences in the degree of formality of the employment structure and labour institutions will have to adopt different priorities and combinations of instruments. When there is a low degree of informality, wage policies, training and such mechanisms as unemployment insurance will, of course, have a greater impact.

In view of these characteristics of poor urban households, it may be assumed that with sustained annual per capita GDP growth rates in the order of 5% for a period of no less than five years, accompanied by annual growth in earned income of around 3%, levels of urban poverty could be lowered by between 20% and 30%. This could be achieved by reducing unemployment in poor households with at least one person out of work and above all by raising earned income.

In the longer term, poverty alleviation would logically follow a decline in the number of dependents (chiefly minors) per household with increasing participation of women in the labour force.

---

[4] In order to calculate accurately the weight of the last of these factors, it should be borne in mind that three out of the seven poor households where the income of the main breadwinner is low also have a large number of dependents, which aggravates the situation.

Table I.5

**PERCENTAGE BREAKDOWN OF POOR URBAN HOUSEHOLDS
BY CHIEF DETERMINING FACTORS** a/

Countries	Low earnings and limited education			One or more members out of work	Large number of minors in relation to adults	Other factors and combinations	Total
	Total	Alone	Combined with large number of dependents				
Argentina	33	13	20	37	10	20 b/	100
Bolivia	67	41	26	10	12	11	100
Brazil	73	46	27	13	9	5	100
Chile	71	47	24	15	10	4	100
Colombia	75	51	24	10	8	6	100
Costa Rica	53	27	26	15	14	18 b/	100
Honduras	74	41	33	10	11	5	100
Mexico	83	48	35	8	7	2	100
Panama	59	32	27	20	13	8	100
Paraguay	72	42	30	11	10	7	100
Uruguay	68	27	41	20	10	2	100
Venezuela	61	29	32	20	9	10	100
Simple average	66	37	29	16	10	8	100

Source: ECLAC, *Social Panorama of Latin America. 1996 Edition* (LC/G.1946-P), Santiago, Chile, 1997, chapter I. United Nations publication, Sales No. E.97.II.G.4.
a/ Data are from around 1994. See box for definitions of indicators used.
b/ A high percentage of poor households consist of senior adults, including low-income retirees and pensioners.

> **Box I.3**
>
> **INDICATORS USED TO CHARACTERIZE URBAN POVERTY**
>
> Three factors were taken into consideration in analysing the characteristics of urban poverty in the mid-1990s: demographic situation, unemployment and low income associated with limited human capital. For purposes of analysis, a threshold was defined for each factor and the households were classified accordingly.
> **Demographic situation:** this refers to the dependency ratio, i.e., the number of children and adolescents in the home relative to the total number of adults of a fully economically active age. Households with a high dependency ratio are those where the number of minors aged 0 to 17 years, divided by the number of persons aged 18 to 59 is greater than or equal to two.
> **Unemployment factor:** this refers only to open unemployment and takes account of the presence in the household of at least one unemployed person, either the head or another member.
> **Low income and limited education:** this is estimated on the basis of earned income and the number of years of education of the head of the household or main breadwinner. The low-earnings line is 2.5 times the value of the per capita poverty line of each country, while persons with less than 10 years of schooling are considered as having low education levels.
>
> **Source:** ECLAC, *Social Panorama of Latin America, 1996 Edition* (LC/G.1946-P), Santiago, Chile, 1997, chap.I. United Nations publication, Sales No. E.97.II.G.4.

b) Poverty and occupational category

A high percentage of a household's resources comes from the earnings of its economically active members.[5] Hence, it is of interest to determine to what extent different occupational categories are affected by poverty.

Poverty is closely associated with low-productivity job categories, but is also widespread among government employees and wage earners of medium-sized and large businesses. In over half of the countries of the region, from 30% to 50% of private-sector wage earners live in poor households. However, there are wide variations between countries, from under 10% in Argentina and Uruguay to over 60% in Honduras. In Chile, Costa Rica and Panama, the percentage is between 10% and 20% while in Bolivia, Brazil, Colombia, Mexico, Paraguay and Venezuela, it falls between 30% and 40%.[6]

---

[5] Around 70% of the income of urban households at all income levels is earned income. Of that, wages and salaries account for two-thirds.

[6] In this analysis of the correlation between employment and poverty, no account is taken of what occurs with groups where the incidence of poverty is greater than among employed persons, i.e., the economically inactive who receive benefits (retirees and pensioners) and the unemployed. This accounts for the fact that the poverty ratio among employed persons is lower than the ratio for the population as a whole.

Table I.6
PERCENTAGE OF EMPLOYED POOR IN EACH OCCUPATIONAL CATEGORY AND PERCENTAGE OF TOTAL POOR [a] [b]
URBAN AREAS, 1994
(Percentages)

Country	Total employed [c]	Public-sector wage earners [d]	Non-professional, non-technical private-sector wage earners		Domestic employees	Non-professional, non-technical own-account workers
			Businesses:			
			With over 5 employees	With up to 5 employees [d]		
Argentina (Greater Buenos Aires)	5	-	5	7	10	3
	100	-	52	22	10	16
Bolivia	37	30	40	51	30	41
	95	12	19	19	4	41
Brazil	37	-	31	47	55	41
	91	-	27	29	12	23
Chile	18	-	21	28	23	16
	92	-	46	20	8	18
Colombia	34	15	41	-	31	42
	97	4	58	-	5	30
Costa Rica	12	5	11	19	25	20
	94	11	28	18	9	28
Honduras	66	42	71	83	56	79
	96	7	33	14	5	37
Mexico	29	-	33	-	56	27
	95	-	71	-	7	17
Panama	18	6	16	30	28	25
	98	9	30	19	14	26
Paraguay (Asunción)	27	13	38	36	29	33
	90	5	34	15	11	25
Uruguay	6	2	6	7	13	9
	97	8	32	13	16	28
Venezuela	32	38	29	48	41	32
	91	21	26	14	5	25

Source: ECLAC, *Social Panorama of Latin America. 1996 Edition* (LC/G.1946-P), Santiago, Chile, 1997, chapter I. United Nations publication, Sales No. E.97.II.G.4.

[a] The upper row shows the percentage of those employed in each occupational category who live in households below the poverty line.
[b] The lower row shows the percentage of poor persons employed in each category in relation to total employed.
[c] The total does not usually add up to 100 since figures exclude employers and professional and technical workers.
[d] In Argentina, Brazil, Chile and Mexico, public-sector workers are included among wage earners of establishments with over five employees. For Colombia and Mexico, micro-enterprise wage earners are also included in this category.

The percentage of poor non-professional, non-technical private-sector wage earners in medium-sized and large firms does not differ substantially from that of poor unskilled own-account workers, many of whom are in the informal sector. In some countries (Chile, Mexico and Paraguay), poverty is more prevalent among wage earners than among unskilled own-account workers.

Consequently, a high percentage of total employed poor are formal-sector wage earners. In Argentina, Chile and Mexico, the percentage is over 40%. In Brazil, Colombia, Panama, Paraguay and Uruguay, urban poverty actually affects a higher percentage of wage earners of medium-sized and large businesses than of unskilled own-account workers.

The incidence of poverty among public-sector wage earners is high, although in most of the countries their wages have improved in the current decade.[7] In Bolivia, Costa Rica, Panama and Uruguay these wage earners account for 10% of total employed urban poor; in Venezuela, one out of every five employed poor persons works in the public sector.

In low-productivity sectors, income inadequacy is most common among micro-enterprise wage earners and domestic employees. In most of the countries, these two groups account for 25% to 40% of total employed poor. Their share is somewhat less in countries with a high proportion of own-account workers, such as Bolivia and Honduras, where around 40% of urban poor are unskilled own-account workers.

This pattern of poverty among urban workers is, unsurprisingly, closely associated with low earned income. In the mid-1990s, non-professional, non-technical wage earners in businesses with over five employees received an average income 3.6 times the level of the per capita poverty line. This figure was 16% lower than the average income of the employed population as a whole (4.3 times the poverty line) and only 12% higher than the figure for low-skilled, own-account workers.

Wage earners employed in micro-enterprises received a monthly income equivalent to only 2.5 times the poverty line, an amount which represents a minimum threshold above which one may enjoy a certain degree of well-being and have a good chance of keeping above the poverty line. Domestic employees, who account for 6% of urban employed, received an average income equivalent to 1.4 times the poverty line. One out of ten employed poor persons belonged to this occupational category.

From the foregoing, it may be inferred that a high percentage of wage earners, even among those in medium-sized and large businesses in the formal sector, still have substandard jobs and no security that they will remain above the poverty line. In 7 of the 12 countries analysed, it was noted that between 30% and 50% of private-sector wage earners working in establishments other than micro-enterprises lived in poor households. In three countries, the percentage varied between 10% and 20% and only in two (Argentina and Uruguay) was it around 5%.

A high proportion of public-sector employees have low incomes and are thus affected by poverty, a situation which, clearly, hinders the process of State reform and modernization. In Bolivia, Honduras and Venezuela, between 30% and 40% of civil servants were below

---

[7] Between 1990 and 1994, the percentage of total employed persons corresponding to public-sector employees declined by between three to four percentage points in eight countries. In five, their average income increased significantly (ECLAC, 1997).

the poverty line; in Colombia and Paraguay, this applied to around 15% and in Costa Rica and Panama, to 5%. In Uruguay, on the other hand, only 2% lived in poor households.

3. Rural poverty

a) The severity of rural poverty

Despite the fact that most poor people in the region live in urban areas, it should be recalled that poverty rates are highest in the rural areas. In the poorest countries and also in some where development is more advanced but unbalanced,[8] poverty is predominantly rural and rural areas suffering from poverty are the source of migration which swells the numbers of urban poor.

In countries where poverty is predominantly rural, putting an end to the cycle is essential if it is to be eradicated from the country as a whole. In countries where poverty is primarily urban, and even in those which have recently made strides towards alleviating it, rural poverty is the great challenge of the end of the century, in view of the special difficulties identified below (see table I.7). Nevertheless, there have recently been concrete cases that demonstrate that rural poverty can be overcome by empowering the rural poor to assume a key role in their own development.

b) The dual heterogeneity of rural poverty

The heterogeneity of poverty is evident in the differences between urban and rural poverty. The latter is distinct from urban poverty in the importance of the following factors:
- lack of (or limited) possession of land;
- population dynamics, especially fertility rates;
- lack of education and the high rate of functional illiteracy (several times the urban rate);
- geographical isolation and lack of communications;
- lack of public services; and
- the impact of environmental degradation on the production base of the rural poor.

But rural poverty itself is heterogeneous: it varies in severity from country to country and from area to area, according to the following factors (see table I.8):

---

[8] In Brazil, Colombia and Venezuela, the rural indigence (extreme poverty) rate is double the urban rate, while, in Mexico, it is triple. In Mexico, most of the poor live in rural areas, while in the other three countries, this is true of the indigent.

- climatic zones and agricultural potential of the land; and
- type of work (poor wage earners of big agribusiness concerns, poor peasants and workers involved in non-farm activities); frequently, rural households include individuals from all low-income occupational categories and apply diversified survival strategies.

Table I.7
LEVELS OF RURAL POVERTY

Percentage of rural households below the poverty line	Countries
Over 66%	Guatemala, Honduras
Between 34% and 66%	Brazil, Colombia, Mexico, Panama, Peru, Venezuela
Up to 33%	Argentina, Chile, Costa Rica, Uruguay

Source: Based on ECLAC, *Social Panorama of Latin America. 1996 Edition* (LC/G.1946-P), Santiago, Chile, 1997, table 16 of the Statistical appendix. United Nations publication, Sales No. E.97.II.G.4.

Table I.8
RECENT TRENDS IN RURAL POVERTY BY AREA OF PREDOMINANCE

Predominance of poverty	Countries where the percentage of rural poor is increasing more slowly or decreasing faster than that of urban poor	Countries where the percentage of rural poor is decreasing more slowly or increasing faster than that of urban poor
Poverty predominantly rural	Colombia Guatemala Honduras	Costa Rica Mexico
Poverty predominantly urban	Brazil	Chile Panama Venezuela

Source: ECLAC, *Social Panorama of Latin America. 1996 Edition* (LC/G.1946-P), Santiago, Chile, 1997, table 16 of the Statistical appendix. United Nations publication, Sales No. E.97.II.G.4.
Note: The period covered is from the mid-1980s to the mid-1990s.

c) **Recent changes in the structure of rural poverty in Latin America and the Caribbean**

Table I.8 contains a summary of the changes in rural poverty in nine countries, from the second half of the 1980s to the first half of the 1990s and reveals a number of different trends. However, it is clear that rural poverty is not always less responsive than urban poverty to economic growth and social policies. In the very countries that have a high poverty rate there have been greater advances among the rural than among the urban poor; it has proven possible to tap the unused potential of many rural poor and to improve their access to services and the means of production.

d) **Current demographic trends and the dynamics of rural poverty**

For countries where the vast majority of the rural population are poor, it is of interest to consider the point at which the country entered demographic transition, as this helps to explain the difficulties in alleviating poverty. In seven countries[9] where the fertility rate is over 4%, the lack of real alternatives to the use of children as family workers has contributed to the inter-generational propagation of poverty in a sort of "demographic trap". This involves the division of family land among many siblings, a practice that tends to result in soil depletion and many small holdings; an increase in the number of poor landless families; and perpetuation of survival strategies based on the only asset controlled by poor householders: their own labour and that of their children.

According to projections by the Latin American Demographic Centre (CELADE), between 1995 and 2000 the rural population will continue to grow in 12 of 20 countries in the region (CELADE, 1995). In five countries, including the poorest,[10] this growth is expected to be over 1% per year. However, while these demographic growth rates are related to high percentages of rural poverty, they have not been an obstacle to its reduction. Of the four countries for which there is empirical evidence pointing to a recent reduction in the proportion of inhabitants living in poverty, three have a growing rural population.

e) **Rural poverty and occupational category**

Among the economically active population in rural areas, non-professional, non-technical own-account workers suffer the highest incidence of poverty with between 50% and 80% of workers affected. This category of workers represents between one third and one half of total employed rural poor (see tables I.9 and I.10).

---

[9] Bolivia, El Salvador, Guatemala, Haiti, Honduras, Nicaragua and Paraguay.
[10] The exception is Costa Rica, a country where despite the fact that the majority of the population is rural, only one fourth is poor.

Table I.9
INCIDENCE OF POVERTY IN SELECTED OCCUPATIONAL CATEGORIES [a]
RURAL AREAS
(Percentages)

Country	Year	Total population	Total employed	Public-sector wage earners [b]	Private-sector wage earners in non-professional, non-technical occupations			Non-professional, non-technical own-account workers	
					In establishments employing more than 5 persons	In establishments employing up to 5 persons	Domestic employees	Total	Agriculture, forestry and fisheries
Brazil [c]	1990	62	55	-	34	58	55	62	65
	1993	61	55	-	41	62	54	55	55
Chile	1990	40	26	-	31 [d]	-	23	22	24
	1992	33	22	-	24 [e]	30	21	18	20
	1994	32	21	-	22	27	14	22	25
Colombia	1994	62	55	-	55 [e]	-	57	61	59
Costa Rica	1990	27	17	-	13	23	22	24	27
	1992	28	16	-	11	21	25	22	25
	1994	25	14	7	3	20	23	21	24
Guatemala	1989	78	70	-	72	74	64	71	76
Honduras	1990	88	83	-	71	90	72	88	90
	1992	84	78	-	73	81	68	83	87
	1994	81	73	40	65	79	74	78	81
Mexico	1989	57	49	-	53 [f]	-	50	47	54
	1992	55	47	-	43 [e]	59	37	47	55
	1994	57	47	-	53 [e f]	-	53	46	54
Panama	1989	57	46	-	22	45	42	61	67
	1991	51	40	-	24	43	43	52	57
	1994	49	38	6	23	39	40	52	61
Venezuela	1990	47	31	-	35	37	44	32	37
	1992	44	28	-	10	35	35	27	34
	1994	56	42	27	50	50	53	42	44

Source: ECLAC, *Social Panorama of Latin America. 1996 Edition* (LC/G.1946-P), Santiago, Chile, 1997, table 19 of the Statistical appendix. United Nations publication, Sales No. E.97.II.G.4.
[a] Refers to the percentage of employed persons in each category residing in households below the poverty line.
[b] In 1994, public-sector wage earners were also considered separately.
[c] The figures given in the columns for establishments employing more than 5 and up to 5 persons correspond to wage earners with and without an employment contract ("carteira"), respectively.
[d] Refers to all wage earners.
[e] Includes public-sector wage earners.
[f] Includes wage earners in the public sector and in establishments employing up to 5 persons.

Table I.10
BREAKDOWN OF TOTAL EMPLOYED RURAL POPULATION LIVING IN POVERTY, BY OCCUPATIONAL CATEGORY
(Percentages)

Country	Year	Public-sector wage earners [a]	Private-sector wage earners in non-professional, non-technical occupations			Non-professional, non-technical own-account workers		Total [b]
			In establishments employing more than 5 persons	In establishments employing up to 5 persons	Domestic employees	Total	Agri-culture	
Brazil [c]	1979	-	6	25	2	66	62	99
	1987	-	8	29	3	59	52	99
	1990	-	9	25	4	60	53	98
	1993	-	7	35	3	53	48	98
Chile	1990	-	69 [d]	-	3	27	23	99
	1992	-	41	30	3	25	21	99
	1994	-	36	21	2	41	35	100
Colombia	1994	-	47 [d]	-	4	45	24	96
Costa Rica	1981	-	29	36	10	20	14	95
	1988	-	20	28	8	36	28	92
	1990	-	25	23	6	41	27	95
	1992	-	24	23	7	38	24	92
	1994	5	20	28	7	35	19	95
Guatemala	1986	-	22	16	2	59	49	99
	1989	-	22	12	2	62	52	98
Honduras	1990	-	11	17	2	68	51	98
	1992	-	15	12	2	66	48	95
	1994	3	14	15	2	65	49	99
Mexico	1984	-	43 [d]	-	2	53	45	98
	1989	-	50 [d]	-	3	45	38	98
	1992	-	21	28	2	44	33	95
	1994	-	50 [d]	-	3	45	35	98
Panama	1979	-	13 [d]	-	2	80	73	95
	1986	-	11	16	4	64	54	95
	1989	-	7	10	3	78	69	98
	1991	-	9	9	3	75	65	96
	1994	3	10	15	4	68	56	100
Venezuela	1981	-	15	7	2	68	53	92
	1986	-	19	9	2	63	52	93
	1990	-	28	14	3	48	39	93
	1992	-	35	13	4	40	32	92
	1994	5	23	19	6	45	31	98

Source: ECLAC, *Social Panorama of Latin America. 1996 Edition* (LC/G.1946-P), Santiago, Chile, 1997, table 21 of the Statistical appendix. United Nations publication, Sales No. E.97.II.G.4.

[a] In 1994, public-sector wage earners were also considered separately.
[b] The totals are less than 100% owing to the exclusion of employers, professionals and technicians, and public-sector wage earners, except in 1994.
[c] The figures given in the columns for establishments employing more than 5 and up to 5 persons correspond to wage earners with and without and employment contract ("carteira"), respectively.
[d] Includes wage earners in establishments employing up to 5 persons.

In second place are the private-sector non-professional, non-technical wage earners working in establishments with up to five workers. Here again, the incidence of poverty ranges from 50% to 80%. These wage earners account for between one fifth and one third of the employed rural poor.

Among the non-technical wage earners working in establishments with over five employees in rural areas, the incidence of poverty is lower, although in a number of countries the rates are fairly high. This group accounts for between one fifth and one third of the employed rural poor.

Lastly, the incidence of poverty is high among domestic employees, although they account for a very low percentage of total rural employed, i.e., between 2% and 4% in most countries.

The increasing number of medium-sized and large modern agricultural concerns and the emergence of non-farm activities in rural areas, have generated some high-quality rural jobs in various countries of the region. Much of this progress is associated with the growing presence of medium-scale entrepreneurs and modern capitalized farmers, professionals or semi-professionals and skilled workers, not necessarily of rural origin. However, an assessment based on the occupational/educational level of workers, with emphasis on non-professional, non-technical occupations, shows that low-skill jobs are present in every sector: the peasant farming sector,[11] traditional agricultural enterprise and non-farm paid employment. As in the case of urban poverty, which cuts across formal occupational sectors including large companies and public-sector establishments, the incidence of rural poverty in most countries does not vary much from one category to another; so far, neither the wages paid to farm workers nor the earnings of non-farm workers (either own-account or wage-earning) have been able to offer unskilled workers from peasant families a secure means of escaping poverty.

These similarities between the different occupational categories open to the unskilled rural population suggest high labour mobility between these subsectors and, above all, the existence of highly diversified strategies for household survival. According to some estimates, the majority of peasant households derive the greater part of their income from off-the-farm activities.

Owing to discrimination, there is more rural poverty among indigenous peoples, who suffer great disadvantages with respect to access to land and various basic needs such as education; rural women are also affected and, in poor rural families, they are usually discriminated against in the distribution of consumption.

Today, the poor rural woman increasingly chooses to abandon her background and traditional practices. Reversing earlier trends, the rural-urban migration of women currently exceeds that of men, except in those countries where armed conflicts have led to international emigration by men. The available evidence suggests that education is one escape route for poor rural women and may allow them to aspire to paid employment off the farm and in non-rural activities.

---

[11] According to the standard definition in use, this refers to agricultural own-account workers.

f) **Changing agricultural production patterns**

Significant changes may be expected in rural production and occupational patterns as a result of trade liberalization and the recent flurry of trade agreements. This situation has revived the old debate as to whether peasant farmers can become competitive agriculturists. Prospects for integration and globalization have only served to sharpen differences of opinion. Liberalization and agreements for the reduction of reciprocal protectionism are opening up markets to all agricultural producers; but the entry of new suppliers onto the world market increases competition.

Some peasants may modernize, switch to new crops, acquire new know-how and compete successfully under the new circumstances, but this is only possible if they receive support during the transition period. At a time of sluggish economic activity and cut-backs in farm jobs —resulting from automation combined with slow growth in demand for food products— those with the least access to material and financial resources and know-how will tend to adopt strategies that combine subsistence farming with paid jobs in agribusiness and non-farm activities in urban as well as rural areas.

The combination of dangers and opportunities generated by rapid changes in rural economies of the region gives rise to a paradoxical situation. On the one hand, peasant agriculture in its present form offers little scope for applying the knowledge received through formal education, while on the other hand, educational levels of rural youth have been improving steadily. There are already some countries where only 10% of young people are functionally illiterate (with zero to three years of schooling), and even in countries where rates are higher, there have been steady improvements. In the case of Chile and Panama, most rural young adults already have seven or more years of education to their credit. Young rural women, for whom the improvement in educational coverage has been particularly remarkable, now have a potential role to play in overcoming rural poverty by increasing their labour productivity.

Recent developments attest to the fact that rural poverty can indeed be reduced. Statistics show that improvements in public education coverage in rural areas have played a key role in improving productivity among new rural cohorts who have managed to escape from poverty. The challenge now for Governments is to create new facilities for supporting the efforts of both farm and non-farm rural workers. Only by providing support to new forms of rural business cooperatives will it be possible to resolve the above-mentioned problem of persons who have the skills and potential but who, so far, have lacked the necessary production structures to develop them fully. This issue will be discussed further in the section on proposed policy guidelines.

4. Household income distribution trends

Relative poverty in Latin America and the Caribbean, like absolute poverty, has changed significantly in recent times. High levels of inequality and rigidity in income distribution have persisted even in countries that have recorded high growth rates. An assessment of the changes in distribution observed between the middle of the 1980s and the 1990s reveals an increase in the inequality of income distribution in most countries of the region.

This situation is a reflection of the ability of the richest 10% of households to hold onto or increase their share while the poorest 40% just manage to maintain theirs or suffer a decline[12] (see table I.11).

Expectations that the recovery of previous production levels or the beginning of a new growth phase would make it possible to reverse the retrogression in income distribution patterns that developed in the 1980s have not been borne out in fact. The dynamic economic upturn of the first half of the 1990s (1990-1994), approaching full capacity in some cases, has not been reflected in a reduction in income concentration. Of the five countries with annual growth rates of over 5%, two (Argentina and, to a lesser degree, Costa Rica) saw an increase in income concentration, two others (Chile and Panama) showed a degree of inequality that remained at practically the same high level as at the beginning of the decade, and only one (Uruguay) continued to make marked improvements in income distribution.

Among the countries with lower annual growth rates, on the order of 3% to 4%, changes in income distribution over the period varied significantly. In Bolivia and Honduras and, to a lesser extent, Mexico there was some moderation in the level of concentration, whereas in Paraguay and Venezuela it increased, and in Colombia it is thought to have remained the same. In Brazil,[13] both the bottom 40% of the distributive structure and the highest-income decile registered an increase in their shares. This was reflected in a slight improvement in urban income distribution, whereas in the rural zones, there was a regression (see figures I.2, I.3 and I.4).

Argentina's high growth rate in the 1990s (7.7% per year up to 1994) resulted in a very marked increase in income for the richest 10% of households between 1992 and 1994, and a considerably smaller increase for households in the four poorest deciles. Thus, the improvement in distribution achieved in the first two years of the decade was lost. The figures for Greater Buenos Aires, which probably are representative of the trend for the urban population as a whole, indicate an increase in the Gini coefficient and in the income gap between the richest 10% and the poorest 40%. Hence, the decline in poverty deriving from economic growth in Argentina was not associated with any positive change in income distribution. Moreover, the sharp deterioration recorded since late 1994 has probably caused a regression in this regard due to the country's high and rising unemployment, which has been concentrated in the households of the first four income-distribution deciles.

---

[12] Data from household surveys used to work out income distribution probably underestimate to a greater extent the income of the top strata, through either omission or understatement. Hence, an effort was made to compare the values of the different income flows declared in the surveys against national account statistics of each country and adjust them to ensure that the amounts of profits and returns on investment of the richest households were compatible with those accounts. Despite this, the income of the highest strata may have been underestimated.

[13] As explained in chapter I, the figures for Brazil only go up to 1993. The surveys currently underway may reveal some reduction in the level of concentration.

Table I.11
**CHANGES IN INCOME DISTRIBUTION IN URBAN AREAS,
1986, 1990, 1992 AND 1994**[a]

Country	Gini coefficient[b]				Variation in share of total income between 1990 and 1994		Share of income in 1994 compared with share in 1986	
	1986	1990	1992	1994	Poorest 40% of households	Richest 10% of households	Poorest 40% of households	Richest 10% of households
Argentina (Greater Buenos Aires)	0.41	0.42	0.41	0.44	decreased	unchanged	lower	same
Bolivia	-	0.48	0.47	0.43	increased +	decreased +	-	-
Brasil [c]	0.54	0.54	0.51	-	increased	decreased	higher	lower
Chile	0.49	0.47	0.47	0.48	unchanged	increased	higher	higher
Costa Rica	0.36	0.35	0.36	0.36	unchanged	increased +	same	same
Colombia [d]	0.46	0.45	0.45	0.51	decreased	increased +	same	lower
Honduras	-	0.49	0.46	0.46	increased	decreased	-	-
Mexico	0.32	0.42	0.41	0.41	increased	decreased	lower	higher
Panama	0.43	0.45	0.45	0.45	increased	increased	lower	higher
Paraguay (Asunción)	0.40	0.36	0.39	0.42	decreased	increased +	same	higher
Uruguay	0.39	0.35	0.30	0.30	increased	decreased +	higher	lower
Venezuela	0.38	0.38	0.38	0.39	unchanged	increased +	same	higher

Source: ECLAC, *Social Panorama of Latin America. 1996 Edition* (LC/G.1946-P), Santiago, Chile, 1997, chapter. II. United Nations publication, Sales No. E.97.II.G.4.
[a] The "+" sign indicates an increase or decrease in share of three percentage points or more.
[b] The Gini coefficients were calculated on the basis of the per capita household income distribution, by decile.
[c] The most recent figure available is for 1993.
[d] To 1992, the figures apply to the eight main cities; after 1992, they apply to all urban areas.

POVERTY AND DISTRIBUTION   Chapter I - 47

Figure I.2
INCOME SHARE OF THE POOREST 40% [a]
(Urban areas)

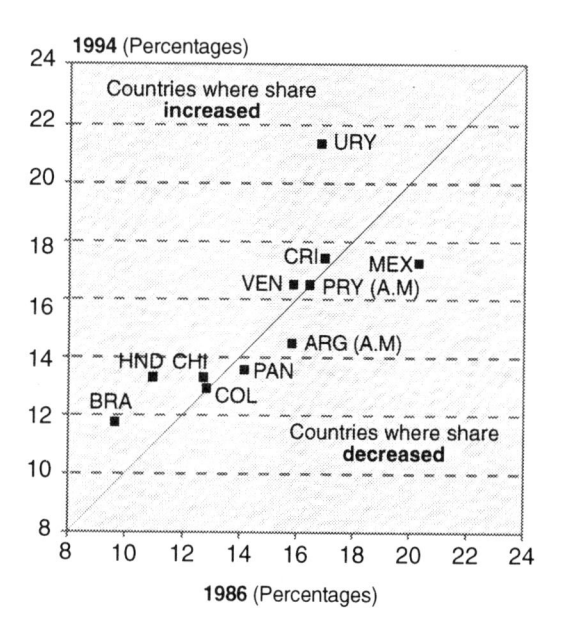

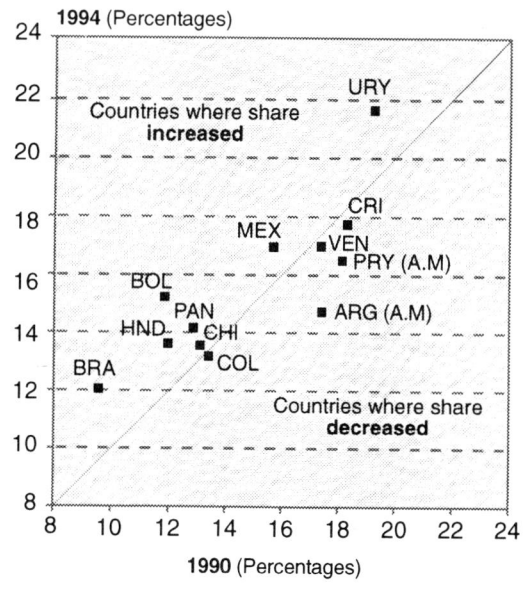

SOURCE: ECLAC, *Social Panorama of Latin America. 1996 Edition* (LC/G. 1946-P), Santiago, Chile, 1997, figure II.1. United Nations Publication, sales No. E.97.II.G.4.

[a] Percentage of total income received by the 40% of households with the lowest incomes.

Figure I.3
INCOME SHARE OF THE RICHEST 10%[a]
(Urban areas)

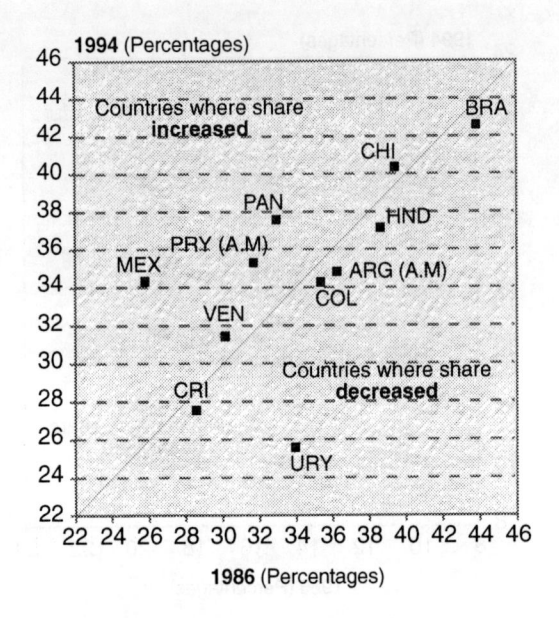

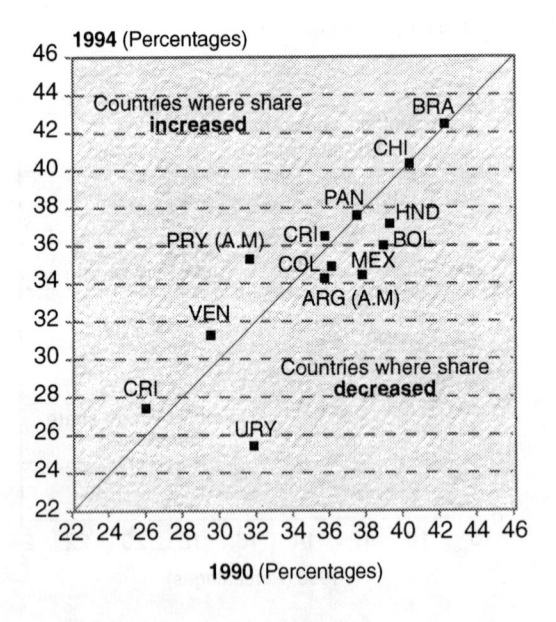

1994 (Percentages) vs **1986** (Percentages)

Countries where share **increased**: BRA, CHI, PAN, HND, PRY (A.M), MEX, ARG (A.M), COL, VEN, CRI

Countries where share **decreased**: URY

1994 (Percentages) vs **1990** (Percentages)

Countries where share **increased**: BRA, CHI, PAN, HND, BOL, PRY (A.M), CRI, COL, MEX, ARG (A.M), VEN

Countries where share **decreased**: CRI, URY

SOURCE: ECLAC, *Social Panorama of Latin America. 1996 Edition* (LC/G. 1946-P), Santiago, Chile, 1997, figure II.2. United Nations Publication, sales No. E.97.II.G.4.

a Percentage of total income received by the 10% of households with the highest incomes.

POVERTY AND DISTRIBUTION   Chapter I - 49

Figure I.4
CHANGES IN INCOME DISTRIBUTION: 1986, 1990 AND 1994 [a]
(Urban areas)

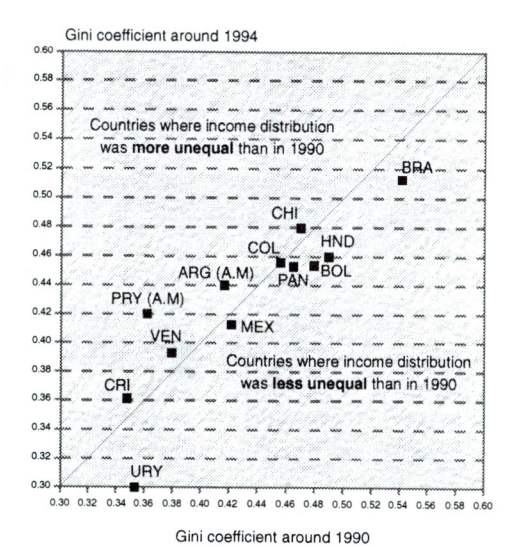

SOURCE: ECLAC, *Social Panorama of Latin America. 1996 Edition* (LC/G. 1946-P), Santiago, Chile, 1997, figure II.3. United Nations Publication, sales No. E.97.II.G.4.

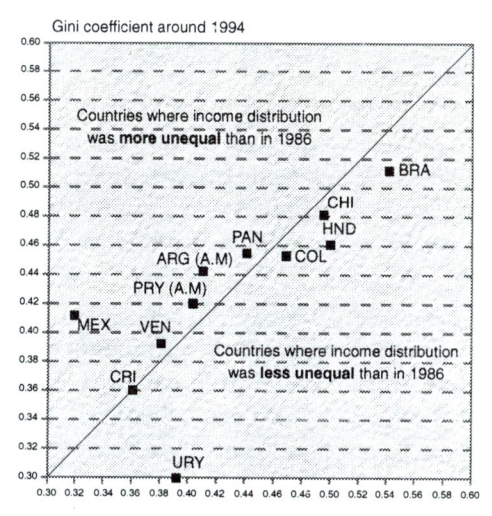

[a] The Gini coefficients were calculated on the basis of the per capita household income distribution, by decile.

In Costa Rica, immediately after the deterioration in distribution between 1990 and 1992, rapid economic growth resulted in a much greater increase in income for the top decile than for the poorest 40%. By the end of the period, and contrary to the experience of its urban counterpart in Argentina, the bottom 40% had held onto its share of income, and the overall situation was therefore less negative. Nevertheless, in Costa Rica as well, the growth-based decline in urban poverty coincided with an increase in the income gap between the groups at opposite ends of the scale.

The strong and sustained economic growth experienced by Chile in the 1990s has not been accompanied by any improvement in income distribution. The share of the poorest 40% remained the same, while that of the top decile increased. The only other countries in which the richest 10% of households has as large a share as in Chile are Brazil and Colombia; in these three countries, this decile receives over 40% of total urban income,[14] although in Chile, the lower strata have a larger share (see tables I.12 and I.13).

Chile is a particularly interesting case for an analysis of income distribution trends. It was the first country in the region to embark upon a structural reform process, and its reform programme has been the most radical as well. It is also the country that has experienced the most prolonged swiftly-paced growth process since the mid-1980s. At the same time, social expenditure has reached increasingly high levels in recent years. However, it is interesting to note that following a slight improvement —up to 1992— in the share of the poorest 40% and the poorest 25%, there has been a slow but persistent erosion of the share of the poorest decile and in the share of the poorest 25%, whereas the share of the richest 10% has continued to climb. This accounts for the fact that the high levels of inequality prevalent in the mid-1980s have persisted, while the significant decline in poverty derives mainly from economic growth. These most recent trends also reflect the difficulties involved in bringing about a more rapid increase in income for households forming what is known as the "hard core" of poverty.

Uruguay remains a noteworthy exception in the region, not only because the level of inequality is low, but also because there has been a constant trend towards income deconcentration since the middle of the last decade.[15] The degree of inequality in urban income distribution, which was already very low in the mid-1980s, continued to decline up to 1992. During that period, the share of the four poorest deciles grew by almost five percentage points (from 17% to 21.9%), while the richest decile recorded a six-point reduction in its share (from 32.4% to 25.9%). The slowdown in growth seen in the two following years (1992-1994) curbed this trend but did not result in any loss in social equity, since the different strata maintained their respective income shares. Thus, Uruguay has been the only country in the region to reduce poverty appreciably in the first half of the 1990s by combining the positive effect of growth with progressive income distribution, and this has been reflected in a more rapid improvement for households in the lower strata than in those of the highest.

---

[14] In 7 out of the remaining 10 countries for which comparable data are available, the highest decile accounts for close to or less than 35% of urban income; in the other three, the figure is on the order of 37% (see table I.12).

[15] At 0.3% in urban areas, the Gini coefficient for per capita household income distribution in Uruguay is closer to the indexes of industrialized countries with intermediate degrees of inequality than to those of the other Latin American countries.

POVERTY AND DISTRIBUTION   Chapter I - 51

Table I.12
CHANGES IN HOUSEHOLD INCOME LEVELS AND DISTRIBUTION

Country	Year	Average household income [a]		Gini coefficient [b]		Poorest quartile's income share [c]		Income share of poorest 40%		Income share of richest 10%		Average income of richest 10% as multiple of average income of poorest 40%		Households with below-average income	
		Urban	Rural	Urban	Rural	Urban	Rural	Urban	Rural	Urban	Rural	Urban	Rural	Urban	Rural
								(Percentages)						(Percentages)	
Argentina (Greater Buenos Aires)	1980	4.56	-	0.365	-	9.3	-	18.0	-	29.8	-	6.7	-	66	-
	1986	4.30	-	0.406	-	8.8	-	16.2	-	34.5	-	8.5	-	74	-
	1990	3.59	-	0.423	-	8.4	-	14.9	-	34.8	-	9.3	-	72	-
	1992	4.62	-	0.408	-	7.3	-	15.2	-	31.6	-	8.3	-	71	-
	1994	4.91	-	0.439	-	6.8	-	13.9	-	34.2	-	9.8	-	72	-
(urban areas)	1994	4.53	-	0.438	-	7.0	-	14.4	-	34.6	-	9.7	-	73	-
Bolivia [d] (17 cities)	1989	1.77	-	0.484	-	5.4	-	12.1	-	38.2	-	12.6	-	71	-
(9 cities)	1992	2.06	-	0.467	-	6.5	-	13.3	-	38.3	-	11.5	-	73	-
	1994	2.15	-	0.434	-	7.5	-	15.1	-	35.4	-	9.3	-	74	-
Brazil	1979	3.21	1.30	0.493	0.407	5.6	8.1	11.7	16.6	39.1	34.7	13.3	8.4	74	72
	1987	3.43	1.50	0.543	0.472	4.4	6.6	9.7	13.9	44.3	40.0	18.2	11.5	76	75
	1990	3.24	1.62	0.535	0.458	4.5	7.1	9.6	14.4	41.7	38.0	17.3	10.5	75	74
	1993	2.74	1.83	0.512	0.476	5.5	6.2	11.8	13.4	42.5	41.9	14.5	12.5	76	73
Chile [e]	1987	2.56	1.80	0.485	0.387	6.1	9.3	12.6	17.7	39.6	34.1	12.6	7.7	74	74
	1990	2.68	2.93	0.471	0.486	6.6	6.8	13.4	13.8	39.2	45.1	11.7	11.6	74	80
	1992	3.10	2.72	0.474	0.415	6.7	8.5	13.6	16.6	40.5	37.4	11.9	9.0	75	76
	1994	3.46	2.75	0.479	0.414	6.4	8.7	13.4	17.1	40.3	38.4	12.1	9.0	74	76
Colombia (8 major cities)	1980	2.05	-	0.518	-	4.9	-	11.0	-	41.3	-	15.0	-	75	-
	1986	2.36	-	0.455	-	5.7	-	13.0	-	35.3	-	10.9	-	72	-
	1990	2.59	-	0.450	-	6.6	-	13.6	-	34.9	-	10.2	-	73	-
	1992	2.44	-	0.454	-	5.9	-	12.9	-	34.5	-	10.7	-	72	-
	1993 [f]	2.51	1.44	0.518	0.505	5.1	3.6	11.2	10.0	43.8	37.6	15.6	15.1	77	72
	1994 [f]	2.52	1.53	0.505	0.494	5.3	3.7	11.6	10.0	41.9	34.6	14.5	13.8	76	72
Costa Rica	1981	2.95	2.50	0.328	0.355	9.5	7.9	18.9	17.2	23.2	25.6	4.9	6.0	65	66
	1988	2.57	2.30	0.364	0.358	8.3	7.8	17.2	17.0	27.6	26.3	6.4	6.2	68	66
	1990	2.56	2.30	0.345	0.351	8.2	7.8	17.8	17.6	24.6	24.5	5.5	5.6	65	65
	1992	2.49	2.30	0.362	0.358	7.9	7.7	17.0	17.3	26.9	25.2	6.4	5.8	67	66
	1994	3.09	2.59	0.363	0.372	8.3	7.6	17.4	17.1	27.5	28.5	6.3	6.6	69	69
Guatemala	1986	1.55	1.01	0.464	0.472	5.8	6.1	12.5	13.1	36.4	39.5	11.6	12.1	72	76
	1989	1.89	1.00	0.479	0.432	5.4	6.4	12.1	14.4	37.9	35.1	12.5	9.7	73	73
Honduras	1990	1.27	0.70	0.487	0.465	5.4	6.1	12.2	13.1	38.9	37.4	12.8	11.4	73	75
	1992	1.16	0.80	0.461	0.415	6.4	6.8	13.2	15.0	35.4	29.9	10.8	8.0	71	71
	1994	1.08	0.88	0.459	0.467	6.2	5.1	13.3	12.1	37.2	36.2	11.2	11.9	73	71

Chapter I - 52 SUMMIT ISSUES

Table I.12 (concl.)

Country	Year	Average household income[a]		Gini coefficient[b]		Poorest quartile's income share[c]		Income share of poorest 40%		Income share of richest 10%		Average income of richest 10% as multiple of average income of poorest 40%		Households with below-average income	
		Urban	Rural	Urban	Rural	Urban	Rural	Urban	Rural	Urban	Rural	Urban	Rural	Urban	Rural
						(Percentages)								(Percentages)	
Mexico[g]	1984	2.33	1.75	0.321	0.323	10.5	10.6	20.1	20.3	25.8	26.4	5.1	5.2	70	71
	1989	2.54	1.57	0.424	0.345	8.5	9.6	16.0	18.7	36.9	27.4	9.1	5.9	75	70
	1992	2.74	1.75	0.414	0.341	8.7	10.0	16.6	19.4	34.8	28.9	8.4	6.0	73	72
	1994	2.76	1.68	0.405	0.330	9.0	11.0	16.8	20.1	34.3	27.1	8.2	5.4	74	71
Panama	1979	2.65	1.67	0.399	0.347	7.0	9.5	15.5	17.8	29.1	28.1	7.5	6.3	67	67
	1986	2.89	2.42	0.430	0.451	6.2	6.8	14.2	13.6	33.0	38.8	9.3	10.6	70	76
	1989	2.86	1.90	0.460	0.432	6.0	7.6	13.2	15.0	36.2	36.1	10.9	9.7	73	73
	1991	2.72	2.14	0.448	0.431	5.9	7.5	13.3	15.0	34.2	35.6	10.3	9.5	71	72
	1994	3.40	2.16	0.451	0.411	6.4	7.7	13.8	15.5	37.4	33.1	10.9	8.5	73	71
Paraguay (Asunción)	1986	1.81		0.404		8.0		16.3		31.8		7.8		71	
	1990	1.92		0.357		9.4		18.6		28.9		6.2		68	
	1992	2.02		0.391		7.8		16.2		29.2		7.2		68	
	1994			0.417		8.3		16.2		35.2		8.7		74	
(urban areas)	1994			0.423		5.7		16.1		35.2		8.7		73	
Uruguay	1981	3.91		0.379		9.3		17.7		31.2		7.1		69	
	1986	3.50		0.385		8.7		17.3		32.4		7.8		72	
	1990	3.29		0.353		10.9		20.1		31.2		6.2		70	
	1992	3.73		0.301		11.9		21.9		25.9		4.7		67	
	1994	4.06		0.300		11.8		21.6		25.4		4.7		67	
Venezuela	1981	2.90	2.00	0.306	0.288	10.0	10.2	20.2	20.5	21.8	20.5	4.3	4.0	66	67
	1986	2.53	1.80	0.384	0.370	8.0	9.0	16.3	17.6	28.9	29.2	7.2	6.7	70	69
	1990	2.18	1.80	0.378	0.316	8.2	10.1	16.8	19.8	28.4	23.8	6.8	4.8	69	68
	1992	2.30	1.93	0.380	0.331	8.0	9.2	16.4	19.2	28.1	25.0	6.8	5.2	70	68
	1994	1.90	1.58	0.387	0.349	8.4	9.3	16.7	18.6	31.4	29.3	7.5	6.1	71	69

Source: ECLAC, *Social Panorama of Latin America. 1996 Edition* (LC/G.1946-P), Santiago, Chile, 1997, table 23 of the Statistical appendix. United Nations publication, Sales No. E.97.II.G.4.

[a] Average monthly per capita household income divided by the per capita poverty line.
[b] Calculated on the basis of per capita household income distribution by deciles.
[c] Percentage of total income received by the 25% of all households having the lowest incomes.
[d] Both the 1989 and 1992 surveys include the eight departmental capitals and El Alto. The 1989 survey also includes eight other cities, which represented 8.2% of the total.
[e] Calculations based on 1987, 1990, 1992 and 1994 CASEN (national socio-economic survey) data. Estimates adjusted for the latest figures for the household income and expenditure account from the Ministry of Planning and Cooperation (MIDEPLAN).
[f] Beginning in 1993, the geographical coverage of the survey was extended to nearly the entire urban and rural population of the country. Until then, the survey covered approximately half the urban population.
[g] The data are from national household income and expenditure surveys (ENIG).

Table I.13
URBAN INCOME DISTRIBUTION [a]

Country	Year	Poorest 40%	Next 30%	20% below the richest 10%	Richest 10%
Argentina [b]	1980	14.9	23.6	26.7	34.8
	1992	15.2	25.0	28.2	31.6
	1994	13.9	23.4	28.6	34.1
	1994 [c]	14.4	22.9	28.1	34.6
Bolivia	1989	12.1	21.9	27.8	38.2
	1992	13.3	22.0	26.4	38.3
	1994	15.1	22.3	27.2	35.4
Brazil	1987	9.7	18.1	27.9	44.3
	1990	9.6	19.3	29.4	41.7
	1993	11.8	19.1	26.6	42.5
Chile [d]	1990	13.4	21.2	26.2	39.2
	1992	13.6	20.7	25.2	40.5
	1994	13.3	20.5	25.9	40.3
Colombia	1990	13.7	22.5	28.9	34.9
	1992	12.9	23.5	29.1	34.5
	1993 [e]	11.2	19.9	25.1	43.8
	1994 [e]	11.6	20.4	26.1	41.9
Costa Rica	1990	17.8	28.7	28.9	24.6
	1992	17.0	27.8	28.3	26.9
	1994	17.4	26.8	28.3	27.5
Honduras	1990	12.2	20.8	28.1	38.9
	1992	13.2	22.1	29.3	35.4
	1994	13.3	23.0	26.5	37.2
Mexico [f]	1989	16.2	22.0	24.8	36.9
	1992	16.6	22.1	26.5	34.8
	1994	16.8	22.8	26.1	34.3
Panama	1989	13.2	22.7	27.9	36.2
	1991	13.3	24.3	28.2	34.2
	1994	13.8	23.3	25.5	37.4
Paraguay [g]	1990	18.6	25.7	26.8	28.9
	1992	16.2	24.8	29.8	29.2
	1994	16.2	23.0	25.6	35.2
	1994 [c]	16.1	22.6	26.1	35.2
Uruguay	1990	20.1	24.6	24.1	31.2
	1992	21.9	26.2	26.0	25.9
	1994	21.6	26.3	26.7	25.4
Venezuela	1990	16.8	26.1	28.7	28.4
	1992	16.4	26.2	29.3	28.1
	1994	16.7	24.9	27.0	31.4

Source: ECLAC, *Social Panorama of Latin America. 1996 Edition* (LC/G.1946-P), Santiago, Chile, 1997, table II.1. United Nations publication, Sales No. E.97.II.G.4.

[a] Refers to the percentage share of total urban household income of strata classified by per capita income.
[b] Metropolitan area of Greater Buenos Aires.
[c] Urban total.
[d] Special tabulations of data from national socio-economic survey (CASEN) conducted in 1990, 1992 and 1994.
[e] As from 1993, the geographical coverage of the survey was extended to include virtually the entire urban population of the country. Up to that time, the survey had covered about half of the urban population.
[f] Special tabulations of data from the national household income and expenditure survey (ENIG).
[g] Metropolitan area of Asunción.

In Colombia, there was little change in the country's high levels of inequality between 1986 and 1992. The moderate growth achieved in the first half of the 1990s coincided with a loss of income share on the part of the bottom 25% and 40% without any variation in the share of the top decile. The possible effect on income distribution of the acceleration of the growth rate that occurred after 1992 cannot be assessed owing to a lack of data. Nevertheless, estimates for 1993 and 1994 indicate that there may have been a slight decrease in inequality in both urban and rural areas.

In Brazil, the 15% decline in the income of urban households between 1990 and 1993 did not exacerbate the problem of unequal distribution, whereas the 13% increase in rural zones did have that effect, with the share of the top decile rising by three percentage points and that of the poorest 40% slipping by one point.

Income distribution patterns in the 1990s in Venezuela attest to the top stratum's ability to secure a larger proportion of incremental income during periods of growth and to avoid losing any ground in recessionary phases. Indeed, during the three-year period 1990-1992, when the annual economic growth rate stood at close to 8%, the share of the poorest 40% diminished slightly, while the share of the highest decile increased. What is more, between 1992 and 1994, when the economy was contracting, the richest 10% again increased its share, this time by three percentage points, an even more significant gain. This gain accentuated the inequality, bringing it back up to where it had been in 1986 (see table I.12).

A review of changes in income distribution between 1985 and 1994 shows that, with the exception of Uruguay, countries that recorded high growth rates (for more or less protracted periods) following their recovery from the preceding recession did not make any progress in terms of equality.

Changes in the shares of the top decile and the poorest 40% over the decade reveal a worsening pattern of income distribution in Argentina, Mexico, Panama, Paraguay and Venezuela. The level of income disparity between households in the highest and lowest strata in Chile and Costa Rica remained fairly constant, although in Chile both groups showed a slight increase in their income shares. In Colombia, too, the level of inequality was similar to what it had been a decade earlier.

The rigidity of the structure of income distribution is evident from the fact that the share of the top decile increased in five countries, remained unchanged in two and declined in only one.

Thus, it may be concluded that despite the reduction in poverty in a number of countries, it has not been possible to reinforce the positive effect of the growth that occurred between 1990 and 1994 by reducing overall inequality. This is due to various factors, including: i) persistently high unemployment rates and failure to create sufficient new high-productivity jobs at wages above the minimum threshold for escaping poverty; ii) the tendency for wages to lag behind in cases of increased productivity, which has a regressive effect that is most evident in the more dynamic sectors; iii) the growing income disparity between workers with different levels of skills, due to the sharp rise in demand for and wages of highly skilled workers.

II. PRODUCTIVE JOB CREATION

1. Moderate, unstable growth

The average growth rate registered thus far in the 1990s is proving to be too slow to bring about an improvement in the employment situation or in wages. In addition to being moderately paced (averaging 3.1% in 1991-1996), it has been unstable, falling from a high of 5.3% in 1994 to 0.3% in 1995 and then climbing back to 3.4% in 1996. Hence, the coefficient of variation for GDP growth has been nearly 50% for the period between 1991 and 1996.

The ECLAC secretariat has estimated that, in order to make lasting progress towards changing production patterns and achieving greater social equity at one and the same time, annual growth rates on the order of 6% will have to be attained (ECLAC, 1996a). Moreover, that pace of growth will need to be maintained over time, since excessive variability in the level of economic activity discourages investment and employment, especially now that the region is moving towards more flexible forms of hiring and firing.

Despite high interest rates, the domestic saving rate is too low. Among other factors, exchange rate lags mask signals for the expansion for export and import-substitution activities by stimulating imports and expenditure on non-tradables. Thus, financial and currency markets have been hindering the attainment of a more stable form of growth and this, in turn, has been blocking more significant gains in employment and wages. Not surprisingly, this situation has given rise to a tendency to shift responsibility for employment matters to labour policy; this approach is clearly a limited one, however, since labour policy addresses only one dimension of employment issues.

In 1996 the region was able to resume a moderate pace of growth much more quickly than had been expected, given the repercussions of Mexico's financial crisis on external finance. Generally speaking, however, the performance of the labour market, while differing from country to country, was fairly poor. Unemployment continued to climb, reaching 8%.

Low-productivity (and low-paying) jobs expanded the most, with 8 out of every 10 new jobs falling into that category. Although the region made gradual progress in terms of stabilization, in many countries real wages grew slowly or not at all.

The growth rates of Guyana, Chile, El Salvador and Peru topped 5%; eight countries registered rates of between 3% and 4% and another 14 countries had rates below 3% (see table II.1). As a result, per capita GDP (measured in 1990 dollars) was higher in 1996 than it had been in 1980 in only 10 Latin American countries. Within this group, the cumulative variation has been considerable —over 30%— only in Colombia (36%) and Chile (56%). In the cases of Argentina (1.5%), Brazil (0.6%), Costa Rica (1.6%) and Paraguay (0.6%), per capita GDP is practically the same as it was in 1980, while in Uruguay (14%), the Dominican Republic (17%) and Panama (10%), the increase ranges between 10% and 20%. In the Caribbean, economic growth in the 1990s has generally been even slower than in Latin America, with the exceptions of Guyana, Belize and Saint Lucia, all of which have recorded annual GDP growth of over 4%.

In contrast, when the levels of per capita GDP for 1996 and 1980 (in the same currency) are compared, the results show the Caribbean to be in a better position than Latin America. Although the average figure for the subregion denotes a cumulative decrease of 14.8%, this result is heavily influenced by the performances of Trinidad and Tobago (-30%), which accounts for 22% of the Caribbean's population, and of Suriname (-8%), which has 7.5% of the subregion's total population. In the case of the other Caribbean economies, which do not appear to have been seriously affected by the economic crisis that swept over the rest of the region during the 1980s, per capita GDP is higher than it was in 1980, in some instances by quite a large margin, as in the cases of Saint Kitts and Nevis (136%), Saint Lucia (98%), Saint Vincent and the Grenadines (93%), Dominica (78%), Antigua and Barbuda (74%) and Grenada (74%) (see figures II.1 and II.2).

On average, economic growth in the 1990s has not only been fairly slow, but has also been somewhat unstable, and this has prevented it from translating into stronger gains in the labour market. As may be seen from table II.2, only Chile, El Salvador, Colombia, Guatemala and Bolivia have achieved annual GDP growth rates of over 4% while avoiding sharp fluctuations. Another group of countries (Peru, Argentina, Panama and the Dominican Republic) have similar average growth rates but have registered a considerably greater degree of variability.

The growth rates of most of the Latin American economies, however, have been both slow and unstable during the 1990s (see table II.2), and this has been a crucial factor in holding back progress in connection with labour-related issues.

Table II.1
ECONOMIC GROWTH IN THE 1990s
(Average annual GDP growth rates, 1991-1996[a])

Over 5% per year

Guyana	8.1
Chile	7.1
El Salvador	5.6
Peru	5.1

4%-5% per year

Argentina	4.7
Panama	4.5
Colombia	4.4
Belize	4.3
Dominican Republic	4.3
Saint Lucia	4.2
Guatemala	4.1
Bolivia	4.0

3%-4% per year

Uruguay	3.8
Costa Rica	3.7
Ecuador	3.4
Honduras	3.4
Saint Kitts and Nevis	3.3[b]
Saint Vincent and the Grenadines	3.0

1%-3% per year

Paraguay	2.9
Brazil	2.7
Nicaragua	2.4
Venezuela	2.4
Dominica	2.1[b]
Mexico	2.0
Grenada	1.8[a]
Trinidad and Tobago	1.7

Under 1% per year

Jamaica	0.9[b]
Suriname	0.9[b]
Antigua and Barbuda	0.7
Barbados	0.6
Haiti	-2.4
Cuba	-4.8

Source: ECLAC, on the basis of official figures.

[a] The figures for 1996 were taken from ECLAC, *Preliminary Overview of the Economy of Latin America and the Caribbean, 1996* (LC/G.1947-P), Santiago, Chile, 1996. United Nations publication, Sales No. E.96.II.G.13.

[b] 1991-1995.

Figure II.1
PER CAPITA GDP, 1996
(Cumulative variation since 1980)

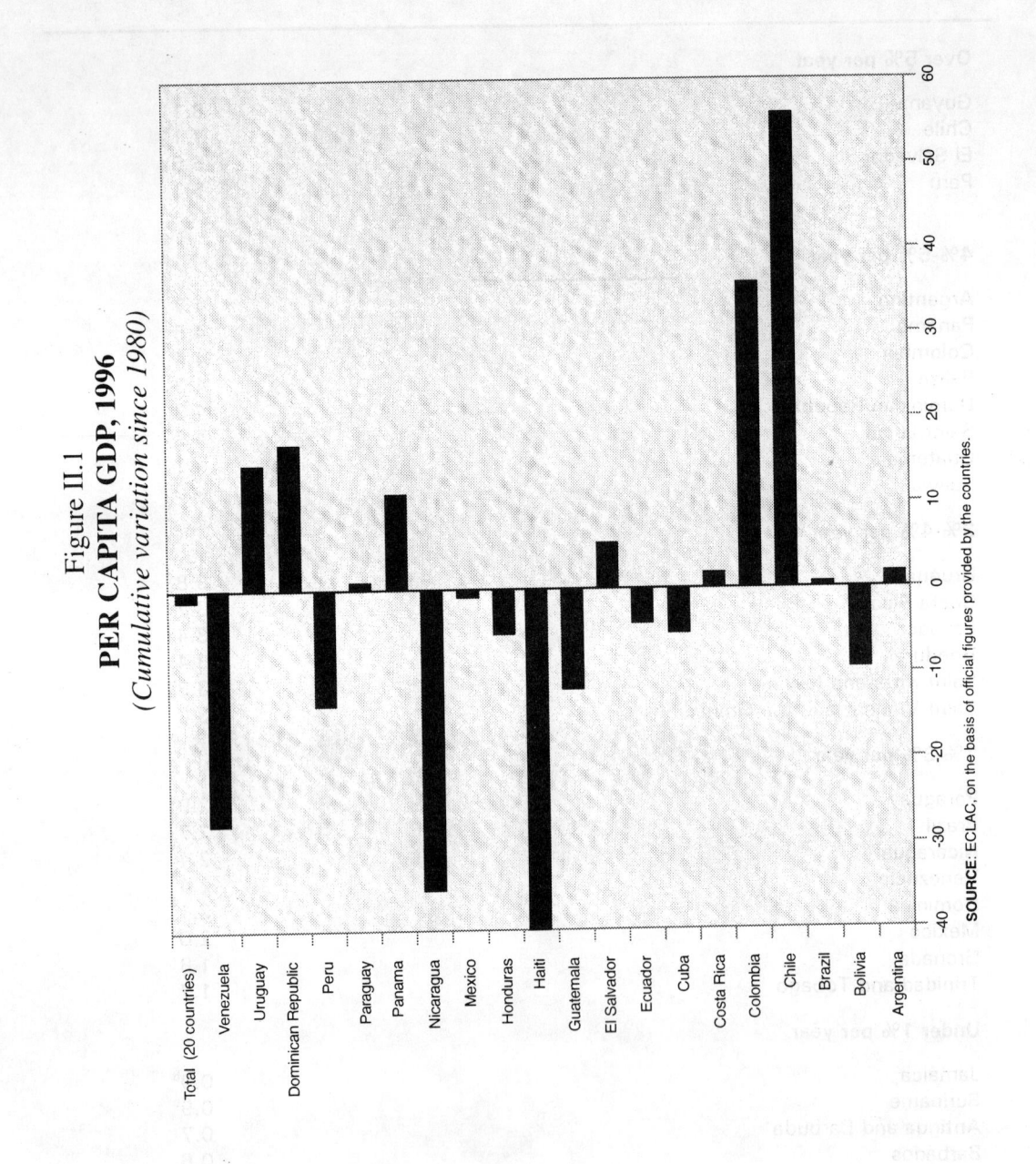

SOURCE: ECLAC, on the basis of official figures provided by the countries.

PRODUCTIVE JOB CREATION

Figure II.2
PER CAPITA GDP, 1996
(Cumulative variation since 1980)

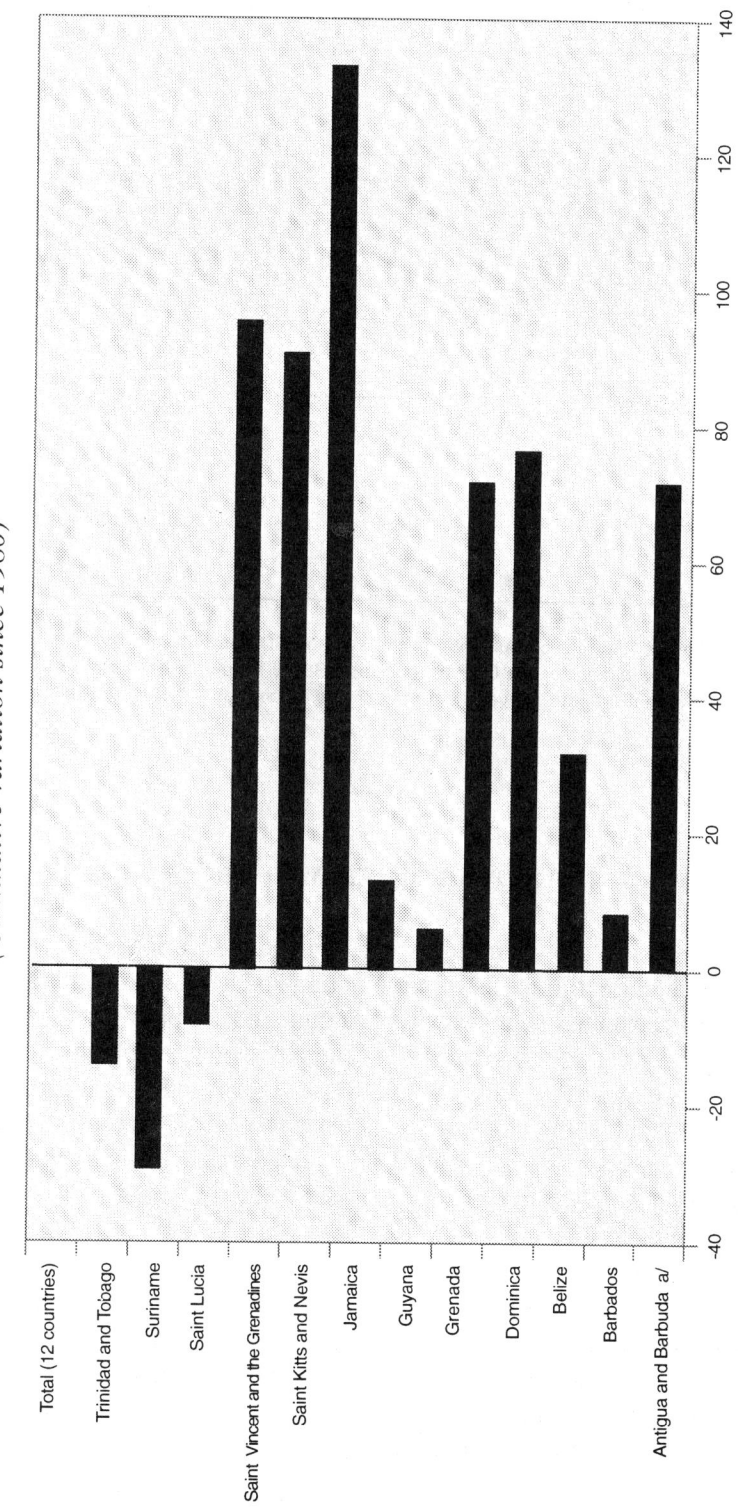

Total (12 countries)	~-13
Trinidad and Tobago	~-13
Suriname	~-30
Saint Lucia	~-7
Saint Vincent and the Grenadines	~95
Saint Kitts and Nevis	~90
Jamaica	~135
Guyana	~15
Grenada	~5
Dominica	~73
Belize	~77
Barbados	~32
Antigua and Barbuda a/	~72

SOURCE: ECLAC, on the basis of official figures.
a/ Based on figures expressed in terms of factor cost.

Table II.2
RATE AND VARIABILITY OF GROWTH IN THE 1990s a/

LOW, UNSTABLE GROWTH		HIGH, UNSTABLE GROWTH	
Uruguay	(3.8; 0.9)	Peru	(5.1; 0.9)
Costa Rica	(3.7; 0.6)	Argentina	(4.7; 1.0)
Ecuador	(3.4; 0.6)	Panama	(4.5; 0.5)
Honduras	(3.4; 0.8)	Dominican Rep.	(4.3; 0.5)
Paraguay	(2.9; 0.4)		
Brazil	(2.7; 0.9)		
Nicaragua	(2.4; 1.0)		
Mexico	(2.0; 2.0)		
LOW, STABLE GROWTH		**HIGH, STABLE GROWTH**	
		Chile	(7.1; 0.3)
		El Salvador	(5.6; 0.3)
		Colombia	(4.4; 0.4)
		Guatemala	(4.1; 0.2)
		Bolivia	(4.0; 0.3)

^a   In each pair of figures, the first corresponds to the average GDP growth rate for 1991-1996 and the second to the coefficient of variation for the GDP growth rate. Solely for purposes of classification, growth has been considered to be high if the rate is over 4% per year and to be stable if the coefficient of variation is 0.4 or less.

2. Employment: growth and trends[16]

The new foundations for growth in Latin America and the Caribbean appear to have had no more than a limited effect in terms of job creation and average remunerations. One reason for this is that the region has been growing at a quite modest pace which, even assuming the continuation of historical patterns, does not generate enough employment to absorb all new entrants into the economically active population (EAP). Another is that the restructuring of the production system favours more capital-intensive activities, thereby reducing the elasticity of employment relative to output. This has prompted a shift of workers out of "modern", relatively high-productivity activities into activities exhibiting differing degrees of informality and low productivity.

The rising productivity of "modern" activities is being counteracted by the expansion of the informal sector; as a net result of these trends, increases in average productivity have been negligible. This has also affected real wage levels (particularly in the case of minimum wages), which have shown little or no improvement. In fact, in 1996 the labour situation suffered a setback, with unemployment mounting and both the purchasing power of wages and productivity failing to make any headway.

---

[16] This section is based on ILO (1994, 1995 and 1996).

Owing to the impact of the demographic transition, the total population growth rate has been lower in the 1990s (1.8% per year) than it was in the 1980s (2.0% per year), and much the same kind of change has been seen in the working-age population. In addition, rural-urban migration has continued, and as a result nearly 80% of the region's workforce is now concentrated in urban areas, as compared to 70% in 1980. Finally, the labour force participation rate climbed gradually between 1985 and 1995, primarily as a consequence of the increasing number of women entering the labour market.

Output and employment in non-agricultural activities in Latin America and the Caribbean rose in 1990-1995 at average annual rates of 3% and 2.9%, respectively. As a result, average productivity per worker remained flat, edging upward by an average annual rate of just 0.1% (see table II.3).

The labour market has therefore become more urban, the percentage of women in that market has increased, and the growth of the labour force has slowed from 3.8% per year in the 1980s to 3.3% in the 1990s. Thus, during the period spanning the introduction of economic reforms, the pressure exerted by the labour supply has eased, since fewer new jobs have been needed in order to absorb entrants into the workforce.

Employment has increased more slowly than the non-farm EAP (3.2% per annum), thereby driving up open unemployment from 5.7% of the region's EAP in 1990 to 7.3% in 1995 and 7.7% in 1996.[17] Moreover, the informal sector consolidated its position as the main source of job creation. At the start of the decade, 51% of non-agricultural employment was in the informal sector. This figure had risen to 56% by 1995 and is believed to have increased slightly again in 1996, given the deterioration of the employment situation seen during that year. Thus, between 1990 and 1995, 84 out of every 100 new jobs were in informal activities. Meanwhile, public-sector employment shrank from 15.3% to 13% of total employment between 1990 and 1995 and employment in the modern private sector expanded very little as it responded to variations in the pace of growth and the degree of maturity and continuity exhibited by economic reforms. The average rate of growth has been slow, and job creation in this sector has therefore been slow as well, although differences are to be observed which are proportionate to the amount of time that has passed since the introduction of economic reforms and measures to restructure production.

The highest unemployment rates have been in the Caribbean (between 15% and 21%), although it should be noted that this subregion uses a different methodology for measuring unemployment than the rest of the region. If the same methodology were to be used, the rates in the Caribbean would be considerably lower, although they would still be higher than those of Latin America. Within Latin America, unemployment in 1995-1996 was highest in Argentina, Panama and the Dominican Republic, which all had rates above 15%, and Uruguay, where the rate was nearly 12%. The lowest levels were found in Bolivia and Brazil (around 5%). In the rest of the countries, unemployment rates ranged between 6% and 8% (Paraguay, Chile and Mexico) and between 8% and 10% (Peru and Colombia) (see table II.4).

---

[17] The figure for 1996 is a preliminary estimate, since information is not yet available on a number of countries. As of the end of the third quarter of 1996, the average unemployment rate was 8% of the workforce.

Chapter II - 62   SUMMIT ISSUES

Table II.3
GROWTH AND PERFORMANCE OF THE LABOUR MARKET
(Annual growth rates, 1990-1995)

	GDP	EAP	Employment	Real wages	Productivity
Chile	7.2	2.5	3.7	4.4	3.3
Peru	5.7	3.4	3.5	4.8	2.2
Argentina	5.2	3.2	1.0	0.2	4.1
Panama	5.0	6.4	7.3	-	-2.1
Colombia	4.5	3.3	3.7	1.5	0.8
Costa Rica	4.4	4.0	4.0	0.4	0.4
Bolivia	4.0	3.2	4.0	1.6	-0.1
Ecuador	3.8	4.6	4.4	-	-0.6
Dominican Republic	3.7	3.6	4.6	-	-0.9
Uruguay	3.6	1.9	4.0	0.8	2.1
Honduras	3.4	5.6	5.8	0.1	-2.3
Venezuela	3.2	3.8	4.0	-7.5	-0.8
Paraguay	3.0	5.6	5.8	-0.3	-2.7
Brazil	2.5	2.7	2.6	5.1	-0.1
Trinidad and Tobago	1.4	2.2	2.9	-	-1.5
Jamaica	1.0	1.6	1.4	-	-0.4
Mexico	0.8	3.9	3.1	0.8	-2.2
Barbados	-0.5	2.0	0.9	-2.6	-1.4
Total	3.0	3.2	2.9	-	0.1

Source: International Labour Organization (ILO), *Panorama laboral'96*, Regional Office for Latin America and the Caribbean, 1996, based on information provided by ECLAC and official figures from the countries.

Table II.4
URBAN UNEMPLOYMENT
(Average annual rates)

	1980	1985	1990	1991	1992	1993	1994	1995	1996[a]
Latin America and the Caribbean (Regional average)	6.2	7.3	5.8	5.8	6.3	6.3	6.4	7.3	7.7
Argentina (Total urban rate)	2.6	6.1	7.5	6.5	7.0	9.6	11.5	17.5	17.2
Bolivia (Department capitals)	...	5.8	7.3	5.8	5.4	5.8	3.1	3.6	3.5
Brazil (Six metropolitan areas)	6.3	5.3	4.3	4.8	5.8	5.4	5.1	4.6	5.7[b]
Chile[c] (Metropolitan Region)	11.7	17.2	6.5	9.3	7.0	6.2	8.3	7.4	7.2[d]
Colombia[e] (Seven metropolitan areas)	10.0	13.9	10.5	10.2	10.2	8.6	8.9	8.9	11.4[f]
Costa Rica (Total urban rate)	6.0	6.7	5.4	6.0	4.3	4.0	4.3	5.7	...
Ecuador[e] (Total urban rate)	5.7	10.4	6.1	8.5	8.9	8.9	7.8	7.7	...
El Salvador (Total urban rate)	...	...	10.0	7.9	8.2	8.1	7.0	7.0	7.5[g]
Guatemala (Nationwide total)	2.2	12.1	6.5	6.4	5.7	5.5	5.2	4.3	...
Honduras (Total urban rate)	8.8	11.7	7.8	7.4	6.0	7.1	4.0	6.0	6.3
Mexico (Total urban rate)	4.5	4.4	2.7	2.7	2.8	3.4	3.7	6.3	5.7[b]
Nicaragua (Nationwide total)	...	3.2	11.1	14.2	17.8	21.8	20.7	18.2	16.1
Panama[e] (Metropolitan Region)	9.9	15.6	20.0	19.3	17.5	15.6	16.0	16.2	16.4
Paraguay[h] (Asunción metropolitan area)	4.1	5.2	6.6	5.1	5.3	5.1	4.4	5.3	...
Peru[i] (Lima metropolitan area)	7.1	10.1	8.3	5.9	9.4	9.9	8.8	8.8	8.7
Uruguay (Montevideo)	7.4	13.1	9.2	8.9	9.0	8.4	9.2	10.8	12.6[d]
Venezuela (Total urban rate)	6.6	14.3	11.0	10.1	8.1	6.8	8.9	10.9	11.9[g]

Source: ECLAC, *Preliminary Overview of the Economy of Latin America and the Caribbean, 1996* (LC/G.1947-P), Santiago, Chile, 1996. United Nations publication, Sales No. E.96.II.G.13.

[a] Preliminary figures.
[b] January/October.
[c] From 1991 on, the data have been drawn from a new sample.
[d] January/September.
[e] Includes hidden unemployment.
[f] Average for the rates in March, June and October.
[g] First half of the year.
[h] From 1994 on, the figures shown correspond to the total urban rate.
[i] The data for 1995 and 1996 have been taken from a new survey and refer to the first half of each year.

The available figures for the Caribbean (which, as mentioned, uses a different methodology from the rest of the region) indicate that open urban unemployment stood at 16% in the third quarter of 1996 in Barbados, Jamaica and Trinidad and Tobago. This represents a substantial decrease in the case of Barbados from the 23% and 24% levels recorded in 1992 and 1993. Unemployment in Jamaica has tended to hold at around 16%, but this level constitutes a reduction for Trinidad and Tobago, which had rates of nearly 20% between 1991 and 1993.

Unemployment was highest among women and young people. The specific rates exceeded the average by 10%-20% in the case of women and by 50% in the case of young people.[18]

In Latin America, the growth of informal employment has tended to drive down average labour productivity. Between 1990 and 1994, employment expanded by 4.9% per year in informal occupations and by 1.2% in modern activities. The average productivity of the informal sector declined even in countries where output per worker rose. Thus, productivity gains in the modern sector appear to have outpaced the region's average rate of productivity growth.

In the 1990s, the employment situation has improved —i.e., unemployment and informal activity have decreased— in countries that have attained economic growth rates nearing 6%. Growth rates below or similar to the increase in the urban EAP (between 3% and 4.5%) have been enough to lower unemployment, but not to reduce informal activity. With economic growth rates below these levels, it appears to be impossible to bring about a reduction even in unemployment.

In the countries with the highest annual economic growth rates (such as Chile, Peru, Argentina and Panama), the employment situation has improved (except in Argentina, where the expansion of employment has been slow and the unemployment rate rose between 1993 and 1995).[19] In these countries, employment has been expanding faster than the EAP and major gains in productivity have been made, except in Panama, where employment has risen sharply. The combination of a reduction in unemployment with increases in real wages and in labour productivity is most notable in Chile and Peru, which are precisely the countries with the highest growth rates.

The countries with moderate economic growth rates (Colombia, Costa Rica and Bolivia) have managed to make a partial improvement in the situation by lowering unemployment. This reduction has largely been based on a rapid expansion of informal employment, however, which has led to decreases in job quality and productivity.

Employment has risen in all the countries; nevertheless, trends in unemployment, informal activities and real wages have differed. The countries can be divided into three different groups in terms of the performance of their labour markets.

---

[18] In 1996, 25%-30% or even more of the labour force between the ages of 15 and 20 (or 25, depending on the age groups used by the different countries) was unemployed in Argentina, Colombia, Uruguay and Venezuela.

[19] In the case of Argentina, the problem is how to establish a direct link between growth and employment, and even between economic reform and labour performance. In 1993-1994, the country experienced both rapid economic growth (an average rate of 6%) and high urban unemployment (10.5%).

In countries with higher-quality jobs, such as Chile and Peru, not only have employment levels risen, but open unemployment has been reduced, the extent of informal activity has held steady or declined, and real wages and average labour productivity have increased. Argentina has recorded the largest increase in labour productivity, but this achievement has been accompanied by a lacklustre performance in terms of employment, no more than a small increase in real wages and rising unemployment since 1993.

In countries located in the mid-range in terms of job quality —the majority of the countries in the region— the number of jobs has risen but in some cases there have also been increases in unemployment or in informal activity or both, as well as downturns in wages or productivity.

In countries where job quality is poor, the situation in the labour market has deteriorated even though employment has expanded. With very low growth rates, this deterioration has been manifested in increases in both unemployment and in the percentage of the labour force in the informal sector, and labour productivity has slipped. In Mexico and Venezuela, the expansion of the informal sector has been coupled with downturns in minimum wages and average labour productivity.

3. Job creation

Job creation during the 1990s has been concentrated in the informal sector,[20] thereby stalling the growth of average labour productivity. In most of the countries, this sector's share of employment is now greater than it was in 1990 and in 1985; in fact, the percentage of total employment accounted for by the informal sector swelled from 51.6% at the start of the decade to 56% in 1995. In the formal sector, on the other hand, the growth of employment has been sluggish and productivity has been advancing more swiftly. As a result, the productivity gap separating these two sectors has been widening.

Informal jobs, most of which are in low-productivity, poorly-paid activities, have registered a slower increase in earnings than high-paying jobs and than the average. The expansion of the informal sector has helped to mitigate poverty by boosting the employment rate for poor households, but it has also had a negative effect in terms of social equity because, by widening the wage gap, it has made the distribution of income more unequal and, by concentrating the growth of employment in low-productivity activities, has lowered average productivity as well. As a result, it has hampered efforts to enhance competitiveness.

Of every 100 new jobs created in 1990-1995, 84 were in informal activities. Thus, out of the approximately 16 million jobs created in Latin America and the Caribbean in 1990-1994, 13.4 million were in the informal sector, which thus came to account for 56% of the total working population of the region (including those working in domestic service jobs).

The fastest-growing category of informal employment has been that of micro-enterprises (an annual growth rate of 5.2% in 1990-1995), and today this sector accounts for

---

[20] This sector is composed of own-account workers, unpaid family workers and persons employed in micro-enterprises and in domestic service.

22.5% of total employment in the region, versus 20.2% in 1990. Informal own-account workers have also increased in number (at an annual rate of 4.4%) and now make up 26.5% of the region's total working population, which is almost two percentage points more than in 1990. Employment in domestic service has climbed by 3.9% per year, with 7.1% of the working population employed in that sector at the present time as opposed to 6.7% in 1990.

The informal sector has grown the most in Bolivia (at an annual rate of 6.4%), Costa Rica (5.1%), Ecuador (5.4%), Honduras (5.9%), Panama (7.7%), Paraguay (7.2%) and Venezuela (8.0%). The countries where informal employment has increased the least have been Argentina (3.4% per annum), Colombia (3.8%) and Uruguay (2.3%). In the rest of the countries, informal employment has expanded at an annual rate of 4.5% during the 1990s.

Micro-enterprises have been the fastest-growing informal employers in Argentina, Bolivia, Chile, Colombia, Costa Rica, Ecuador, Honduras, Mexico, Peru and Venezuela; in Paraguay and Uruguay, the largest increase has been in own-account workers, and in Brazil and Panama, it has been in domestic service.

The fact that employment has grown more swiftly in the informal sector than in the modern sector has had a detrimental impact on the countries' average productivity levels. This effect has been the most marked in those cases (Brazil, Panama and Paraguay) in which the expansion of informal-sector employment has been concentrated in the lowest-productivity occupations, such as those of own-account informal workers and domestic service.

It is estimated that during 1990-1994, the modern sector created nearly 2.5 million new jobs as the net result of the private sector's contribution of nearly 2.7 million jobs and a decrease of 200,000 jobs in the public sector.

Public-sector employment contracted between 1990 and 1995 (-0.6% per year) and its share of the total shrank from 15% to 13%. In recent years the modern private sector has maintained a pattern of strong gains in productivity, modest increases in output and decreasing employment (-6.4% in manufacturing). The growth of employment in the modern sector of the economy has therefore come to depend essentially on the expansion of employment in construction and services, which has not been rapid enough to offset the decreases registered in employment in manufacturing and the civil service.

4. Remunerations

The current situation with regard to labour income is marked by low wages (as wages fall behind the real levels of the 1980s) and widening income differentials within the occupational structure.

In 1990-1994, real wages in the manufacturing sector rebounded in a majority of the countries, with the annual rate of increase for the region as a whole amounting to 2.6%. Even so, manufacturing wages were still nearly 5% lower in 1994 than they had been in

1980.[21] The recovery in the purchasing power of wages has primarily been due to a reduction in inflation rather than to the behaviour of the labour market or to institutional mechanisms.

Average real remunerations have followed differing patterns from one country to the next but have shown a nearly across-the-board increase during the 1990s. Despite this upturn in real wages, however, in a number of cases wage levels are still lower than they were in 1980 (see figure II.3).

The available data indicate that this upward trend in wages was interrupted in 1996, although pay levels did continue to climb in Barbados, Brazil, Chile and Colombia. One reason for this is that the favourable effect on wages of a slowdown in inflation weakens as the inflation rate descends; another is that, as lower inflation rates are reached, the intervals between wage adjustments tend to lengthen, thereby slowing the rise of real wages. An additional factor is the competitive readjustments being made by modern firms, which involve staff cuts and the introduction of more flexible wage schemes.

Out of a sample of 17 Latin American countries, 13 of them had a lower minimum wage in real terms in 1995 than in 1980. The only countries where real minimum wages were higher in 1995 than in 1980 were Colombia, Costa Rica, Panama and Paraguay, and this continued to be the case in 1996 (see figure II.4).

As noted earlier, in 1994 average wages in the manufacturing sector were 5% lower in real terms than they had been in 1980. During this same period, the level of output per worker in the modern sector rose by 15.4% (1% per year). This indicates that real wages have not kept step with productivity but have instead fallen behind. This lag was reduced somewhat during the economic recovery of 1990-1994, but a downward trend re-emerged in 1995 and 1996.

The halting growth of real average wages is the net effect of rapid rates of increase in the wage levels of persons employed in the most dynamic activities within the modern sector and the slow growth or even decline of remunerations in all other activities. For example, the earnings of persons employed in the informal sector and at the bottom rungs of the employment ladder within the modern sector are not only substantially lower than they were before but have also been shrinking further. Moreover, a downward trend in the real minimum wage —a variable that has some impact on poverty levels— has been observed in no fewer than nine countries during the past two years.

Using 1980 as a reference point, the figures show that the purchasing power of the minimum wage in 1995 was 28% lower than it was then. Indeed, the lag in the minimum wage is significantly greater than the lag in industrial wages.

The recovery in different wage levels has been very uneven, thus widening the wage gap. On average, informal workers earn only half as much as manual and non-manual workers in modern enterprises do and, what is more, work longer hours; in other words, if the statistics are corrected for the number of hours worked, then the labour income distribution is even more unequal than it would otherwise seem.

---

[21] In 1995 the wage situation was worse than in 1994, as manufacturing wages fell in 8 out of the 14 countries for which information was available. In 1996, wages in the manufacturing sector plunged (by almost 15%) in Mexico and Venezuela.

Figure II.3
REAL AVERAGE REMUNERATIONS
(*Average annual indexes, 1990=100*)

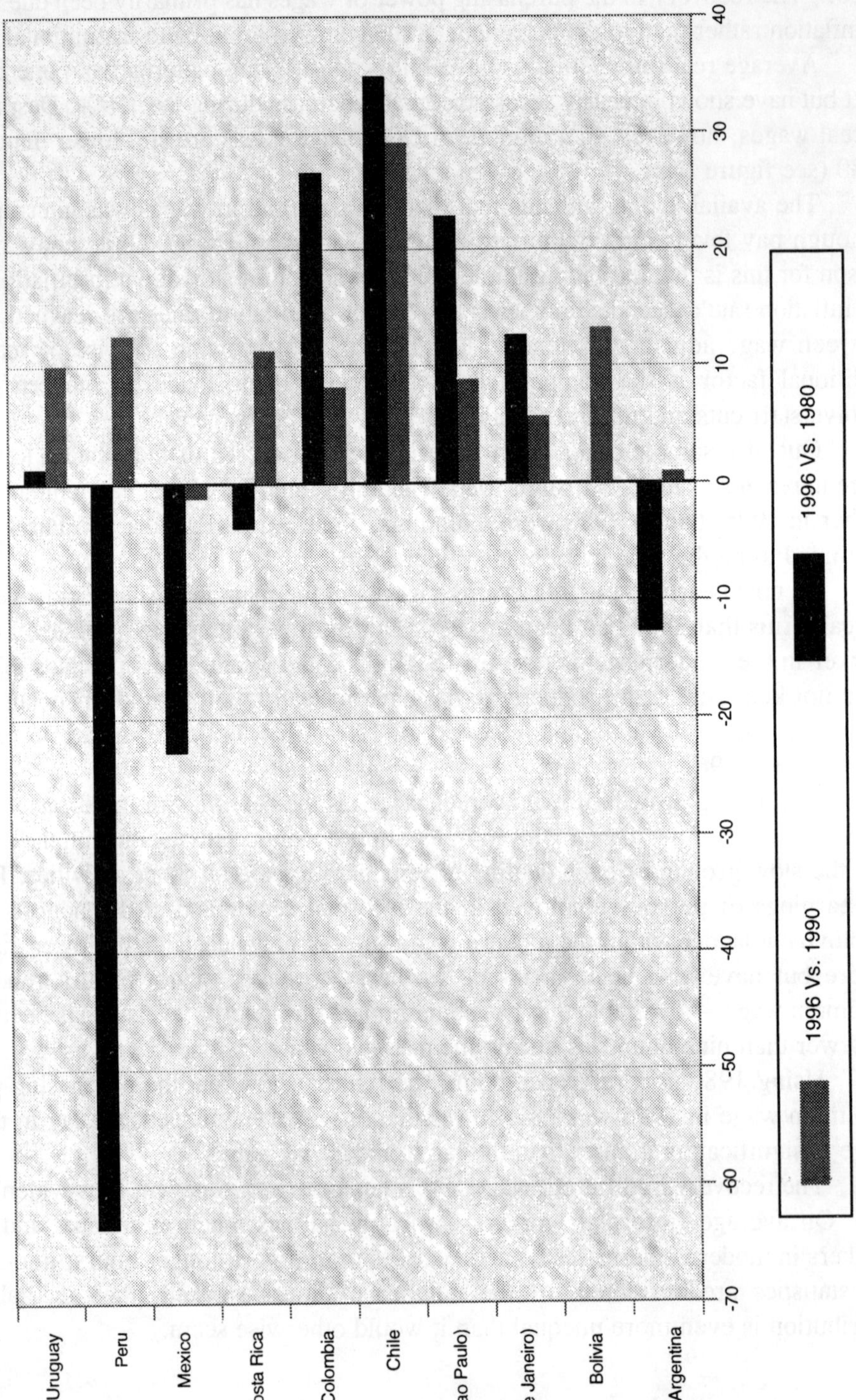

SOURCE: ECLAC, on the basis of official figures.

Figure II. 4
REAL URBAN MINIMUM WAGE
(Average annual indexes, 1990=100)

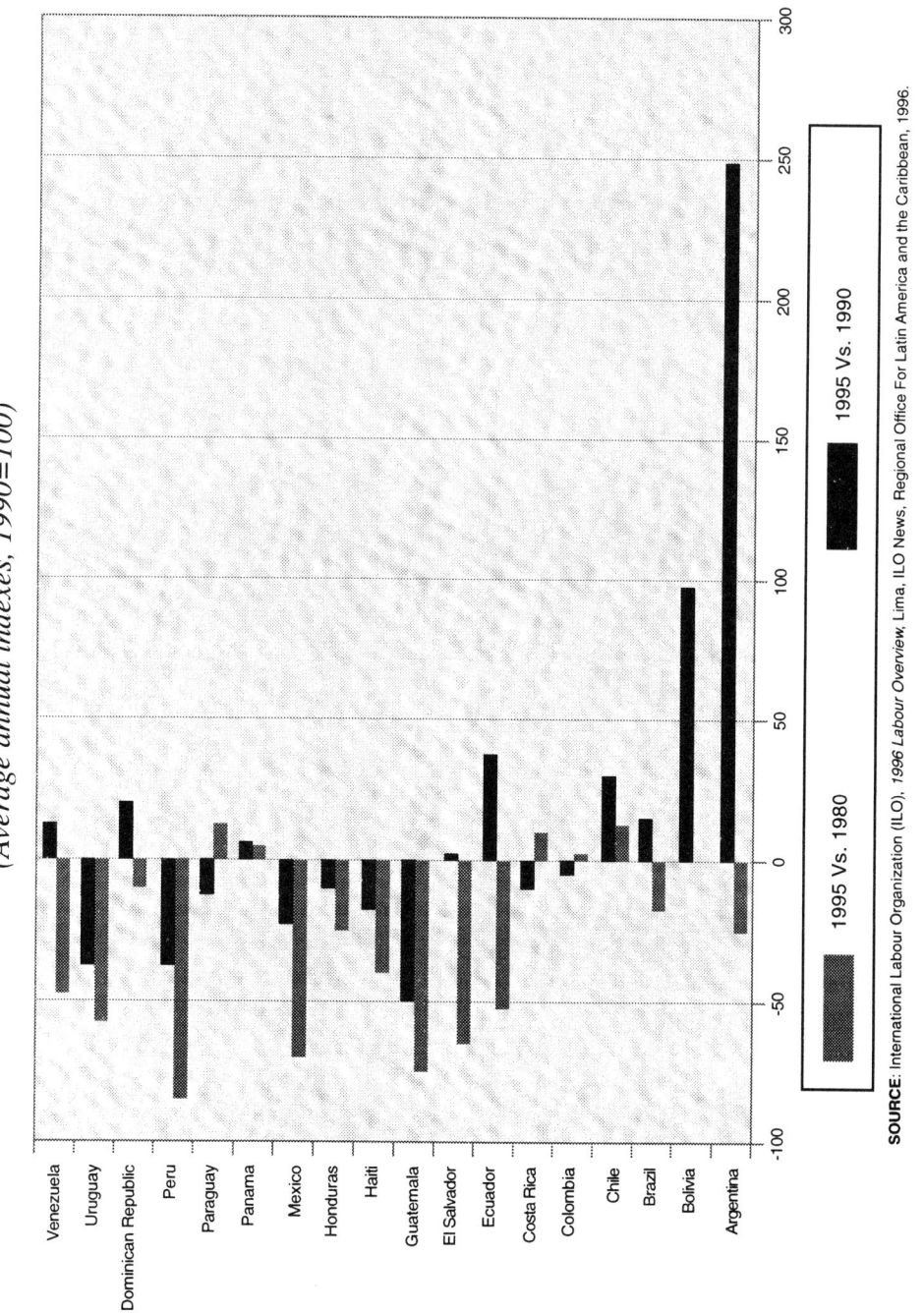

SOURCE: International Labour Organization (ILO). *1996 Labour Overview*, Lima, ILO News, Regional Office For Latin America and the Caribbean, 1996.

Informal-sector earnings that provide a level of household income which is just barely sufficient to cover a family's basic needs make it necessary to turn to labour survival strategies involving the acceptance of substandard forms of employment by women and the premature entry of young people into the labour market, all of which strengthens the vicious circle of poverty. In the presence of low growth rates and a lack of occupational dynamism for protracted periods of time, such strategies tend to harden into permanent behaviour patterns which lessen these sectors' chances of taking advantage of employment opportunities opened up by expansionary phases of the economic cycle.

Another argument which serves to underscore the centrality of growth is that employment demand has shown itself to be more sensitive to variations in levels of economic activity than to variations in the cost of labour. Apparently, wages have only a slight effect on job creation capacity, with a nominal wage increase of 10% translating into a decrease of only 0.4% in industrial employment. Indeed, the data do not support the idea that "lower wages" equals "more employment". The output elasticity of employment, which fluctuates between 0.09 and 0.22, is significantly greater than the wage elasticity of employment, which ranges between 0.1 and 0.13.[22]

The declining trend value of the elasticity of employment relative to output may be due to the fact that, at the present time, the greater openness of the countries' economies, together with corporate reorganization and the use of new technologies, is weakening job creation in the modern sector. In order to attain greater competitiveness in situations where the local currency is overvalued, it becomes necessary to make large increases in productivity, which may be difficult to accomplish quickly without resorting to personnel cuts.

5. Labour income disparities

The broad income gap separating highly-skilled workers from those in low-skill occupations and the fact that this gap is widening in countries whose economies are growing constitute decisive factors in the inequality of income distribution in Latin America.

The distance separating the incomes of professional and technical personnel from those of workers in low-productivity sectors increased by between 40% and 60% in 1990-1994. This was due to the rapid improvement of the labour incomes of skilled manpower and the reduction or lack of growth in pay levels for workers not taking part in the modernization of production, who account for a large percentage of total employment.

The recovery of production levels and the resumption of economic growth —at rates nearing full capacity— are being achieved with smaller increases in employment than were to be expected given the swift pace of expansion in some countries. Hence, it has been difficult to reduce open unemployment and underemployment in the lower income strata. The

---

[22] The average figure for the elasticity of employment relative to output for the period 1990-1995 (an estimated 0.18) is substantially lower than the figure yielded by similar correlations (nearly 0.50) for the same countries in earlier years (ILO, 1996).

number of employed persons per household remains lower in these strata than in middle- and high-income households.

A breakdown of the increase in employment by sector of activity and occupational category also reveals a growing heterogeneity in the types of jobs being created. The use of new business management methods and of state-of-the-art machinery and equipment have created pockets of high productivity in the most dynamic sectors which are spearheading growth in some countries. These sectors mainly employ professional, technical or highly specialized workers, whose wages have begun to rise rapidly, climbing more steeply than wages in activities having average productivity levels and certainly more than the average for the sectors in which they are employed.

On the other hand, as noted earlier, a large number of new jobs are being created in low-productivity sectors. The rapid expansion of capital in the most dynamic industries —which attract a very large share of total investment and are not labour intensive— impedes a greater dissemination of technical progress that would boost the productivity of the economy's technologically backward sectors. This has tended to perpetuate the heterogeneity of productivity levels typically found in the region, one of whose manifestations is a high degree of income dispersion in the labour market, which is in turn an important component of inequality in general.

The maintenance or increase in this scattered distribution of labour income is a major factor in the rigidity of the income distribution structure which has continued to be a feature of recent economic growth in many countries. Wage trends for workers at different skill levels show that in 8 out of 10 countries the gap between the average income of professional and technical workers and that of manual workers employed in low-productivity sectors is widening (see table II.5).

Real wages in professional and technical categories rose sharply in Chile, Paraguay, Uruguay and Venezuela; with the exception of Paraguay, these countries also recorded high GDP growth rates (as much as 8% or even higher in some years) during the first half of the decade.

In some countries, the widening gap between the earned incomes of highly-skilled workers and unskilled workers has stemmed from a more marked decline in the incomes of those employed in low-productivity sectors. This has been the case, for example, in the urban areas of Bolivia and Brazil.

In Colombia, Mexico, Paraguay and Venezuela, the increase in the incomes of professional and technical personnel has coincided with a steep drop in the incomes of relatively unskilled workers, thereby exacerbating existing inequalities.

The income gap between skilled and unskilled wage earners in the formal sector has also tended to widen. With the exception of Bolivia, the average incomes of civil servants and of private-sector wage earners working in medium-sized and large establishments have climbed much more slowly than the incomes of professional and technical workers.

These greater disparities have also contributed to the perpetuation —and, in some countries, exacerbation— of the overall inequality of income distribution.

Table II.5
AVERAGE INCOMES AND LABOUR INCOME DISPARITIES
(Urban areas, 1990-1994)

Country	Year	Average income [a] of:			Income disparities [c]	
		Professional and technical workers (1)	Public employees and private wage earners in firms employing more than five persons (2)	Workers in low-productivity sector [b] (3)	(1)/(2)* 100	(1)/(3)* 100
Bolivia	1989	7.6	3.9	3.4	195	224
	1994	7.2	3.9	2.3	185	313
Brazil	1987	7.7	4.8	3.4	160	226
	1993	7.5	4.4	2.3	170	326
Chile	1990	6.6	4.1 [d]	3.9 [e]	161	169
	1994	8.4	4.8 [d]	4.1 [e]	175	205
Colombia (8 major cities)	1990	6.7	3.3 [d]	3.3 [e]	203	203
	1994	7.9	3.4 [d]	2.7 [e]	232	293
Costa Rica	1990	7.2	5.7	3.2	126	225
	1994	8.2	5.8	3.6	141	228
Honduras	1990	6.5	3.5	1.5	186	433
	1994	4.5	2.4	1.4	188	321
Mexico	1989	5.5	3.5 [d]	4.0 [e]	157	138
	1994	6.3	3.9 [d]	3.1 [e]	162	203
Paraguay (Asunción)	1990	3.9	2.6	2.4	150	163
	1994	6.7	3.2	2.0	209	335
Uruguay	1990	6.0	3.9	2.7	154	222
	1994	9.6	4.9	3.1	196	310
Venezuela	1990	4.2	3.8	3.6	111	117
	1994	6.3	3.4	3.3	185	191

Source: ECLAC, *Social Panorama of Latin America. 1996 Edition* (LC/G.1946-P), Santiago, Chile, 1997. United Nations publication, Sales No. E.97.II.G.4.
[a] Expressed as multiples of the value of the per capita poverty line.
[b] Includes wage earners working in firms employing up to five persons, own-account workers not employed in professional or technical occupations and domestic employees.
[c] Quotient of average incomes.
[d] All public- and private-sector wage earners.
[e] Including only own-account workers not employed in professional or technical occupations and domestic employees.

III. SOCIAL INTEGRATION

An integrated society is one in which its citizens conduct themselves according to socially accepted norms of behaviour and the goals established by the culture are congruent with the opportunity structure for realizing those goals and the training available to individuals to enable them to take advantage of opportunities.

There are always, of course, some behaviours that do not conform to the norms. Non-conformist behaviour may take various forms in different time periods. It can bring about greater social cohesion, but may also unleash processes of disintegration. The latter are often associated with exclusion, that is, with circumstances in which the society fails to provide some of its members with the necessary means (opportunities) to achieve the goals imposed by the culture.

The legacy of past deficiencies adverse to integration in combination with the new risks of disintegration inherent in the current situation make it urgent to provide opportunities for segments of the population who have hitherto been left out of economic growth and social and political development to participate actively in their society. To achieve this goal, ways must be found to provide them with access to productive work for better pay and essential social services, and at the same time to set up appropriate channels through which they can participate in society and exercise full citizenship.

1. Social integration and diversity

It is important to recognize that social integration does not imply homogeneity. A modern society respects the right to individual cultural identity and increasingly values diversity for the creative contribution that each cultural group can make towards overcoming the problems of the society. From this perspective, a society can share overall norms and goals, while still leaving room for a broad range of specific goals at the individual and group levels. This concept is especially relevant to Latin America and the Caribbean, whose societies are and see themselves as multi-ethnic and multicultural.

The region is far from achieving high levels of social integration: poverty, unemployment and underemployment, inequitable income distribution and social segmentation with regard to education are prevalent structural phenomena.

Against this background of exclusion, a new reality is taking shape through globalization and economic opening and will undoubtedly have an impact on the region's societies.

There are two ways of viewing the situation. Some feel that economic opening and globalization will in the future create greater opportunities for all, as innovations in technology and communications help individuals to realize their potential. Others feel that the new trends will usher in a period of uncertainty, in which the old pathways of social mobility will disappear, while the new will open slowly and remain virtually closed to large segments of the population; hence, in this view, exclusion and marginalization will tend to increase and weaken the social fabric.[23]

Globalization is challenging the traditional notion of social integration, both through economic shifts and through the new influences brought in by the culture and entertainment industry. Social gaps are widening, but at the same time there is a proliferation of networks uniting multiple groups. Societies are fragmenting, but are also being enriched by diversity.

Public perception of the opportunities for attaining socially accepted goals is critical. One indicator of this attitude is how widely the public believes the benefits of growth are being distributed. In a recent survey, over two thirds of those polled in Brazil, Paraguay and Mexico (78%, 76% and 68%, respectively) consider wealth either somewhat or very unfairly distributed; of those surveyed in Venezuela, Argentina and Uruguay, 66% share that view; while in Chile the figure is 61% (Huneeus, 1996, p. 28).

The region's experience of development seems to have been marred by frustrated expectations; there is a perception that opportunities for development and personal realization have not been spread equitably. On the one hand, expectations have been raised as people internalize the aspirations publicized by the mass media, in school and in political debate; on the other hand, opportunities for social mobility and consumption have not been generated to match those aspirations.[24]

The problem is particularly acute among young people who are emerging from a long process of education with high expectations of good earning potential, only to find that they have few opportunities of obtaining productive employment. Moreover, as a group they have greater than average access to information and stimuli about the new and varied goods and services that constitute symbols of social mobility and yet are out of their reach. It is no

---

[23] Disintegration can occur even in countries that are considered highly integrated, Uruguay, for example, whose society has been described as having a "relatively high level of equity, effective social democracy, symmetry in day-to-day relationships, an absence of barriers to easy communication between people at different income levels, solid political democracy and a high level of integration based on the combination of equity and democracy" (Kaztman, 1996).

[24] In comparison with the other developing regions, Latin America has the highest percentage of television receivers per 1,000 inhabitants and the poorest income distribution. In Brazil, which has the largest total number of poor and the least equitable income distribution, there were 213 television sets per 1,000 inhabitants in 1990, a figure typical of an industrialized country.

accident, then, that in many Latin American cities both political and criminal violence often involves young people who are unemployed or poorly employed.

2. Situations that undermine social integration

There are some critical problems in the region that threaten social integration in a variety of ways.

a) The first of these is the accretion of pockets of "hard-core" poverty, a term applied to social groups living in conditions that prevent them from finding productive employment and make it hard for them to communicate with other groups, so that they lack the skills they need to participate actively in modern society and are thus excluded from real citizenship. It is often hard to find a way of reaching these groups through social policies.

These marginal poor are identified by their reduced capacity to take advantage of the existing opportunity structure. Their lifestyle is marked by the absence of a project to incorporate themselves into the larger society, low self-esteem and few expectations of improving their level of well-being.

The hard-core poor include both the disruptive and the disheartened —the two emotional faces of disintegration. Among the former are urban youth who typically have dropped out of school, live in poorly constituted family groups where they receive inadequate socialization, reside in marginal areas and lack jobs. As a group they are prone to common crime, have a high incidence of anomic behaviour and often resort to violence to resolve conflicts. The second group —the disheartened— include older people without adequate economic resources or support networks; female heads of household who have poorly paid employment; rural people without access to credit, training, modern technology and markets; and ethnic minorities who have been uprooted from their traditional cultures without being assimilated into modern society.

b) Another threat to social integration is ethnic discrimination, the roots of which go back centuries in some countries of the region. Denying value to the identity of some ethnic or cultural group makes it difficult for its members to assume a full, recognized role in society. When this denial of the "different other" derives from attitudes of an ethnic group belonging to the dominant culture, the result is invariably blockage of access to material resources and to information and knowledge essential to achieving minimum levels of physical well-being.

Ethnic discrimination may even result in the destruction of the culture and identity of a given group, either as a deliberate policy or as the unintentional effect of attitudes of disdain transmitted through the communications media and the school system. Those discriminated against may internalize such attitudes and deny their own identity.

Essential prerequisites for overcoming ethnic discrimination are the dissemination of knowledge about the non-dominant cultures and the recognition that achieving social integration does not mean that all members of multicultural nations must necessarily share the same concept of success. Social mobility, for example, is a personal goal, one among other legitimate personal goals, and a society may not demand that an individual abandon his or her individual ethnic and cultural identity in order to be upwardly mobile.

c) Another critical set of problems relates to the family group, the basic unit for socialization and transmission of individual behaviours. When the heads of the household have low levels of education or regularly display violence or irresponsibility towards the rest of the family, this situation tends to lower the probability that the children in the household will attain good levels of education and behave responsibly in the future. Parents are the formative models for norms and standards, and they inculcate habits and create the links between their children and the world of work and the culture at large. They thus constitute essential social capital for facilitating the social integration of children and adolescents. In Latin America and the Caribbean, statistics on intra-family violence and paternal irresponsibility towards children are alarming, both because of the high incidence of such behaviour and because it tends to be transmitted from generation to generation.

d) Another issue of concern is residential segregation. A large percentage of children and adolescents live in the many makeshift settlements in the region. The typical isolation of such settlements is not helpful —indeed, is a major obstacle— to interchanges of all kinds with the rest of society. This situation fosters disintegration, generates feelings of not belonging to society at large, and creates subcultures with their own norms of coexistence and networks of reciprocity limited to the settlement, all of which have the additional effect of making it harder to move into the labour force later on. The inhabitants of such settlements are deprived of access to legitimate avenues for achieving the goals their society extols, and this situation generates deviant conduct. An extreme example is provided by the children in marginal neighbourhoods in Medellín who act as hired assassins.

The difficulties faced by those who live in makeshift settlements in satisfying their minimum needs and their lack of access to normal channels for obtaining justice and protection as citizens leads them to adopt socially unacceptable means of survival and to resort to illegal expedients to earn income, expedients such as affiliation with organized crime, drug trafficking, neighbourhood violence and even murder as a means of settling accounts or acquiring power and profit.

e) In many countries of the region, urban violence is increasing. It exacts a high toll in both human and economic terms by generating a climate of public insecurity, corroding the bases of citizenship and discouraging investment. In some countries, this problem has reached critical proportions, a fact recorded in the vital statistics and reflected in the basic norms of social behaviour (see box III.1).

There is also a strong correlation in the region between urban concentration, the accretion of pockets of hard-core urban poverty and an increase in violence. The rise in urban homicide rates that accompanies urban growth is an alarming indicator of the problems of social disintegration, since "Latin American cities are young and growing rapidly, and are therefore constantly undergoing changes in their culture, their administrative and political systems and their socio-territorial organization", all of which produces cities that are "highly fragmented by economic gulfs, cultural rifts and social inequalities" (Carrión, 1995).

At the present time, 74% of the people of Latin America and the Caribbean live in urban areas; by the year 2000 it is estimated that the urban population of the region will be the world's largest, as a result of late but extremely rapid urbanization. Simultaneously, over the past decade, urban violence in Latin America has grown at an unprecedented pace. In Colombia, for example, homicide rates tripled during the period 1983-1992; in Peru they increased by a multiple of five between 1986 and 1991; in Panama they doubled in the three-year period 1988-1990. It is also disturbing that in some countries where violence did not use to be a major cause of concern, public opinion today has changed as result of increased threats to physical safety in daily life (see figures III.1, III.2 and III.3).

Box III.1

VIOLENCE IN COLOMBIA

The rate of homicides in Colombia is among the highest in the world (along with those of Brazil, Mexico and Panama). Around 1990, 37% of male deaths were ascribed to external causes. Among young men, violence is the main cause of death.

The impact of the violence in the country is felt in the socio-political sphere, in the world of drug trafficking and in the life of the ordinary citizen. During the period 1984-1994, between 545,000 and 628,000 persons, approximately 2% of the population, were displaced as the result of violence. In the metropolitan area of Cali, the homicide rate per 100,000 inhabitants increased from 32 to 89 between 1980 and 1992. In Medellín, between 1980 and 1986 the number of homicides were twice the figure for Cali, and during the past decade there were more than 40,000 such deaths. In the Valle del Cauca area, 64% of crimes are crimes of violence and 16% are homicides. Of the women included in the prevalence, demography and health survey conducted in Colombia in 1990, one of every five said that she had been beaten at least once, and one of every ten said that she had been sexually forced.

Source: Episcopal Conference on Colombia, "Derechos humanos y desplazamiento interno en Colombia", Bogotá, Colombia, 1995; Alvaro Guzmán and others, "Violencia urbana en Cali durante 1993: una primera aproximación", *Boletín socioeconómico*, No. 27, Cali, June 1994, pp. 17-32; Association for Family Welfare/Institute for Resource Development, "Colombia: encuestas de prevalencia, demografía y salud 1990", Bogotá, Colombia, 1991, pp. 165-179.

---

f) Another situation with serious potential for social breakdown is the nexus of drug trafficking, corruption and violence. Although these three phenomena are not equivalent, they are often interconnected, and the most corrosive aspect of their combined impact is that they undermine the basic norms of coexistence and erode governability. The majority of people identify precisely these three —corruption, drugs and crime— as the most pressing political problems today (see figure III.4). In seven of the eight countries covered by the Latinobarómetro survey, over 50% of those surveyed think that drug addiction, drug trafficking, corruption and crime have increased greatly over the last five years (Huneeus, 1996).

g) Lastly, lack of access to justice is a serious problem that undermines social integration in many ways: loss of public confidence in the institutions of justice and public protection and safety; substandard conditions and poor security in prisons; lack of access to legal defense for low-income individuals and, in many cases, lengthy periods of detention because of the slow pace of legal proceedings; and last but not least, a general perception that some groups in society enjoy impunity, or that access to justice depends on income level.

Lack of confidence in the system of justice and law and order breeds deviant behaviour and undermines the value system of the community, thereby making coexistence more problematic. Creating and strengthening public confidence requires a transparent, fair and

Figure III.1
CHILE: PERCEPTION OF INCREASE IN CRIME IN 1996 OVER THE PAST YEAR

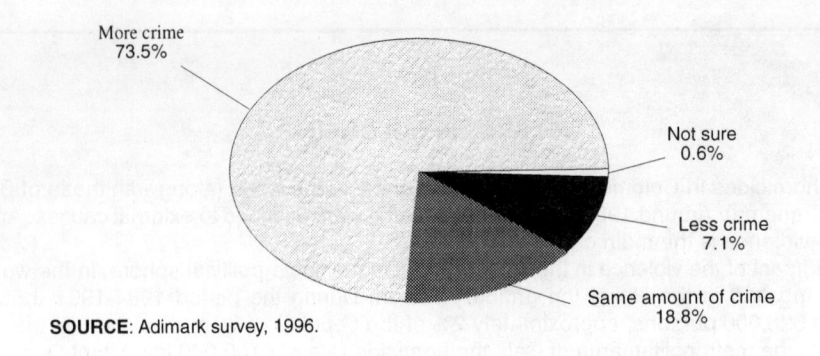

- More crime: 73.5%
- Not sure: 0.6%
- Less crime: 7.1%
- Same amount of crime: 18.8%

SOURCE: Adimark survey, 1996.

Figure III.2
CHILE: PERCEPTION OF INCREASE IN VIOLENCE OF CRIMES IN 1996 OVER THE PAST YEAR

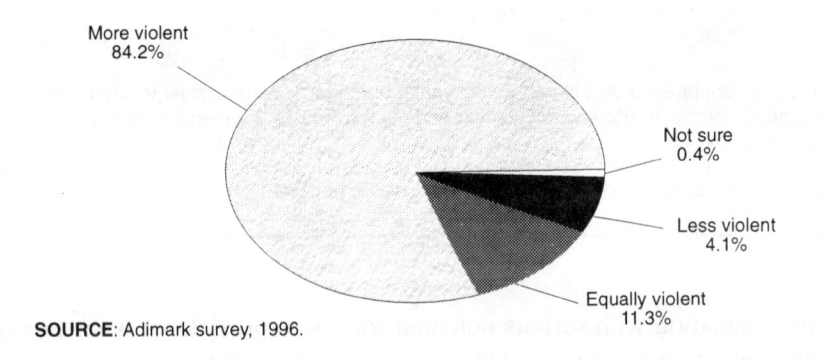

- More violent: 84.2%
- Not sure: 0.4%
- Less violent: 4.1%
- Equally violent: 11.3%

SOURCE: Adimark survey, 1996.

Figure III.3
CRIME OVER THE LAST FIVE YEARS

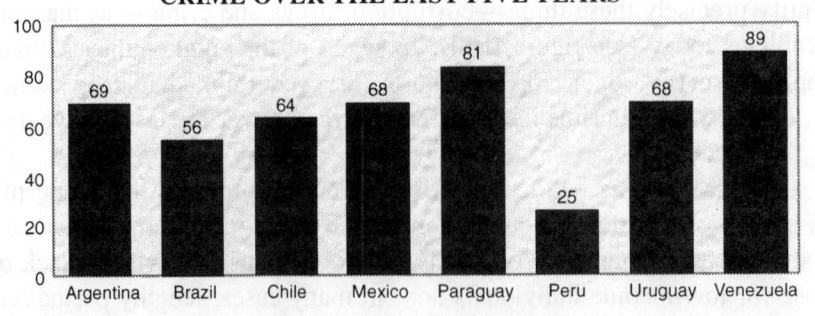

Country	%
Argentina	69
Brazil	56
Chile	64
Mexico	68
Paraguay	81
Peru	25
Uruguay	68
Venezuela	89

Question: As I read you this list of problems, for each tell me whether you think it has increased a great deal; has increased somewhat; has decreased a great deal; has decreased somewath; or has remained the same over the last five years.
Crime: graph depicts "have increased a great deal" responses only.

SOURCE: Latinobarómetro survey, 1995.

Figure III.4
MOST PRESSING PROBLEMS
Political problems

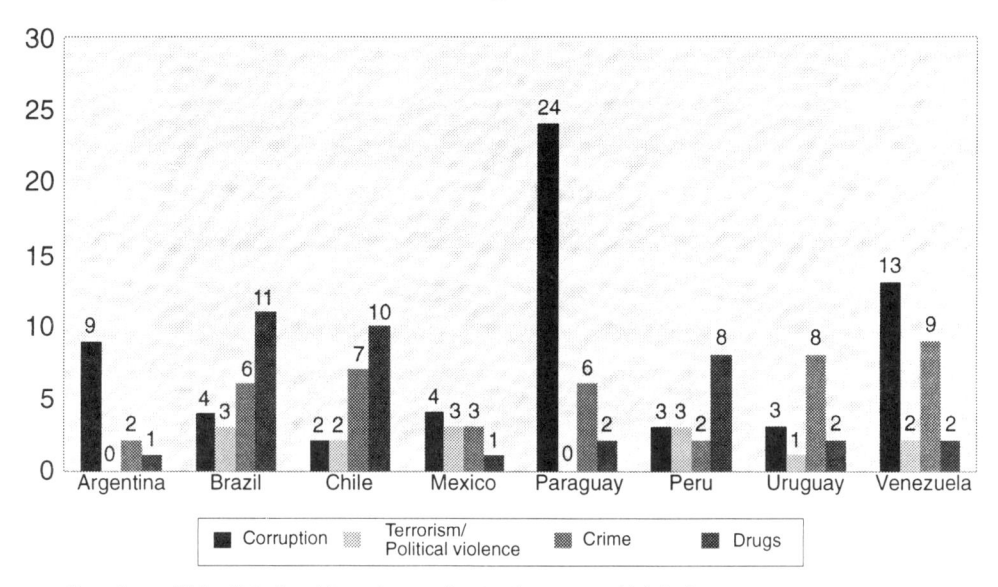

Country	Corruption	Terrorism/Political violence	Crime	Drugs
Argentina	9	2	0	1
Brazil	4	3	6	11
Chile	2	2	7	10
Mexico	4	3	3	1
Paraguay	24	0	6	2
Peru	3	3	2	8
Uruguay	3	1	8	2
Venezuela	13	2	9	2

Questions: Of the list of problems I am going to show you, which is the most important?
Political problems only.

SOURCE: Latinobarómetro survey, 1995.

effective judicial system that does not erect barriers against the poorest groups; a system of law and order that ensures protection and respect for the physical integrity of individuals; and a penal system that avoids both impunity and the moral degradation of those in detention.

The above-mentioned phenomena have generated a "public insecurity syndrome", that is, a general feeling of insecurity that derives from the perception that antisocial behaviour is on the rise and from lack of confidence in the institutions (the judiciary and the police) that should be keeping a check on such behaviour.

What is more, the consequences go beyond perception and influence patterns of life. A widespread sense of insecurity leads people, for example, to restrict their visits to public spaces, avoid going out at night or entering certain neighbourhoods, remain shut up their houses and seek entertainment in the privacy of their homes (see figure III.5). The net effect is to reduce interactions with people of different social origins and to depress the spontaneous sociability that results from encounters in public places. Social classes and groups associate only with their peers and develop a feeling of distrust towards all others, those who are "different". The shape of the city changes, as gated communities and condominiums proliferate and many opt to live in apartments rather than houses. Expenditure rises on theft insurance, guard services, and weapons for personal protection. Commercial activities start to be concentrated in big shopping centres or malls, because they are perceived as being safer in terms of muggings and accidents. This behaviour is accompanied by an increased fear of poor and marginal individuals as potential criminals.

To sum up, the process of development in the region over the course of its history has created pathways of social mobility and progressively incorporated some social groups; to

Figure III.5
CHILE: HABITS ADOPTED DURING THE PAST YEAR TO AVOID CRIME
(Percentages)

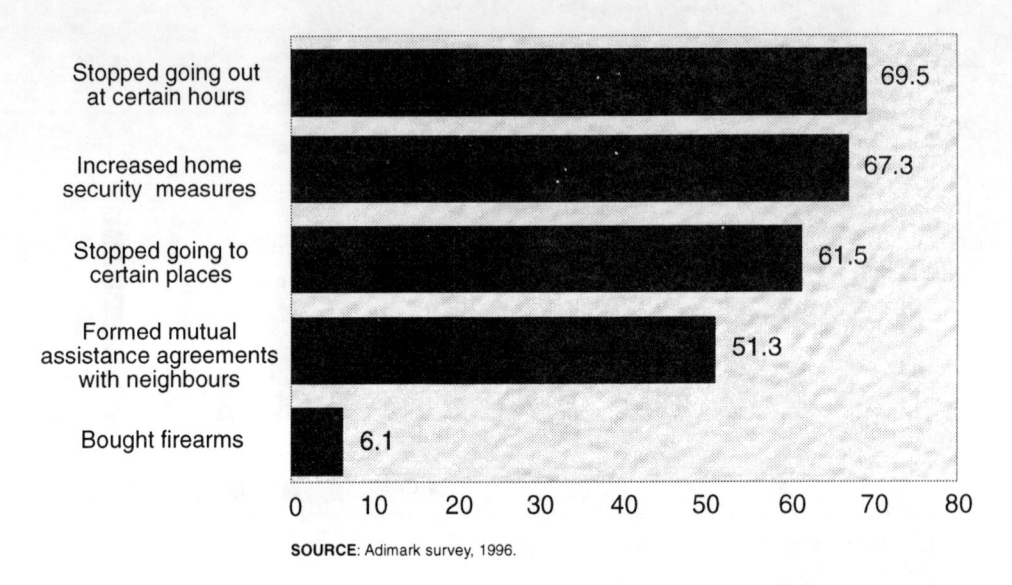

Habit	Percentage
Stopped going out at certain hours	69.5
Increased home security measures	67.3
Stopped going to certain places	61.5
Formed mutual assistance agreements with neighbours	51.3
Bought firearms	6.1

SOURCE: Adimark survey, 1996.

date, however, it has not succeeded in creating fully integrated, equitable and non-exclusive societies. The globalization process now under way is creating new strains in the region; while greater integration is achieved on the symbolic level —through expanded access to communications and information media—, at the same time large segments of the population are becoming more thoroughly excluded.

What results are societies in which many people perceive a wide gap between expectation and reality, a perception that sets the stage for social and political conflict that could weaken the still fragile structures of democracy. In order to give a positive turn to these conflicts, the problems here discussed, which are tending to fragment the region's societies, must be overcome: the persistence of large pockets of "hard-core" poverty; ethnic discrimination; the breakdown of the family; residential segregation; lack of access to justice; urban violence; growing drug use, drug trafficking and corruption; and the remoteness and lack of transparency of government.

It can be said in general that this set of problems, many of them closely interrelated, weaken or destroy a sense of a common identity, the acceptance of common norms of behaviour and the exercise of effective citizenship, while reinforcing patterns of exclusivity and distrust of public institutions. Achieving a greater degree of social integration therefore depends heavily on the recreation of pathways of social mobility that are adapted to the changes now in progress; on a development approach that generates greater equality of opportunity by combining growth with equity; on a public sphere that recognizes and values diversity and encourages civil society to take an active role; and on a political system that represents and balances the demands and interests of all citizens.

PART TWO:
REFORMS NOW UNDER WAY

IV.   Economic reforms

V.   Social reforms

PART TWO:

IV. ECONOMIC REFORMS

1. An overview

The process set in motion by economic and political reforms in the region can be interpreted as a search for a progressive institutionalization of open, competitive market economies coupled with attempts to introduce adjustments in the interests of greater social equity within a context of increasing democracy.

Against this backdrop, rapid progress is being made towards new economic structures defined in terms of the interaction of firms, agents of production, markets, sectoral policies and regulatory mechanisms. What is different now is that most —if not all— of the above elements are in the process of readapting to new national and international circumstances. It therefore stands to reason that they all find themselves in an unstable balance or are in transition towards a longer-term equilibrium.

This accounts for the marked asymmetry that exists between changes in policy (the rules of the game) which have occurred at a fairly rapid pace, and the belated response in terms of organizational readjustments. At a time when the regional development strategy is undergoing a substantive shift in direction, this general lack of institutional flexibility not only prevents the region from taking full advantage of new opportunities but also makes it impossible to ensure that the body or process that is being reformed will function properly. This is one of the factors which makes an examination of public policies and State reform so urgent.

a) Latin America is undergoing an intense transformation

Never before has a form of democratic pluralism existed in so many countries of the region at the same time. Above and beyond any weaknesses or constraints that may mark the exercise of democracy, these participatory regimes appear to be taking hold and consolidating, as they must in order to fulfil one of the intrinsic requirements of modernization.

Economic reforms are enabling the region to move forward in terms of macroeconomic stabilization and international competitiveness on the basis of fiscal discipline, trade and financial liberalization, the operation of market mechanisms, greater confidence in private investment and new incentive regimes and regulatory frameworks. Taken as a whole, their shortcomings notwithstanding (of which more will be said below), these reforms are engendering a fundamental transformation of the regional development process.

b) **International linkages are expanding and substantial progress is being made towards regional integration**

The economies of the region are moving towards a much stronger outward orientation based, to a great extent, on a more intensive development of natural resources. The export ratio increased from 14% of GDP in 1980 to 21% in 1990 and to 25% in 1995. This dynamism is in part a reflection of the expansion of trade within the Latin American and Caribbean region, which has been stimulated by a number of trade agreements and the further development of integration schemes. This trend has also been accompanied by a notable upsurge in intraregional investment in conjunction with an increasing level of competitiveness on the part of a growing number of firms and industries and significant progress in terms of businesses' ability to gain access to foreign markets. Progress has also been made in the areas of export diversification and the application of technical progress in the development of natural resources (agriculture, forestry, fisheries, mining and natural resource-intensive industries), as well as in the modernization of financial, telecommunications, energy and transport services.

c) **Economic reforms have achieved a great deal in terms of stability, but are proving less satisfactory in promoting growth and social equity**

The above-mentioned successes notwithstanding, most of the economies continue to operate within a framework of vulnerability and moderate growth, and their results in the social sphere are still clearly unsatisfactory. The political institutional structure is subject to tensions stemming not only from the difficulty of making an orderly transition to new patterns of development, but also from the questions being raised in many countries about the transparency and integrity with which public affairs are conducted in situations where civil society does not always have effective supervisory and safeguard mechanisms at its command.

As a result of economic reforms, the countries of the region have made considerable headway with respect to stabilization and, as mentioned, the implementation of thorough-going structural reforms. However, the social costs of stabilization and reform have generally been high. Hence, with few exceptions, GDP growth rates have been moderate (3% per annum in 1990-1996), thus falling below both historical levels (5.5% per annum in 1945-

1980) and the levels which ECLAC has estimated to be necessary in order to deal with existing technological and equity lags (6% a year). Consequently, as has been demonstrated in preceding chapters, only in exceptional cases has it been possible to identify tangible successes in terms of growth and poverty reduction. More uncommon still are situations where the simultaneous achievement of these goals has been coupled with improvements in income distribution.

Moreover, the region's economies continue to function within a framework of vulnerability. In most cases, macroeconomic stability has been achieved at the cost of high balance-of-payments current account deficits, sometimes financed with volatile capital that is liable to take flight should any event occur which shakes investors' confidence. This phenomenon has at times combined with the fragility of the relevant financial systems to drive up the cost of public finance.

Savings rates, and especially investment coefficients, which fell sharply in the 1980s, are making a quite slow recovery in the 1990s and in the vast majority of the countries have not yet regained their pre-crisis levels.

In summary, the consolidation of the transformation process will hinge on two factors: on the one hand, the possibility of establishing a complementary relationship between growth and social equity; and on the other, the ability to ensure that economic and social policy stances are founded upon solid institutional arrangements.

d) The intense economic restructuring process is producing new winners and losers

The processes of adjustment, macroeconomic stabilization and structural reform initiated in the wake of the external debt crisis acted as a powerful screening device that forced each economic agent to seek ways of adapting to new price signal scenarios and forms of regulating production activity.

The segments of the production system that were most affected by these changes in the ground rules and in regulatory frameworks were those branches of industry whose output was destined for the domestic market, small and medium-sized enterprises and State-owned enterprises in general. The sectors that were most successful in adapting to the new circumstances were export industries, natural resource- based activities, large locally-owned conglomerates and many transnational corporations.

The structural heterogeneity characteristic of the region's production systems has been accentuated by the widening productivity gap between large firms at the forefront of the modernization process and the broad range of activities that are falling behind in this same process. The productivity gains that are being made are occurring in the modern manufacturing sector, export agriculture, large-scale mining firms, the energy sector, the telecommunications industry and financial services, and tend to be concentrated both across and within sectors. These circumstances exacerbate internal productivity gaps and heighten the degree of economic concentration in the production structure. In the absence of a more determined effort to provide training, adjust the production structure and promote the dissemination of technology, the increase in these differentials lays the foundations for even greater social inequality and affects the economy's growth potential, since they curb the propagation of linkages, the dissemination of technical progress and the effectiveness of exports as an engine of development.

These sharp productivity differentials between the bulk of firms and the front runners in each sector are mirrored in widening wage differentials and a sharp lag in pay levels for low-skill jobs.

The type of productive restructuring now in progress has not yet translated into the creation of a sufficient number of jobs. In view of the impact of wages and employment in terms of the level of inequality, such a situation has been reflected in the fact that, in many countries, social equity indicators have still not regained their pre-crisis levels. With the downturn in employment and the rise in inequality and poverty caused by the recession and adjustment stemmed, if not always surmounted, the current growth phase has seen only a very slow increase in good-quality jobs, and relative pay rates for jobs at differing skill levels have tended to grow further apart.

e) **The second half of the 1990s may witness more discontent among the populace**

Even before the Mexican financial crisis, the global economy was already showing signs of major weaknesses. Initially, due to the very magnitude of the crisis, society and particularly the poorest groups within it came to attach a great deal of value to the attainment of stability. Nonetheless, the social lags mentioned earlier have led to growing displays of dissatisfaction on the part of various segments of the population.

It would not necessarily be correct to link this discontent with populist movements. For one thing, there have been growing signs of social asymmetry in the way in which the costs and benefits of economic restructuring are being distributed. Even more importantly, however, there are no explicit, institutionalized mechanisms for lending credibility to the stated intention of dividing up the fruits of future growth equitably.

This becomes all the more evident when, as now, a vigorous economic restructuring process is under way. What appears to be taking place in most cases is a relative deterioration in compensatory social policies and only marginal —though recently expanding— efforts to revitalize policies for making development more accessible.

From this viewpoint, today's challenge would appear to be how to combine the advantages of market competition with those to be derived from cooperation among the relevant agents, both at the inter-firm level and between Government and the private sector. This holds true with respect to macroeconomic, microeconomic and sectoral policies as well, but is of fundamental importance in respect of policies aimed at building a social consensus among various actors as to the main direction or paths which the development process should take.

2. Employment and labour reforms

a) **The sphere of reform**

In 1990-1995, a number of countries in Latin America reformed their labour laws, and especially those sections dealing with employment contracts, dismissal and collective bargaining (see table IV.1).

ECONOMIC REFORMS

Table IV.1
ISSUES ADDRESSED BY LABOUR REFORMS, BY COUNTRY, 1990-1995

Issue	Argentina	Bolivia	Brazil	Chile	Colombia	Costa Rica	Paraguay	Peru	Uruguay	Venezuela
Hiring	X	X		X	X			X		
Dismissal				X	X	X	X	X		
Collective bargaining	X		X	X				X		X
Minimum wage										X
Size of pensions				X	X					
Vacation							X	X		
Maternity leave						X				X
Rights of nursing mothers						X	X			
Gender-based discrimination			X							
Sexual harassment						X	X			
Youth labour								X		
Unions				X				X		
Union rights			X			X	X			
Strikes								X		
Social security				X	X				X	X
Accident insurance	X			X						
Unemployment insurance					X					
Occupational safety				X					X	
Forced labour			X							
Smoking in the workplace						X				
Special regimes									X	X
Public-sector workers' associations				X						X

Source: ECLAC, *Social Panorama of Latin America. 1996 Edition* (LC/G.1946-P), Santiago, Chile, 1997, table VI.1. United Nations publication, Sales No. E.97.II.G.4.

These reform efforts have taken differing directions, with no one single trend predominating, although the idea of making hiring and firing procedures more flexible has been in evidence in most recent amendments. Labour reforms have sought to boost hiring by making it easier to dismiss workers or to hire them on a temporary basis and by establishing regulations governing collective bargaining. In some countries, there have been attempts to reduce labour costs and revamp unemployment funds (e.g., the elimination of "double retroactivity" in Colombia); furthermore, in cases where workers are dismissed without just cause, the amount of severance pay has been reduced or the grounds for dismissal have been broadened. Some of the reforms carried out in Argentina, Bolivia, Chile, Colombia and Peru fit into this general pattern. In some countries, the existence of strong labour unions has hindered employer-led efforts to make labour laws more flexible.

On the other hand, legislation has also been enacted to improve working conditions and minimum wages for workers as a whole, as well as to protect particular types of workers by, for example, regulating the hiring of temporary workers, wage earners in small and medium-sized enterprises and domestic employees. In addition, laws have been passed to defend union rights, protect women from discriminatory practices, abolish child labour and regulate youth labour (Brazil, Chile, Costa Rica, Peru and Venezuela).

It is generally agreed that the growing flexibility of the labour market in most countries of Latin America has primarily been a response to de facto situations rather than the result of explicit regulations, and that the changes that have taken place in the job market are out of step with labour regulations. Regulations have been introduced which modify certain aspects of labour relations, but, except in a few cases, comprehensive legislative reform efforts that would systematically address the many different facets of those relations in their entirety have not been mounted. Thus, the region is confronted with a panorama of stark contrasts between minority groups of workers who enjoy extensive protection and other groups that are, for the most part, not covered by labour legislation, as is the case of workers employed in small-scale and micro-enterprises, and independent, subcontracted and seasonal workers.

The possible effects of increasing labour flexibility and its implications in terms of job creation, labour costs and working conditions are a subject of debate. These issues, along with others concerning the abolition of child labour, the setting of minimum wages and, in particular, unemployment insurance, make up the agenda of labour reforms that are now being implemented or are under discussion in the countries' legislatures or in tripartite talks (see box IV.1). The most controversial issues have to do with setting limits and striking a balance between employers' need for flexibility in dealing with the new realities of global competition and integration, on the one hand, and workers' needs for job stability or protection in situations of growing unemployment, on the other.

In sum, relations between employers and their employees are in vital need of modernization, since, as it becomes increasingly important to gain workers' allegiance, it will become more and more necessary to view them as collaborative partners rather than as adversaries or a mere factor of production. Modernizing labour relations within each firm and making the transition from a confrontational to a cooperative stance involves many aspects, one of the most important of which is the concept of participation as a means of achieving higher levels of productivity and, hence, better pay.

Box IV.1

LATIN AMERICA: PROPOSALS CONCERNING UNEMPLOYMENT INSURANCE

In both developing and developed countries, experiences, alternatives and proposals in regard to unemployment insurance are a topic of discussion. An increasing lack of job security, coupled with high unemployment, has prompted Latin Americans to become interested in examining the various possible types of unemployment insurance systems.

Insurance-based systems and savings-based systems. In an insurance-based system, the risk of becoming unemployed is shared among all the workers who pay into the system. The benefits paid to unemployed persons are covered by the contributions of the employed workers, without any need for prior accumulation of funds. The main disadvantage of such a system lies in the fact that it reduces both incentives to avoid dismissal and interest in finding a new job, since the duration of benefits depends on the length of time the worker is unemployed. International data confirm that such a system results in a rise in unemployment across the board, a lengthening of the period of unemployment and a level of abuse of the system which endangers its continued operation. One possible modification would be to make this system more like a savings-based system by linking the duration of benefits to the number of prior contributions; the disadvantage here is that the worker only qualifies for the benefit if he has already accumulated funds.

Severance pay. Compensatory payments based on years of service that are provided to workers who are dismissed through no fault of their own are also a form of unemployment coverage. This mechanism has the advantage of reducing two sources of abuse that occur in an insurance system. First, as this system imposes a cost on the employer at the time of dismissal, it forestalls situations in which workers and employers agree to temporary dismissals or make resignations appear as though they were dismissals so that the worker can obtain insurance benefits. Second, since the dismissed worker receives the entire amount of compensation, regardless of how long he or she is out of work, there is no reduction in the incentive to look for a new job. The main drawbacks have to do with the worker's length of service with the firm; if this is short, the worker will not have sufficient resources to cope with the period of unemployment, while if he or she has been with the firm for a long period of time, he or she will have an incentive to seek dismissal deliberately in order to obtain the substantial amount of severance pay that has been accrued. In a similar vein, the employer may prod a worker into resigning in order to avoid paying compensation. Lastly, at the level of the firm, mass lay-offs worsen a firm's problems during an economic downturn, thereby threatening its survival and, ultimately, even the payment of compensation. The fact that severance pay acts as a disincentive for dismissal is in the interests of the worker, since it reduces the likelihood of dismissal; however, it is a disadvantage from the point of view of the employer, who takes these costs into account when hiring new workers and reduces their net remuneration accordingly.

Welfare benefits. When unemployment insurance systems do not provide sufficient coverage to supply an unemployed person with the means of subsistence, the State may provide the person with a subsidy. Such benefits are in keeping with the rationale behind social policies designed to meet basic needs; the actual amount of the benefit is very low, equivalent to only a fraction of the minimum wage.

Source: Postgraduate Programme in Economics conducted jointly by ILADES and Georgetown University, *Trabajo de Asesoría al Congreso Nacional (TASC)*, No. 73, Santiago, Chile, October 1996.

b) Job creation programmes

In the 1990s, most of the countries in the region have implemented a variety of reforms and programmes designed to generate employment, increase organizational efficiency, boost productivity and facilitate the adjustment to modernization processes through the incorporation of technological advances. Most of the countries have also made changes in their labour laws, created new training models and modified their labour management modalities through the use of new wage incentives.

In order to mitigate the impact of their economies' difficulties with respect to job creation, the countries have instituted a range of programmes which, for purposes of analysis, can be grouped into five categories on the basis of certain features that they have in common; these programme categories are: the creation of temporary jobs; incentives for private enterprise; on-the-job training and internships; skills training and relocation of workers in declining industries; and training and credit for owners of small-scale and micro-enterprises. These kinds of programmes have been implemented in various combinations in most of the countries of the region. As a general rule, their aims are to train unemployed youth (e.g., the "Chile-Joven", or "Young-Chile" model, now being applied in Argentina, Peru and Venezuela); create opportunities for self-employment by upgrading business skills and providing loan assistance to owners of small businesses and micro-enterprises (revolving fund-type programmes, Brazil's pro-employment scheme); and use tax incentives to encourage private firms to take on workers and provide them with training. These programmes are targeted at specific groups such as men and women who own small businesses, women heads of household, the unemployed and young people. Some are financed by social investment funds created specifically for that purpose; others are funded out of the countries' national budgets, with inputs taking the form of reimbursable loans and tax revenues. Institutional coordination is the responsibility of various ministries (Labour, Agriculture or Education, depending on the nature of the programme) or the national employment service (see table IV.2).

These job programmes highlight such aspects as a better understanding of the relationship between the labour supply and the needs of the labour market; the training of target groups and the creation of jobs for the more vulnerable groups in society; participation by non-governmental organizations; trainer training; consideration of the gender dimension in training; increasing the self-esteem of those undergoing training; and the design of flexible programmes that can be tailored to different social and labour contexts. The factors that make for the success of a programme in one particular country may not necessarily work the same way in others, however.

One of the areas requiring further attention is the lack of prospective data on the labour market, including the type of information needed in order to provide skills training that more fully meets the actual needs of business firms. The processes used to select target groups and intersectoral coordination should also be improved in order to avoid the dispersion of resources and promote more systematic programme monitoring and supervision.

Table IV.2
LATIN AMERICA: APPLIED JOB PROGRAMME MODELS

Type	Objectives	Target population	Institution	Achievements	Problems	Funding	Countries
I. Emergency temporary job creation	To create temporary jobs in infrastructure projects and community services	Unemployed people living in extreme poverty	Social emergency/investment funds	Jobs created for the poorest of the unemployed	Temporary nature of the jobs created, poor job quality	External sources and non-reimbursable loans	Argentina, Bolivia, Brazil, Costa Rica[a], Mexico, Nicaragua, Venezuela
II. Incentives for private enterprise	To give the private sector incentives to hire and train workers	Trainable young and middle-aged people	Ministries of Labour	Enlistment of private sector	Actual number of jobs created	Budget, development banks	Argentina, Brazil, Uruguay
III. On-the-job training and internships	To provide training and promote employment through apprenticeship contracts	Young people who neither attend school nor work	Ministries of Labour and Planning, Employment services, Youth institutes	Training that develops young people's potential	Training not relevant to needs of the labour market	Budget and reimbursable loans	Argentina, Chile, Colombia, Mexico, Peru, Uruguay, Venezuela
IV. Retraining of workers in declining industries	To enhance prospects of obtaining productive employment	People displaced by retooling or reductions in public-sector employment	Ministries of Labour, Employment services	Training and redeployment of workers	Training not relevant to needs of the labour market, high cost	Budget, reimbursable and non-reimbursable loans	Argentina, Bolivia, Chile, Costa Rica, Peru, Uruguay, Venezuela
V. Training and credit for owners of small-scale and micro-enterprises	To enhance access to credit and business management skills	Men and women who own small-scale and micro-enterprises	Ministries of Labour, National employment services	Upgrading of business skills	Problems in keeping businesses in operation without loan assistance	Reimbursable loans, local and foreign banks	Brazil, Colombia, Mexico, Uruguay

Source: Countries' responses to the survey on employment programmes.
[a] Costa Rica finances this programme with the proceeds from a payroll tax and with a portion of sales tax revenues.

c) Unemployment insurance

If workers who have been laid off receive a sufficient income to cover their basic needs for a reasonable period of time, they not only will enjoy a higher standard of living, but will also be better able to conduct a job search, with the result that resource allocation is improved and productivity increases. This is the rationale for unemployment insurance schemes. Nonetheless, unemployment insurance is practically unheard-of in Latin America, and where it does exist, it covers only a small number of workers or provides absurdly low benefits.

In practice, the only real protection that a worker in Latin America has in the event of dismissal is severance pay, which is normally equal to one month's pay for every year of service with the firm. This is an inadequate form of unemployment insurance, however, because, even though it does afford some coverage in the event of dismissal, the sum provided is adequate only after an employee has been with a given firm for a considerable number of years. Now, since 40% of all workers who are laid off or dismissed have less than two years' service, severance pay provides very little protection to a substantial portion of the labour force.

Moreover, severance pay entails three types of casts) it impedes the voluntary transfer of workers to other, more suitable firms, since workers who leave voluntarily are not entitled to compensation, and, even though they might be more highly paid in a different firm, they would run the risk of receiving little or no compensation in the event of dismissal; ii) should there be an economic crisis that makes mass lay-offs necessary, then firms will have to meet this obligation just when they are least able to do so; and iii) severance pay creates perverse incentives, in that it induces some long-time employees to deliberately set out to be fired in order to qualify for compensation, while encouraging firms to threaten dismissal on other grounds with a view to negotiating a lower amount of compensation.

In view of the need to safeguard a worker's income in the event of dismissal and facilitate a more fruitful job search, many observers propose the creation of a genuine unemployment insurance scheme of the kind that exists in developed countries. Objections to this proposal are primarily based on practical considerations rather than on theoretical ones. The concern is that such a scheme would prove to be excessively expensive because it would be unable to deal satisfactorily with the problem of "moral hazard", which in this case would involve distinguishing in an efficient manner between genuine dismissals and dismissals that have been engineered for the purpose of obtaining unemployment insurance. For example, workers may choose to leave a firm of their own free will —whether to have or raise children, or to seek a better job— and then state that they were dismissed (in collusion with their employer, since in this case the payment would come out of the "fund" rather than the employer's pocket). Similarly, many temporary workers —who for personal, family or scholastic reasons only wish to work for a portion of the year— may state that they are seeking work in order to qualify for unemployment benefits. In addition, many people whose actual period without work is brief —most find work within three months— may extend the duration of their eligibility for benefits or make it appear so by working in the informal sector while continuing to draw benefits. Such "leakages" may cause the real cost of an unemployment insurance scheme to be several times greater than the actual cost of covering the genuinely unemployed whom the law is intended to assist.

In view of these pitfalls, several alternative proposals have been put forward: i) offering any worker who is jobless a loan which is to be repaid through automatic deductions from his/her future payslip and which pays an unemployed worker between 50% and 70% of the worker's usual earnings for a period of up to 6 or 8 months; ii) creating an individual fund, financed by workers and their employers, from which a worker may draw compensation in the event of unemployment, voluntary retirement, mandatory retirement or death (survivor's benefits).

Both alternatives involve a measure of self-control that curbs abuse. Both envisage shortening the period during which benefits are paid (e.g., to five months, thus adequately covering the majority of the period of joblessness) in order to reduce the indirect costs of employment and eliminate most of the perverse incentives associated with the payment of unemployment benefits indefinitely.

The chief advantage of the first option is that it adequately meets the needs of the genuinely unemployed, irrespective of the contribution period. The advantage of the second option is that it is simpler to administer than the first, although it does fail to provide adequate coverage for workers who are laid off after less than two years' service with a firm.

V. SOCIAL REFORMS

1. Social expenditure[25]

a) Trends in public social expenditure

In the majority of the countries of the region, the level of public expenditure on social sectors rose during the early 1990s. By contrast with developments up to 1993, in 7 out of the 11 cases where spending increased, the levels achieved were even higher than those observed at the beginning of the 1980s (ECLAC, 1994).

Comparing the two-year period 1994-1995 with 1990-1991, the regional average for per capita public social spending went up in real terms by nearly US$ 50,[26] an improvement of 27.5% (see table V.1).

Particularly substantial increases occurred in Argentina, Mexico, Panama and Uruguay; in these countries social spending rose by more than US$ 90 per capita during the period in question. Increases in Chile, Colombia and Costa Rica were slightly above the regional average. In Bolivia, Guatemala and Paraguay the rise was smaller in absolute terms. Only in Nicaragua was there a definite drop.

During this period public social expenditure as a percentage of GDP (the measure of its macroeconomic priority) went up by an average of 1.8 percentage points. In 9 out of the 11 cases where an increase was noted, it was equivalent to more than 1% of GDP, with the most significant increases occurring in Colombia, Ecuador, Mexico, Panama, Paraguay and Uruguay. By contrast, in Brazil, El Salvador, Honduras and Nicaragua, the proportion of GDP allocated to public social spending remained unchanged or dropped slightly (see figure V.1 and table V.1).

---

[25] This section is based on ECLAC (1997).
[26] Average figures correspond to 1990-1991 and 1994-1995, except in those cases where only information for 1994 was available. Box V.2 describes the institutional coverage of series on social expenditure in each of the countries.

Table V.1
SOCIAL EXPENDITURE
(Averages) [a]

Country [b]	Real per capita social expenditure (in 1987 dollars)		Social expenditure/ GDP		Social/total public expenditure	
	1990-1991	1994-1995	1990-1991	1994-1995	1990-1991	1994-1995
High social expenditure	**333.6**	**424.9**	**15.2**	**17.2**	**52.7**	**60.4**
Uruguay	463.2	624.9	18.9	23.6	63.0	75.1
Costa Rica	334.0	388.6	19.8	20.8	45.5	44.3
Panama	349.9	466.5	17.1	20.0	37.5	44.2
Argentina	548.5	703.8	17.1	18.3	58.0	66.0
Chile	259.1	318.3	13.1	13.4	60.3	63.3
Mexico	156.4	247.3	8.4	13.1	53.3	71.8
Brazil [c]	224.0	224.8	11.6	11.2	51.0	57.8
Moderate social expenditure [d]	**99.1**	**126.6**	**9.0**	**10.9**	**35.5**	**47.4**
Colombia	107.2	164.2	8.2	11.6	33.9	54.0
Nicaragua	97.4	86.4	10.8	10.6	36.2	48.8
Ecuador	92.7	129.3	7.8	10.4	36.5	39.5
Venezuela	215.6	...	8.5	...	32.1	...
Low social expenditure [e]	**42.3**	**54.3**	**4.8**	**5.9**	**31.1**	**33.2**
Honduras	72.2	69.6	7.8	7.6	33.1	29.1
Paraguay [f]	25.9	66.7	2.6	6.6	33.2	43.2
Bolivia	34.4	49.5	4.6	6.3	36.0	32.0
El Salvador	50.1	53.7	5.5	5.3	23.6	25.0
Guatemala	28.7	32.2	3.3	3.7	29.8	36.4
Dominican Republic	36.3	...	4.7	...	36.6	...
Peru	20.6	...	2.1	...	15.9	...
Regional average [g]	**189.6**	**241.7**	**10.4**	**12.2**	**42.1**	**48.7**
Countries with high social expenditure						
Percentage variation in social expenditure	...	27.4	...	13.5	...	14.6
Percentage variation in GDP	...	17.7	...	17.7	...	17.7
Countries with moderate social expenditure						
Percentage variation in social expenditure	...	27.7	...	21.5	...	33.6
Percentage variation in GDP	...	11.7	...	11.7	...	11.7
Countries with low social expenditure						
Percentage variation in social expenditure	...	28.4	...	24.6	...	6.5
Percentage variation in GDP	...	12.3	...	12.3	...	12.3

Source: ECLAC, *Social Panorama of Latin America. 1996 Edition* (LC/G.1946-P), Santiago, Chile, 1997, table IV.1. United Nations publication, Sales No. E.97.II.G.4.

[a] The countries are listed in descending order according to the proportion of GDP allocated to social expenditure in 1994-1995.
[b] Averages for 1990-1991 and 1994-1995 for all countries, except Bolivia, Brasil, Chile, Costa Rica, El Salvador, Mexico and Panama, figures for which correspond to 1994 only.
[c] Central government expenditure only.
[d] Averages do not include Venezuela.
[e] Averages do not include Peru or the Dominican Republic.
[f] Central government budget expenditure only.
[g] Averages do not include Peru, Dominican Republic or Venezuela.

Figure V.1
TRENDS IN SOCIAL EXPENDITURE
1990 - 1991/1994 - 1995

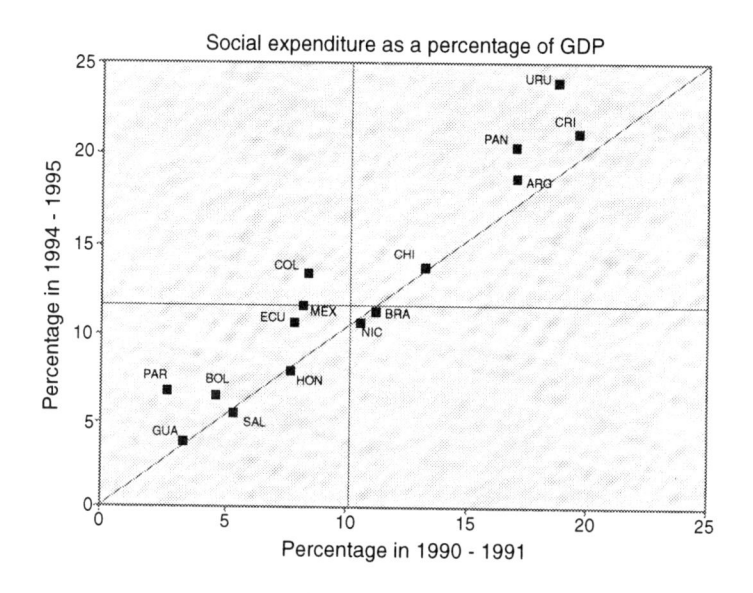

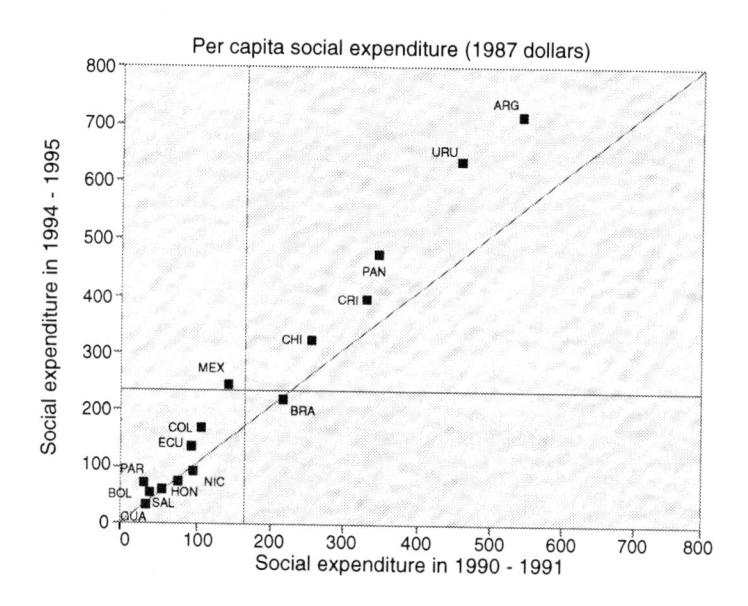

SOURCE: ECLAC, *Social Panorama of Latin America. 1996 Edition* (LC/G. 1946-P), Santiago, Chile, 1997, figure IV.1. United Nations publication, Sales No. E.97.II.G.4.

Note: The vertical and horizontal lines indicate the average for the indicator for the group of countries analysed, in 1990 - 1991 and 1994 - 1995 respectively.

To date in the 1990s, using 1980 as the reference year, distinct trends in public social spending are observable, and these are described in box V.1. In addition, trends in per capita spending in each country between 1980 and 1995 are shown in figure V.1.

Box V.1

TRENDS IN SOCIAL EXPENDITURE IN LATIN AMERICA DURING THE 1990s

Trend		Countries
1.	Predominantly upward, exceeding levels prevailing at beginning of the 1980s (figures V.2a and V.2b)	Argentina Chile Colombia Costa Rica Mexico Panama Paraguay Uruguay
2.	Predominantly upward but without attaining levels prevailing at beginning of the 1980s (figure V.2c)	Bolivia Ecuador El Salvador
3.	Fluctuating or slightly downward (figure V.2d)	Brazil Guatemala Honduras Nicaragua

Source: ECLAC, *Social Panorama of Latin America and the Caribbean. 1996 edition* (LC/G.1946-P), Santiago, Chile, 1997, box IV.1. United Nations publication, Sales No. E.97.II.G.4.

Social spending in the majority of countries moved in the same direction as GDP. GDP growth between 1990-1991 and 1994-1995 was 14.7%, while per capita social expenditure expanded by 27.5% in real terms. Nevertheless, trends varied from country to country depending on initial levels of social spending; in countries with moderate to low levels, spending rose faster in relation to output. Although real per capita social expenditure in the three groups shown went up by nearly 28% during this period, this figure was more than double the growth in output (12%) in countries with moderate to low levels of social spending, but only one and a half times GDP growth (18%) in countries with high levels of social spending (see table V.1).

SOCIAL REFORMS

Chapter V - 99

Figure V.2

TRENDS IN REAL PER CAPITA SOCIAL EXPENDITURE, 1980 - 1994 OR 1980 - 1995

(1987 dollars)

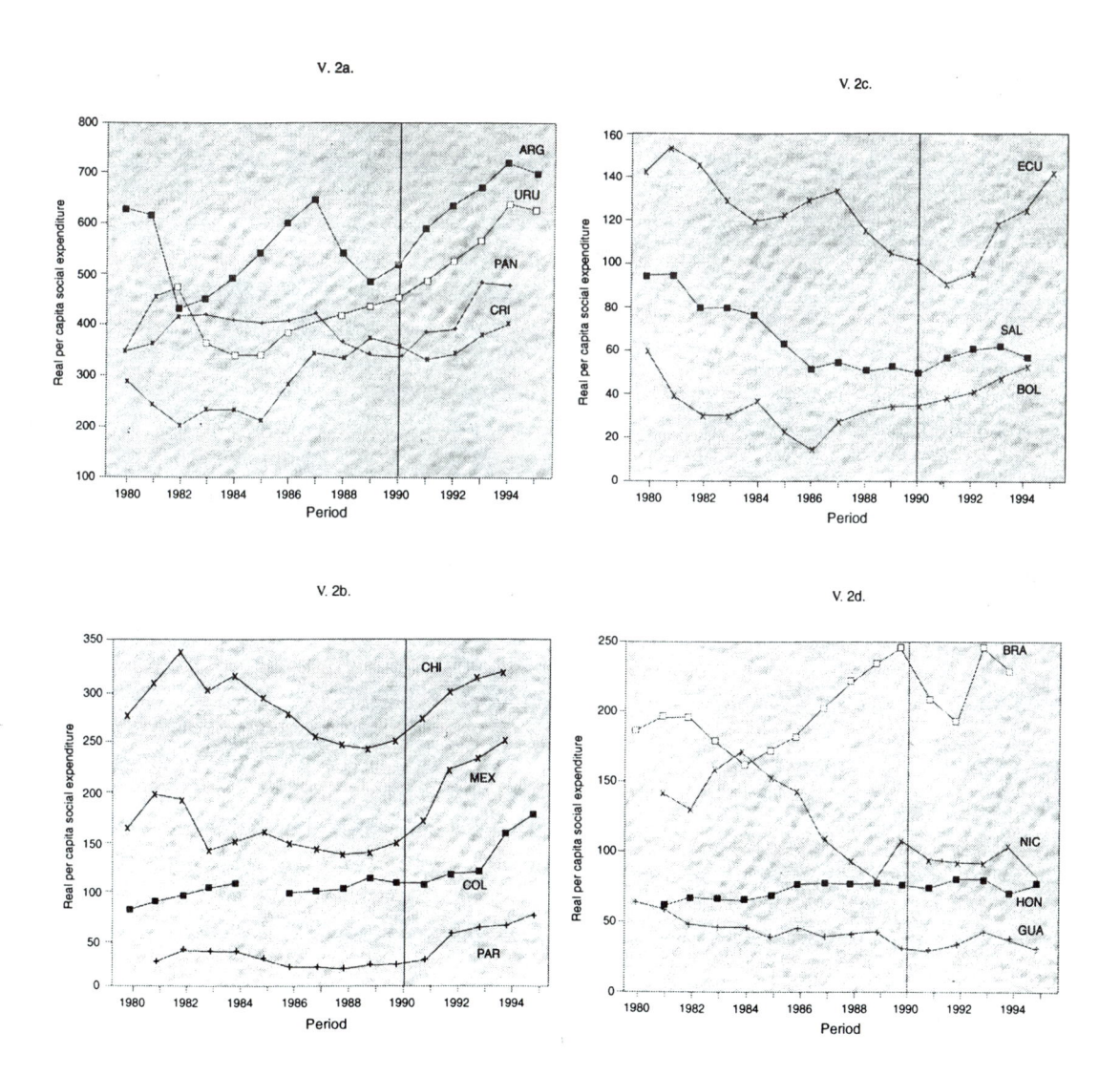

SOURCE: ECLAC, *Social Panorama of Latin America. 1996 Edition* (LC/G. 1946-P), Santiago, Chile, 1997, figure IV.2. United Nations publication, Sales No. E.97.II.G.4.

b) The level of public social expenditure

The perceptible differences among the countries of the region as regards the volume of public social expenditure (see figures V.3 and V.4) make it possible to group them according to their position in relation to the whole (see table V.1). The first group consists of seven countries (Argentina, Brazil, Chile, Costa Rica, Mexico, Panama and Uruguay) in which public social expenditure equals more than 11% of GDP and in per capita terms exceeds US$ 200 in 1987 dollars. The second group consists of four countries (Colombia, Ecuador, Nicaragua and Venezuela) in which per capita expenditure varies between US$ 70 and US$ 200 and total expenditure equals between 8% and 11% of GDP. In the seven countries that form the group with the lowest levels of social spending (Bolivia, Dominican Republic, El Salvador, Guatemala, Honduras, Paraguay and Peru), per capita expenditure is less than US$ 70 and total expenditure equal to less than 8% of GDP.

Both the countries where spending levels were high and those where levels were moderate or low increased their volume of spending at a similar rate —around 28%. However, the biggest increases in spending as a percentage of GDP occurred in the countries with moderate and low levels of expenditure, where the proportion increased by 21.5% and 24.6% respectively, as against 13.5% in the group of countries where social spending levels were high.

Two essential facts emerge from these wide variations in public social expenditure levels in Latin America.[27] The first, striking fact is how small the amounts are in the countries with low and moderate levels of social spending, as compared with industrialized countries and with the countries in the region where social spending levels are higher (see box V.3). Thus, the most urgent task for countries with low to moderate levels of social spending is to boost per capita spending significantly within a relatively short time, while still monitoring the quality of the impact of such spending.

Second, in those countries with the highest per capita social expenditure in the region, in which the percentage of GDP allocated to social sectors is comparable to that in some industrialized countries, the challenge is to improve the efficacy and efficiency with which resources are used. Nevertheless, the amounts these countries spend per capita are still small in relation to the increases in coverage and quality of social services that are needed in order to achieve equitable development. In addition, it is clear that the figures involved are very much lower than those in more developed countries, owing to the vast differences in the size of GDP (see box V.3).

---

[27] The Caribbean countries could not be covered in this analysis since no information was available for them.

SOCIAL REFORMS   Chapter V - 101

Figure V.3

**SOCIAL EXPENDITURE AS A PERCENTAGE OF GDP,
1994-1995**

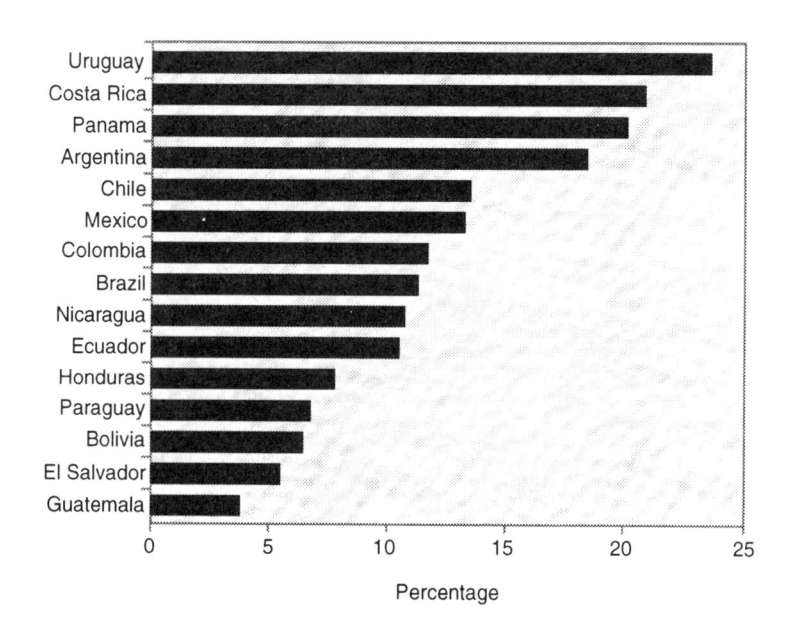

Country	Percentage
Uruguay	~24
Costa Rica	~21
Panama	~20
Argentina	~19
Chile	~13.5
Mexico	~13
Colombia	~12
Brazil	~11.5
Nicaragua	~11
Ecuador	~10.5
Honduras	~8
Paraguay	~7
Bolivia	~6.5
El Salvador	~5.5
Guatemala	~4

Figure V.4

**PER CAPITA SOCIAL EXPENDITURE,
1994-1995**

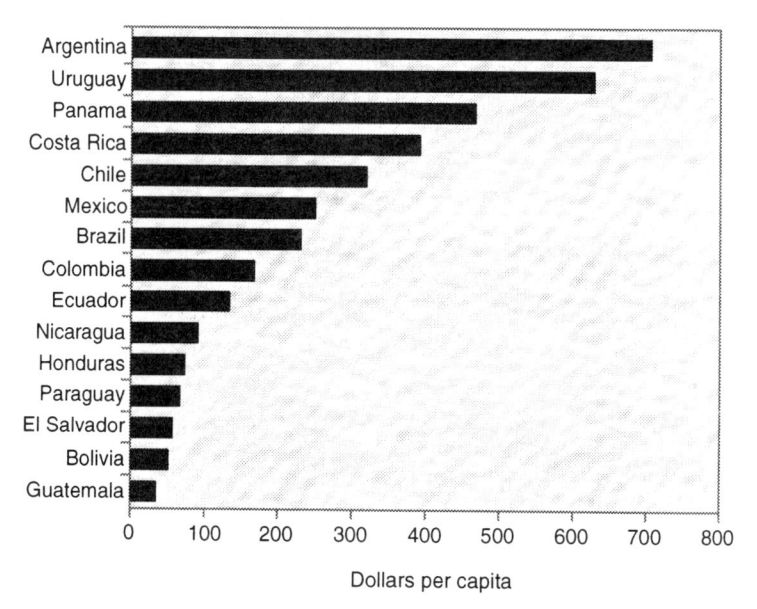

Country	Dollars per capita
Argentina	~720
Uruguay	~640
Panama	~480
Costa Rica	~400
Chile	~320
Mexico	~260
Brazil	~240
Colombia	~180
Ecuador	~140
Nicaragua	~90
Honduras	~70
Paraguay	~70
El Salvador	~60
Bolivia	~50
Guatemala	~30

SOURCE: ECLAC, *Social Panorama of Latin America. 1996 Edition* (LC/G. 1946-P), Santiago, Chile, 1997, figures IV.3. and IV.4. United Nations publication, Sales No. E.97.II.G.4.

Box V.2

METHODOLOGICAL NOTE ON SOCIAL EXPENDITURE STATISTICS

Differences of methodology and institutional coverage make comparative analysis of statistical series on social public expenditure at the regional level difficult. In terms of methodology, the most important differences relate to how expenditure is recorded on the accounts and how social expenditure is defined. In terms of coverage, the differences have to do with how States are structured and whether the figures include local government expenditure.

Public spending can be broken down according to the agencies responsible for it. Thus, a distinction can be made between public expenditure by the financial public sector (FPS) (i.e., the central bank and other State-owned financial agencies) and the non-financial public sector (NFPS) (i.e., central government (CG), public-sector enterprises (PE) and local government (LG)); the latter breakdown applies to two countries.

In 12 of the 18 countries considered, the social expenditure series that have been analysed refer to central government spending. Here again, a distinction can be made between agencies with an autonomous budget structure (AB) and those that depend directly on the treasury (central government budget (CGB)), which is how expenditure is recorded in a further three countries. Lastly, one country takes account of general government spending (GG), which comprises CG and LG.

In sum, by examining the accounting categories used in the available series, it can be stated that in 16 of the 18 countries considered, social spending figures are highly comparable. Strictly speaking, however, the exclusion of social spending at the local level, where there is a significant degree of decentralization of expenditure, result in significant underestimates of total social public spending and thus limits the comparability of figures in cases such as Brazil and Mexico.

The countries are classified below according to the institutional coverage of the available series on social expenditure.

Institutional coverage	Countries
NFPS = CG + PE + LG	Argentina and El Salvador
GG = CG + LG	Ecuador
CG = CGB + AA	Bolivia, Brazil, Colombia, Costa Rica, Chile, Dominican Republic, Guatemala, Honduras, Mexico, Panama, Uruguay and Venezuela
CGB	Nicaragua, Paraguay and Peru

Source: ECLAC, *Social Panorama for Latin America, 1996 Edition* (LC/G.1946-P), Santiago, Chile, 1997, box IV.2. United Nations publication, Sales No. E.97.II.G.4.

> **Box V.3**
>
> **PUBLIC SOCIAL EXPENDITURE IN DOLLARS PER CAPITA AND AS A PERCENTAGE OF GDP**
>
> | Industrialized countries [a] | | | Latin American countries [b] | | |
> |---|---|---|---|---|---|
> | | In dollars per capita | As % of GDP | | In dollars per capita | As % of GDP |
> | Countries with high social expenditure (Sweden, France, Austria, Netherlands) | 7.200 | 31.2 | Countries with high social expenditure | 425 | 17.2 |
> | | | | Countries with moderate social expenditure | 127 | 10.9 |
> | Other countries (United Kingdom, Germany, Spain, Canada, Japan, United States) | 3,600 | 16.4 | Countries with low social expenditure | 54 | 5.9 |
>
> **Source**: ECLAC, *Social Panorama for Latin America, 1996 Edition* (LC/G.1946-P), Santiago, Chile, 1997, box IV.3. United Nations publication, Sales No. E.97.II.G.4.
> [a] Consolidated central government; 1992 figures.
> [b] Figures for 1994-1995.

c) **Social priorities in public expenditure**

During the 1990s, the majority of the countries of the region have increased the proportion of public expenditure allocated to the social sector (see figure V.5). The increase has been greater (33.6%) in countries with moderate social spending and smaller (14.6%) in those where levels of social expenditure were already high. A substantially smaller percentage increase has occurred in countries with low expenditure (6.5%). In 9 out of the 12 countries which raised the priority of the social components of public expenditure, the change brought an increase in real per capita social expenditure and in the proportion of GDP allocated to it.

A positive sign is that, unlike in the 1980s, public spending on social items between 1990 and 1995 was not affected to an appreciable extent by the budget cutbacks experienced by some Governments. Indeed, analysis of the ratios of total public expenditure and social public expenditure to GDP shows that, regardless of the trends observed in total public spending, social spending went up as a percentage of GDP in 11 out of 15 countries. In Bolivia, Costa Rica, Ecuador, Mexico, Paraguay and Uruguay the increase in social spending took place in a context of an expansion in public expenditure as a whole. The countries where social spending as a proportion of GDP expanded while total public expenditure contracted were Argentina, Colombia, Chile, Guatemala and Panama (see figure V.6).

Figure V.5
**SOCIAL EXPENDITURE COMPARED WITH GDP
1990 - 1991 AND 1994-1995**

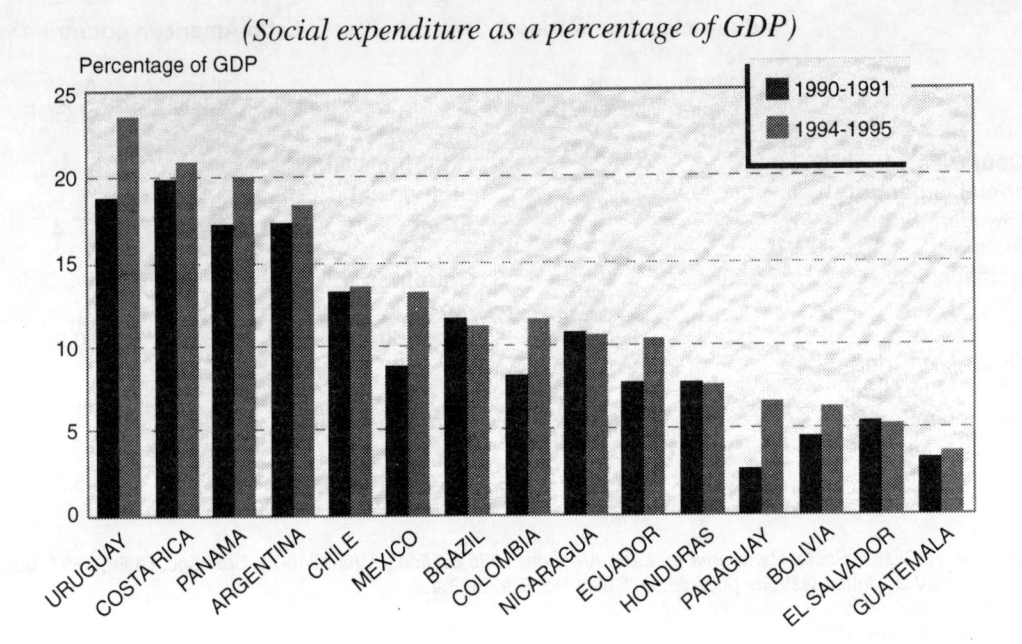

(Social expenditure as a percentage of GDP)

SOURCE: ECLAC, social expenditure database (ECLAC/World Bank project).

The foregoing is borne out by the fact that in the eight countries where total public spending fell as a proportion of GDP between 1990 and 1995, the priority accorded social spending within the fiscal budget went up. Only in Honduras, Costa Rica and Bolivia did the priority fall, but this coincided with growth in total public expenditure (see figure V.7).

d) Social expenditure by sector

The increase in public social spending was attributable mainly to increased spending on education and social security. As regards education, reforms in a number of countries of the region required large outlays of fiscal resources. The growth in social security spending was due principally to adjustments in retirement and other pensions, amortization of liabilities accumulated by the system or expansion of coverage.

The greatest growth in the share of public social expenditure between 1990 and 1995 occurred in education and social security. Real per capita spending on education went up in 12 out of 15 countries, while public spending on social security increased in 10 out of 12 countries (see box V.4). Average growth of real per capita spending in the countries of the

Figure V.6
COMPARATIVE TRENDS IN PUBLIC EXPENDITURE/GDP AND SOCIAL EXPENDITURE/GDP

1990-1991/1994-1995

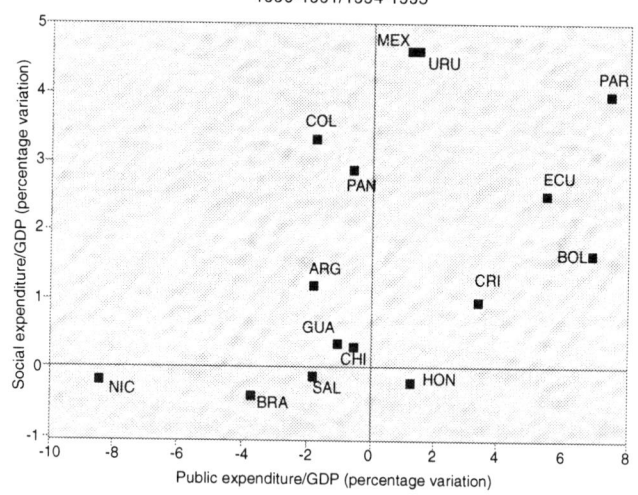

Figure V.7
COMPARATIVE TRENDS IN PUBLIC EXPENDITURE/GDP AND SOCIAL EXPENDITURE/PUBLIC EXPENDITURE

1990-1991/1994-1995

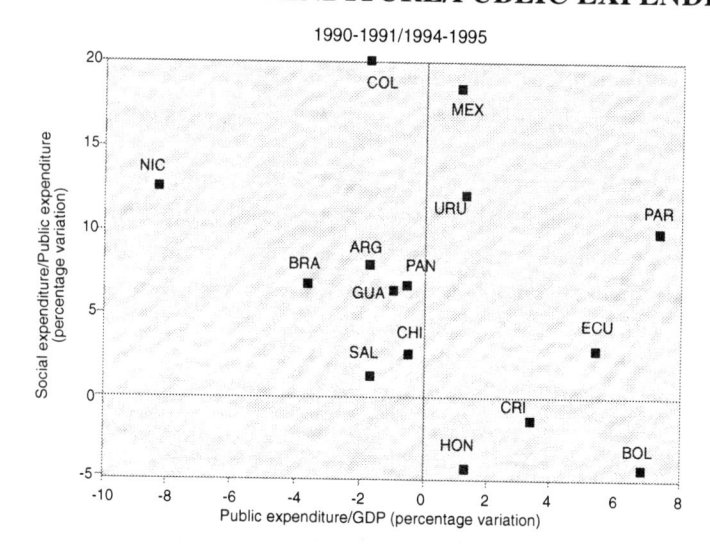

SOURCE: ECLAC, *Social Panorama of Latin America. 1996 Edition* (LC/G. 1946-P), Santiago, Chile, 1997, figures IV.5 and IV.6. United Nations publication, Sales No. E.97.II.G.4.

> **Box V.4**
>
> **THE BASIC COMPONENTS OF EXPENDITURE ON HUMAN CAPITAL**
>
> The resources allocated by Governments to social sectors fall into two categories: resources whose purpose is to offset, temporarily or permanently, particular changes in the population's income levels; and resources that represent a medium- or long-term investment in human capital, insofar as they promote individuals' intellectual and physical development and thus their productive potential. Of special importance within the latter category are resources that are used to satisfy basic needs such as nutrition, health and housing, among others. Although it is difficult to identify precisely which components should be considered investment in human capital —indeed, there is no single definition even of the concept of a basic need— a rough approximation would include all or part of the expenditure on education and health. In some studies, for example, investment in basic health and primary education is classified as "expenditure on human development".
>
> Nevertheless, depending on a country's level of social and economic development, it is necessary to find a broader definition of expenditure on human capital, which means including outlays whose purpose is to meet needs beyond the basic, needs such as secondary and higher education and higher levels of health care. Although total investment in education and health includes components that strictly speaking cannot be considered effective expenditure on human capital, for the purposes of this report this broader definition has been adopted rather than the definition restricting such expenditure to basic education and primary health care.
>
> **Source:** ECLAC, *Social Panorama for Latin America. 1996 Edition* (LC/G.1946-P), Santiago, Chile, 1997, box IV.5. United Nations publication, Sales No. E.97.II.G.4.

region in the first five years of the 1990s was 24.4% on education and around 50% on social security. These improvements made it possible to make up, at least in part, for the spending cuts in these sectors during the 1980s (ECLAC, 1994).

An important consequence of the simultaneous expansion of expenditure on health and on education was that per capita spending on human capital went up in 9 out of 13 countries (see table V.3 and box V.4).

Spending on human capital (education and health) falls in most cases within a range of 20% and 30% of total public expenditure, which means that the level of spending on education and health combined is relatively similar from country to country in the region. Thus, the wide variations in social spending, referred to above, are basically a product of the marked differences in spending on social security.

Per capita spending on human capital is still very low in two thirds of the countries analysed, with less than US$ 100 per person per annum allocated to health and education (see table V.2 and figure V.7). In a number of countries, however, the percentage of GDP and of total public expenditure invested in these sectors is not low in regional terms, which makes it even more essential to ensure adequate management and administration of resources and to improve the quality of social investment. This applies even to countries with higher levels of social expenditure.

Table V.2
PUBLIC EXPENDITURE ON HUMAN CAPITAL

Country	In 1987 dollars per capita		As a percentage of GDP		As a percentage of total public expenditure	
	1990-1991[a]	1994-1995[b]	1990-1991[a]	1994-1995[b]	1990-1991[a]	1994-1995[b]
Argentina	247.4	322.6	7.7	8.4	26.2	30.3
Brazil	80.3	84.4	4.1	4.2	18.1	21.7
Chile	92.3	126.2	4.7	5.3	21.5	25.1
Colombia	46.5	94.8	3.9	6.7	15.1	31.0
Costa Rica	185.9	214.4	11.0	11.5	25.3	24.4
Ecuador	52.2	72.9	4.4	5.9	20.5	22.2
El Salvador	33.3	31.0	3.6	3.1	15.6	14.4
Guatemala	21.5	20.9	2.5	2.4	22.3	23.7
Honduras	64.0	63.6	6.9	6.9	29.4	26.6
Nicaragua	86.2	71.1	9.6	8.9	32.0	40.5
Panama	217.6	257.5	10.7	11.1	23.4	24.4
Paraguay	15.0	43.7	1.5	4.3	19.2	28.3
Peru	20.4	...	2.0	...	15.7	...
Dominican Republic	17.5	...	2.3	...	17.6	...
Uruguay	150.9	174.6	6.2	6.6	20.5	21.0
Venezuela	121.8	...	4.8	...	18.1	...

Source: ECLAC, *Social Panorama of Latin America. 1996 Edition* (LC/G.1946-P), Santiago, Chile, 1997, Table IV.3. United Nations publication, Sales No. E.96.II.G.4.
[a] Figures for the Dominican Republic and Venezuela correspond to 1990 only.
[b] Figures for Bolivia, Chile, Costa Rica, El Salvador and Panama correspond to 1994 only.

Table V.3
SOCIAL INVESTMENT AND EMERGENCY FUNDS FOR THE ALLEVIATION OF POVERTY IN LATIN AMERICA UP TO 1997

Country	Name of fund	Year established/ ended	Administering agency	Sector(s)	Target population	Source of funding
Argentina	Participatory Social Investment Fund	1995 1999	Social Policy Cabinet, Office of the President	Comprehensive programmes	People with unmet basic needs living in working-class areas	World Bank National and provincial budgets
Bolivia	Emergency Social Welfare Fund, Social Investment Fund (FIS)	1986 1990 on-going	Office of the President. Ministry of Sustainable Development and the Environment	Comprehensive programmes covering education, health and nutrition, training and basic sanitation in municipalities accorded priority	Poor people, especially in rural areas	Budget, municipalities, communities, World Bank, Government of the Netherlands
Chile	Solidarity and Social Investment Fund (FOSIS)	1990 on-going	Ministry of Planning and Cooperation	Comprehensive programmes providing training, employment, technical assistance, credit and social advancement	Poor sectors of the population, small businesspeople, women heads of household, young people, farmers and indigenous people	Budget, foreign donors, Government of the Netherlands
Colombia	Co-financing Fund for Social Investment (FIS)	1992	National Council on Economic and Social Planning (CONPES)	Comprehensive programmes offering assistance in the areas of health, education, culture, recreation and sports	Vulnerable groups	Budget
Costa Rica	Fund for Social Development and Family Allowances (FODESAF)	1974 on-going	Autonomous body	Comprehensive programmes for children and adolescents, women, farmers, the elderly and the disabled	Groups targeted by the Plan to Combat Poverty	National budget through a special-purpose tax
Ecuador	Emergency Social Investment (FISE)	1993-1997	Office of the President	Sanitation, education, health, day care centres, orphanages and shelters, production and assistance in production, road improvements and flood protection	784 urban and rural parishes in 191 cantons of the 21 provinces	Inter-American Development Bank (IDB), World Bank, Andean Development Corporation, Government of the Netherlands
El Salvador	Social Investment Fund (FIS)	1990	Office of the President	Projects directed at basic needs, productive management and general education	The poor and the extremely poor	IDB World Bank
Guatemala	Social Investment Fund (FIS)	1993-2001	Office of the President	Education, health and nutrition, water and sanitation, economic infrastructure and the environment and production projects, especially in indigenous communities	Rural population	Budget, soft loans, World Bank, IDB, KfW, Central American Bank for Economic Integration

Table V.3 (concl.)

Country	Name of fund	Year established/ended	Administering agency	Sector(s)	Target population	Source of funding
Guyana	Social Impact Amelioration Program (SIMAP)	1990	Autonomous body	Infrastructure, health and nutrition	Poor people, especially undernourished women	IDB, World Bank
Haiti	Economic and Social Assistance Fund (FAES)	1990	Ministry of Finance and Economic Affairs	Production projects	The rural poor	World Bank
Honduras	Honduran Social Investment Fund (FHIS/PASI)	1990-2005	Office of the President	Small and medium-sized enterprises	Poor people	World Bank, Government of the Netherlands
Mexico	Fund for Municipal Social Development	1995-2000	Ministry of Social Development	Infrastructure, municipal decentralization and credit assistance	People living in higher poverty levels	Federal budget and community contributions
Nicaragua	Emergency Social Investment Fund (FISE)	1990	Office of the President	Infrastructure and employment	People living in extreme poverty, without access to basic services	Ministry of Finance, World Bank, USAID, IDB, KfW, UNDP, Canadian International Development Agency, COSUDE
Panama	Social Emergency Fund (FES)	1990 on-going	Office of the President	Infrastructure and employment	Poor people	World Bank
Peru	National Social Compensation and Development Fund (FONCODES)	1991	President of the Council of Ministers	Social and economic infrastructure	People living in extreme poverty	Budget, foreign donors, World Bank, Government of the Netherlands
Dominican Republic	Fund for the Promotion of Community Initiatives (PROCOMUNIDAD)	1993 1999	Office of the President	Health, education and sanitation infrastructure	Low-income groups with unmet basic needs	Budget, IDB
Venezuela	Social Investment Fund (FONVIS)	1990 on-going	Ministry of Family Affairs	Health, education, provision of equipment, training and technical assistance	Poor people	Budget, IDB, World Bank

Source: ECLAC, *Social Panorama of Latin America. 1996 Edition* (LC/G.1946-P), Santiago, Chile, 1997, table VI.4. United Nations publication, Sales No. E.97.II.G.4.

Analysis of the outlook for spending on human capital indicates that the low levels of pay that prevail in the education and health sectors and the high percentage of total sectoral expenditure they absorb will increase pressure to boost spending in these sectors.

e) Social investment funds[28]

Social investment funds originated as mechanisms for alleviating the adverse social impact of stabilization and adjustment policies, and were therefore initially a short-term emergency measure. They subsequently underwent modification and were eventually incorporated into medium- and long-term social policies; in point of fact, the social investment funds operating in Chile, Panama and Venezuela are on-going in nature. These funds are a relatively new development in the region, since they were modelled on the Emergency Social Welfare Fund (FSE) set up in Bolivia in 1986 (see table V.3). Costa Rica's Fund for Social Development and Family Allowances (FODESAF) established in 1975, is a different kind of institution.

The general aim of the funds is to collect resources, primarily from external sources, and to channel them to specific social programmes and projects, which the institution is not responsible for executing. The role of the funds, then, is one of financial intermediation, which involves the selection, financing and oversight of projects. The sources of financing are varied; funding may come from the national budget (Chile, Colombia and Mexico), multilateral institutions (Bolivia), or non-governmental organizations, either national (Peru) or international (Ecuador). Financing may even be derived from external debt conversion operations (Chile). Among the unresolved problems associated with social investment funds are sustainability over time, for which a constant flow of external resources is required, and capacity-building in project planning.

The funds promote decentralization, social participation and complementarity between the public and private sectors by involving non-governmental organizations, community associations and municipalities in the implementation of activities and sometimes even in their design. Ideally, the funds should be autonomous and operate in a transparent, efficient, rapid and flexible manner.

The main strategy used to transfer resources to the poor has been the creation of temporary jobs in social and economic infrastructure projects (these originally accounted for between 80% and 88% of funding), in addition to social and loan assistance. A smaller proportion of resources has been earmarked directly for productive activities, generally via non-governmental organizations. Now that the flow of funds has begun to stabilize, there is a trend towards a reduction in infrastructure investment and an increase in resources allocated to human resource training.

Officials in charge of the funds need to coordinate their activities with those of the traditional sectoral ministries and other public entities that finance social projects. This kind of coordination is important for increasing the funds' efficiency and enhancing their impact, which has not been great owing to the limited resources at their disposal.

---

[28] This section is based on ECLAC (1997).

Another aspect that merits examination is targeting, since social investment funds often benefit neither the poorest groups in society nor those furthest from urban centres. In addition, the indigent lack the skills to formulate projects and to organize themselves, and this is a major problem in demand-oriented programmes. Moreover, in the execution of infrastructure projects, there is clear discrimination between beneficiaries: men are offered employment, while women and children, groups that have a high incidence of poverty when they reside in female-headed households, receive instead social assistance and services. It is also important to note that job creation projects generate only temporary positions, which do not always meet the country's normal labour standards; hence, they should merely be viewed as a supplement to a more comprehensive social policy.

The absence of impact evaluation of social investment funds is still a problem; this situation is heightened by the current emphasis on reducing administrative costs, which has led to a decision to do without monitoring and evaluation mechanisms. In order for the funds to acquire a more permanent status, they need to become an integral part of public policies and programmes, on the basis of an analysis of the opportunity costs of the resources assigned to them. Excessive bureaucracy should be avoided and stable funding should be provided by the countries themselves.

Perhaps the most important achievement of the social investment funds lies in the fact that they show how, with the necessary political will, it is possible to put an end to the vicious circle of donor distrust, bureaucratic incompetence and low motivation on the part of the poor, while at the same time developing a new "social technology" that expands the opportunities of the extremely needy.

2. Educational reforms

a)   A turning point for education

There is consensus that education is a key area in which to reconcile competitiveness and social equity. An education that meets productive and social needs, is of sufficiently high quality and is completed at the right age is crucial in the achievement of higher productivity, greater social efficiency, increased opportunities for access to well-being and greater cultural and political participation.

Growth with social equity requires competitiveness based on better trained human resources with the potential to add progressively more intellectual value and technical progress to the natural resource base. Without investment in education, the economy will have at its disposal only poor and relatively untrained workers and will be unable to incorporate technical progress.

The above points to the need for a redoubling of efforts. People need to learn more and learn differently. They need to acquire the skills to integrate themselves creatively into the new forms of production and to participate constructively in the various areas of public life. Education is capable of generating the required synergy between productive dynamism, social well-being and democratic institution-building.

The impact of knowledge on competitiveness makes education an essential driving force in development. Hence human resource training is the key to change in the production patterns, in citizenship and in social mobility.

b) The regional situation

Education systems in the region are deficient in quality, efficacy and efficient use of resources, and these deficiencies perpetuate social inequities.

Quality. Despite significant differences between countries overall, only half of the children who begin primary school actually complete it. The region's students perform far worse than their counterparts in the industrialized countries, and also fail to reach the level considered a minimum standard in reading, mathematics and science tests. Many children fail to acquire a basic mastery of their mother tongue and of mathematics, and the secondary education given does not as a general rule equip students to integrate effectively into the modern sector of the economy.

Coverage and repetition rate. While the coverage of education systems is high with respect to the level of development, there is also a high rate of repetition. Of the 9 million children who enter the first level every year (90% or 95% of the cohort), approximately 4 million fail in the first year. Roughly one third of all students repeat a grade each year, and it is calculated that the additional cost of teaching repeaters amounts to US$ 4.2 billion annually.[29]

Equity. The systems for measuring quality of education that have begun to be applied in recent years show a clear segmentation in educational performance, in which students from low-income families are at a disadvantage (see box V.5). Inequality also appears in the way in which education expenditure is distributed; in the late 1980s more than 25% of such spending was allocated to higher education, and currently the highest socio-economic quintile benefits from about 50% of this subsidy, while the lowest quintile benefits from only 5%.[30]

A number of factors need to be taken into consideration if progress is to be made towards improving social equity.

First, **extra-systemic equity** refers to the degree of homogeneity in the ability of students from very diverse socio-economic, family and cultural backgrounds to absorb what the educational system has to offer. Students' educational performance varies greatly depending on their socio-cultural background, especially the educational environment of the home, as determined by the educational level of the parents.

Second, **intra-systemic equity** refers to the degree of homogeneity in the quality —not necessarily the content— of the education offered by schools located in different socio-economic strata and different geographical areas. Mechanisms for measuring the quality of education have revealed segmentation and dissimilar performances in comparisons of students from different socio-economic strata (see tables V.4 and V.5).

---

[29] Based on Rivero (1995) and Puryear and Brunner (1994).

[30] Countries such as Bolivia and Venezuela are currently embroiled in sharp political conflict because their reform agendas envisage a redistribution of social expenditure from tertiary to primary education, in an effort to introduce a greater measure of social equity into public spending on education.

> **Box V.5**
>
> **INEQUITY IN EDUCATIONAL PERFORMANCE AND ATTAINMENT IN CHILE**
>
> The differences in performance on the educational quality measurement system (SIMCE) tests reveal a clear socio-economic split. In 1993, in tests given in the second year of secondary education, municipal schools classified as low socio-economic stratum scored as much as 28% lower than their counterparts of high socio-economic stratum.
>
> The results with respect to overall performance are dramatic. In the poorer half of the population, three quarters of students in the fourth year of basic education are unable to understand what they read. In both Spanish and mathematics students in private schools that charge tuition score on average 20% higher than students who attend subsidized private schools and up to 30% higher than students in municipal schools.
>
> As regards drop-out rates, 91% of students in tuition-charging schools, with greater resources, reach the fourth year of secondary education and 88% graduate, while in municipal schools, with fewer resources, 67% reach that level and 59% graduate. Data from the national socio-economic survey (CASEN) reveal that 96.9% of the fifth quintile enter intermediate education, compared with 73.4% of the first quintile. The same disparity between social strata can be seen in variables such as the number of years it takes to complete school and the drop-out rate at the secondary level.
>
> In terms of investment in education, current average expenditure per student in subsidized schools is only half the estimated cost of ensuring a basic education of acceptable quality and, according to the 1994 CASEN study, five times less than expenditure per student in tuition-charging private schools, while there are ten times as many students in subsidized schools. Only two out of every ten children from low-income households attend kindergarten, and about 4,000 rural schools fail to offer the full eight grades that make up the compulsory basic cycle.
>
> Source: ECLAC, "The strategic role of secondary education in achieving well-being and social equity" (LC/G.1919), Santiago, Chile, 1996.

Table V.4
AVERAGE EDUCATIONAL PERFORMANCE BY SOCIO-ECONOMIC STRATUM LEVEL (GRADE 4 OF BASIC EDUCATION)[a]
(Percentages)

Performance	Low stratum	Medium stratum	High stratum
Language	47.9	58.4	71.9
Mathematics	43.8	49.8	59.0
Total	46.0	54.1	65.5

Source: UNESCO Regional Office for Education in Latin America and the Caribbean, "Medición de calidad de la educación: resultados", vol. 3, Santiago, Chile, 1994.

[a] Argentina, Bolivia, Brazil, Chile, Costa Rica, Dominican Republic, Ecuador and Venezuela.

Table V.5
PERCENTAGE DISTRIBUTION OF STUDENTS ACCORDING TO SOCIO-ECONOMIC STRATUM LEVEL AND OVERALL PERFORMANCE QUARTILE[a]

	Performance quartiles			
Stratum	0-25	26-50	51-75	76-100
Low	8.9	60.6	26.4	2.2
Medium	3.1	40.0	48.0	8.9
High	1.4	15.3	55.1	28.1

Source: UNESCO Regional Office for Education in Latin America and the Caribbean, "Medición de calidad de la educación: resultados", vol. 3, Santiago, Chile, 1994.
[a] Argentina, Bolivia, Brazil, Chile, Costa Rica, Dominican Republic, Ecuador and Venezuela.

Third, **meta-systemic equity** refers to the ability of students from different socio-economic backgrounds to find productive jobs, achieve social mobility and develop their potential, once they have completed their education.

The educational reforms now in progress are aimed essentially at improving intra-systemic equity, which is an easier area for educational policies to tackle. There has however, been some progress made with regard to extra-systemic equity, primarily in the form of bilingual education programmes, increased access to education for the rural population, and community involvement. As regards meta-systemic equity, efforts are being made in some programmes to provide alternatives, both at the basic and intermediate levels, involving non-final interruption of schooling and a continuation of studies in vocational education alternatives.

c) **Expenditure on education**

In the mid-1990s, 11 out of 15 countries increased the per capita resources allocated to education,[31] bringing expenditure to just above average pre-crisis levels, thus reversing the trend in evidence since 1980-1981, which reached its most critical point in the late 1980s. However, the impact of this general recovery has varied substantially from one country to another[32] (see tables V.6 and V.7).

---

[31] At the seventh Regional Conference of Ministers of Education for Latin America and the Caribbean, held in Jamaica from 13 to 17 May 1996, Ministers of Education from 33 of the region's countries made a commitment to increase the level of expenditure on education from the current average of 4.4% of GDP to 6.5% by the end of the 1990s. Moreover, since 1990, the World Bank has increased the funds available for education fourfold.

[32] Countries with higher levels of expenditure (Argentina, Costa Rica and Panama) devote between US$ 80 and US$ 130 dollars per capita annually to education. Next comes a group of countries that spend between US$ 40 and US$ 80 per capita on education (Chile, Colombia, Ecuador, Mexico, Uruguay and Venezuela). Lastly, there is a third group of countries whose spending on education is below the US$ 40 per capita mark (Bolivia, Dominican Republic, El Salvador, Guatemala, Honduras, Nicaragua, Paraguay and Peru).

Table V.6
INCREASE IN PER CAPITA EXPENDITURE ON EDUCATION [a]
(Between 1990-1991 and 1994-1995)

Sector	Real per capita social expenditure (1987 dollars)		Absolute variation (1987 dollars)	Percentage variation
	1990-1991	1994-1995		
Average [b]	46.7	58.1		
Argentina	105.9	145.8	39.9	37.6
Bolivia	22.1	34.6	12.5	56.8
Brazil [c]	26.0	27.3	1.3	5.1
Chile	51.1	67.4	16.3	31.8
Colombia	31.0	46.0	15.0	48.4
Costa Rica	80.7	100.9	20.2	25.0
Ecuador	34.7	50.2	15.5	44.8
El Salvador	19.0	15.8	(3.2)	(16.6)
Guatemala	13.7	14.0	0.3	2.3
Honduras	40.4	37.3	(3.1)	(7.6)
Mexico	53.7	76.5	22.7	42.3
Nicaragua	44.7	36.6	(8.0)	(18.0)
Panama	94.1	113.9	19.8	21.1
Paraguay [d]	11.1	32.4	21.3	192.4
Peru	15.2	...	...	...
Dominican Republic	9.3 [e]	...	...	...
Uruguay	71.7	72.1	0.4	0.6
Venezuela	83.7 [e]	...	...	...

Source: ECLAC, *Social Panorama for Latin America. 1996 Edition* (LC/G.1946-P), Santiago, Chile, 1997, table IV.2. United Nations publication, Sales No. E.97.II.G.4.

[a] Averages for 1990-1991 and 1994-1995 for all countries except Bolivia, Brazil, Chile, Costa Rica, El Salvador, Mexico and Panama, figures for which correspond to 1994 only.
[b] Owing to lack of information, averages do not include Dominican Republic, Peru and Venezuela.
[c] Central government expenditure only.
[d] Central government budget expenditure only.
[e] Includes 1990 only.

Table V.7
DECLINING TREND IN EXPENDITURE ON EDUCATION BETWEEN 1982 AND 1991

	1982-1989	1990-1991
Argentina		
Basic	fell	fell
Higher	fell	fell
Basic education coefficient	stable	rose
Chile		
Basic	fell	fell
Higher	fell	fell
Basic education coefficient	rose	rose
Colombia		
Basic	stable	stable
Higher	fell	stable
Basic education coefficient	rose	stable
Ecuador		
Basic	...	fell
Higher	...	fell
Basic education coefficient	...	fell
Paraguay		
Basic	rose	...
Higher	fell	...
Basic education coefficient	rose	...
Uruguay		
Basic	fell	...
Higher	fell	...
Basic education coefficient	stable	...

Source: ECLAC, Social Panorama of Latin America. 1994 Edition (LC/G.1844), Santiago, Chile, November 1994, chapter IV.

Public spending on education continues to be concentrated at the primary level; in fact, in five out of six countries, primary education accounts for almost half of total expenditure on education. Although arguments can be put forward based on equity and efficiency to justify allocating more resources to primary education, the evidence (ECLAC, 1994a, 1995a and 1997) indicates that for these very reasons equal importance should be accorded to secondary education. Accordingly, efforts should be made to ensure that all children complete both primary and secondary education.[33]

---

[33] In Latin America, it is increasingly necessary to complete secondary education in order to have a probability of 80% or more of avoiding poverty (ECLAC, 1994a).

The countries need to increase both current and capital spending on education. On the one hand, it is necessary to raise teachers' pay which in many countries has lagged behind, even though this item accounts for around 90% of resources spent on education. On the other hand, inadequate investment explains in part the lack of suitable facilities and teaching materials in public schools, and this also has a bearing on the quality and equity of education.

Some of the increased spending on education reflects greater demand for resources to carry out the reforms undertaken by a number of countries in the region in order to tackle the infrastructure deficit and at the same time increase the coverage, quality and equity of educational services.

Countries with low social expenditure, such as Paraguay and Bolivia, have made significant increases in education spending, attributable to the implementation of wide-ranging reform programmes. In some cases, countries have allocated funds from their budgets to match financing granted by international agencies.

Argentina, Colombia and Mexico have also earmarked significantly larger amounts of resources especially in terms of investment, to bolster the educational reforms recently undertaken, which entail decentralization and granting greater autonomy and responsibility to local governments in administering spending.[34] In Chile, the bulk of the increase in education expenditure has gone to salaries, followed by subsidies. Chile has also implemented a programme to improve the quality and equity of education. In Argentina, a programme to evaluate the quality of education and of compensatory initiatives in education has received substantial funding, partly from the Government and partly from multilateral agencies.

d) **Educational reform**

i) **The reform agenda**

With respect to formal education, it is apparent that all of the countries have made definite, steady progress during the past five decades. Thanks to the sustained rise in level of school attendance, a large number of the countries have achieved or are close to achieving total coverage in basic education, have boosted secondary enrolment rates and have steadily reduced illiteracy rates.

The problems facing education systems are also readily apparent: out-of-date curricula, anachronistic teaching methods, social segmentation of access to education and the quality of education offered, misallocation of public resources in the sector, excessive centralization of administration and neglect of teaching as a profession. Consequently, reforms in the region have addressed such areas as the content and process of education, education funding and the mechanisms used to allocate resources, the proper roles of the State and the market in education, teacher retraining, modernization and decentralization of education

---

[34] In Argentina, for example, the Federal Education Act transferred to the provinces and local governments some of the responsibility for generating resources for public primary and —to a lesser extent— secondary education.

administration, monitoring the quality of education supplied, and adapting it to the sociocultural situation of the beneficiaries and the subsequent demands of training in the world of work.

All of these components of the reforms in progress are designed to improve the learning process in basic and secondary education, to enhance efficiency and efficacy in the use of educational resources, and, via different routes, to achieve more equitable access to a good education and higher levels of education.

In order to formulate reform measures that can enhance the quality of education and social equity in terms of educational level, good diagnostic tools are essential. In this regard, attention should be drawn to the efforts made by the countries of the region to create and refine national systems for the periodic evaluation of the quality of education and educational performance (see box V.6).

Educational reform has the support of the authorities, professional educators and public opinion. This is why educational reform has been the most widespread of all reforms, has attracted additional public resources and international loans and is of interest to citizens, who are willing to participate in educational programmes and even to invest a portion of their incomes in them.

In spite of this, educational reform is not free of conflict. Disputes between governments and teachers jeopardize prospects for success, as do controversial moves towards administrative and financial decentralization and resistance by vested interests in higher education to a redistribution of public-sector resources in favour of other levels, especially primary education. The persistence of problems in these areas has raised the issue of whether the reforms are viable.

ii) Educational reform in selected countries

A general overview of some of the educational reforms under way in some of the countries of the region is presented below by way of illustration.

In 1994, **Bolivia** enacted a framework law on educational reform. The 1992 census revealed that the mother tongue of 70% of the population is a language other than Spanish. For that reason reform has focused on multiculturalism and bilingual education, based on the assumption that children who learn to read and write their own mother tongue will then be better equipped to do the same with a second language, in this case Spanish.

The plan involves delegating decision-making to the community, under the coordination of the National Council for Education, a consultative body representing all sectors of society.

Teacher training institutions are also undergoing reform; a system of continuous in-service training for teachers is being instituted and promotion will be made dependent on the results of periodic evaluations.

It is hoped that evaluation and information mechanisms can help optimize the use of resources. With that aim in mind, steps are being taken to implement a system for measuring the quality of education and to create systems for statistical information and for human, physical and financial resources administration.

> **Box V.6**
>
> **NATIONAL SYSTEMS FOR MEASURING QUALITY OF EDUCATION**
>
> An adjusted and disaggregated assessment of the quality of education, defined in terms of a student's level of achievement and performance, can make a significant contribution to the formulation of policies for improving education. National quality measurement systems constitute an essential source of information for decision-making about changes in educational methods and practices. Such systems make it possible to set goals in light of the existing situation, as well as evaluate alternative methods for resource allocation and different combinations of teaching inputs, and in so doing optimize the use of resources for improving educational achievement and outcomes.
>
> With only a few exceptions in the region (including Chile and the English-speaking countries of the Caribbean), the issue of education quality assessment, and particularly the creation of national measurement systems and their evaluation, became part of the education agenda only in the late 1980s. Almost all national assessment systems focus on educational performance after a certain number of years of schooling, in order to assess students' progress and changes in their cognitive capacity. The purpose of these systems is to assess students' skills development and knowledge acquisition, their aptitude for problem-solving and skill acquisition and changes in their attitudes and preferences.
>
> The purpose of evaluating learning at the national level is to assess student performance, monitor progress by schools and school districts towards standard educational goals and identify problems in curricula and teaching methods. The use of results obtained from these systems to redirect resources earmarked for education is still in the very early stages. It is vital that such systems serve as the basis for policy reform instituted in order to raise the quality of education. They can also help to improve education in a variety of ways: by establishing a reference measure for setting standards and monitoring performance; by identifying effective inputs and methods that enable measurable progress to be made in scholastic performance; by mobilizing public opinion in support of education; by providing educators with information so that they can re-evaluate teaching programmes; by instituting mechanisms that provide incentives for good performance by teachers and schools; and by contributing to the analysis of students' difficulties in comprehension and applying knowledge.
>
> **Source:** Violeta Arancibia and Carolina Segovia, "Sistemas nacionales de medición de la calidad de la educación en América Latina y Laboratorio latinoamericano de evaluación de la calidad de la educación", Santiago, Chile, UNESCO Regional Office for Education in Latin America and the Caribbean, May 1996, unpublished.

Colombia's General Education Act (No. 115, 1994) instituted a reform aimed at extending the coverage of primary and secondary education, improving the quality of education and reducing the country's high drop-out and repetition rates.

The law provides for the decentralization of the education system and the creation of local units. The Ministry of Education sets guidelines and promotes initiatives, but does not execute them; that is the responsibility of the departments, which plan, administer and coordinate educational services, and the municipalities, which administer schools. The decentralization of educational services, schools and teaching and administrative staff is a gradual process, one which will advance as the decentralized units demonstrate their technical and institutional capacity. In addition to decentralization, the law provides for mechanisms

Table V.8
EDUCATIONAL REFORM IN SELECTED COUNTRIES OF THE REGION, 1996[a]

Purpose of measures	Argentina	Bolivia	Colombia	Costa Rica	Chile	Paraguay	Peru	Uruguay
Sectoral structure								
Increase coverage of education: pre-school, primary and secondary	X	X	X	X		X	X	X
Restructure educational levels	X					X		
Establish links with vocational training				X		X		
Expand the school day			X	X	X			X
Reduce drop-out and repetition rates	X		X	X		X		
Content of education								
Reform curriculum at the primary and secondary levels	X			X	X		X	X
Promote bilingual education (in combination with indigenous languages)		X				X		
Promote second-language learning (English)	X				X			X
Introduce computers as teaching aids in primary and secondary education	X			X	X			X
Improve instructional materials (books, etc.) and infrastructure	X		X	X	X	X	X	X
Assessment								
Introduce educational quality measurement systems	X	X		X	X	X	X	X
Institute periodic teacher evaluation		X						
Teachers								
Increase the number of trained teachers and level of training	X				X			X
Involve teachers in reform						X		
Increase teacher pay			X		X	X		
Institute training programmes	X	X		X			X	X
Targeting								
Improve equity in terms of access and quality	X			X	X	X	X	
Set up complementary targeted programmes	X			X	X		X	X
Introduce demand-side subsidy mechanisms				X	X			
Decentralization								
Increase competition among educational establishments	X	X	X	X	X			
Delegate administration to local units			X		X	X		
Encourage decentralization in the pedagogical sphere					X		X	
Promote community participation in reform		X	X			X		

Source: Compiled on the basis of official information from the countries.
[a] No distinctions are made with respect to the degree of implementation of the measures.

to facilitate community participation; it recognizes that the family, the society and State share responsibility for education; the Constitution stipulates that the educational community shall participate in the management and administration of schools, as well as in the design, execution and evaluation of the institutional plan for education.

The Government sets out guidelines for schools for organizing and allocating financial resources (their own funding, and funding obtained from enrolments, subsidies, credits, government contracts and donations from the private sector) for the building of facilities and the purchase of textbooks and teaching materials; the Government also provides the private sector with lines of credit to finance libraries, sports facilities and technical improvements.

Public-sector resources are also allocated to grants for basic education, and student loans for higher education. As a redistributive measure, demand-side allowances are granted to 1.6 million poor students and to female heads of household to finance the cost of educating their children.

As part of an initiative termed the "educational leap", the Government is proposing improvements in the quality of basic education, including extending the length of the real school day from 3.5 to 6 hours, increasing teacher pay, supplying textbooks to students attending public schools, and setting up 2,100 libraries and teaching aid centres.

Chile embarked on educational reform early in the previous decade, by decentralizing services to municipalities and granting demand-side subsidies.

The decentralization process is currently being extended to the teaching sphere. Resources are allocated by bidding on projects, and schools are being given greater freedom to prepare their own education plans within the guidelines defined by municipal objectives and the obligatory core curriculum.

The demand-side subsidy is the key funding mechanism and consists of a payment per student to the school, in an amount that varies according to the type of instruction. Supervision of educational establishments was transferred from the Ministry of Education to the municipalities, with the aim of diversifying supply, in the belief that increased competition between schools would make them tailor their services to fit consumer preferences. It is also argued that this method of payment makes it possible to take into account the differences in costs which vary with type of instruction and geographical area. However, attempts are being made to improve the demand-side subsidy as a result of criticisms of its practical application.

With respect to resources, there has recently been a gradual recovery from the 28% decline in public spending on education, which occurred from 1982 to 1990 and had the greatest impact on teachers' real pay.

Steps are also being taken to improve the quality of basic and secondary education. Initiatives in that regard include the system for measuring the quality of education (SIMCE), the programme for better-quality education with greater social equity (MECE) and the programme for improving the quality of basic schools serving low-income groups (the "900 Schools Programme"), which directs resources to the 900 lowest-performing schools in Chile as determined by scores on the SIMCE test. Grants are also given for selected projects submitted by municipal and subsidized schools and targeted programmes for expanding early education, among other things. Schools are starting to use computers as teaching aids, and the goal is to provide coverage to all high schools and at least half of all schools by the year 2000. More active and participatory learning methods are being introduced. Lastly, a programme to lengthen the school day is being gradually implemented, which would result in increasing hours of instruction from 900 to 1,200 annually.

In **Costa Rica,** the Higher Education Council in 1994 approved a programme entitled "Educational policy towards the twenty-first century", which was designed to restore education's role in promoting social mobility, by reducing the disparities in the quality of education students receive between urban and rural areas, marginal and non-marginal urban schools and public and private schools.

Priority has been accorded to formulating a new set of study plans and programmes, including the training of teachers responsible for their implementation, along with the preparation of appropriate teaching materials. In addition, a system for educational assessment has been set up, with a view to creating a new quality-control system to aid the reform process at the Ministry of Education.

In order to increase coverage in the early grades among the most vulnerable groups, the Ministry of Education gave support to 28 education centres serving a total of 26,000 students in marginal urban areas, increasing enrolments by 15% for the 1995 school year in the first and second basic education levels. In addition, students in 1,312 schools were provided with uniforms, shoes and school supplies.

In a bid to counter high drop-out and repetition rates and close the gap between rural and urban areas, assistance was provided to one- and two-teacher schools in vulnerable areas.

A total of 1,400 teachers were trained, and a start was made on the project to establish centres for educational innovation; this project seeks to narrow the social and knowledge gap between rural and urban communities, by training teachers for one-teacher schools, building school facilities and student cafeterias and doubling the number of hours of instruction.

In order to improve the quality of education, a programme to teach a second language has been implemented and the initiative to introduce computer skills into the school curricula has been expanded.

In **Paraguay,** an Advisory Council on Educational Reform was set up within the Ministry of Education and Worship, to assist in the educational reform in progress, which has enjoyed widespread political support within the country. In line with recommendations of this Council, action will be taken to reorganize basic education, delegate responsibilities to schools, promote greater community participation in educational planning, improve coordination between the system of formal education and the world of work and begin a bilingual education programme.

The plan to reorganize the education system involves extending basic education to nine years (three levels of three years each) and instituting pre-school education. The different levels will offer vocational training alternatives; the six years of basic schooling will not be considered final, and there will be a strong push for continuing education.

Many functions previously centralized are now being transferred to the schools, although the process of decentralization to departments and municipalities is still in the early stages. Strengthening the capacity of schools to formulate, develop and evaluate educational projects is one of the fundamental features of the reform.

In this same context, greater community involvement in education is being encouraged, and opportunities for reflecting on education and for planning are being created in each school to get groups of teachers, parents and students to participate in making a diagnosis and in preparing an education strategy for the school that will expand student learning opportunities. "Learning circles", a key tool in teacher training, promote teacher involvement in carrying out the reforms.

Box V.7

EDUCATIONAL REFORM IN JAMAICA

Starting in 1989, the Government of Jamaica has adopted a series of measures designed to accelerate the pace of economic reform. To that end, the Government has created a human resource development programme that targets the poorest groups and places special emphasis on the efficiency and equity of social expenditure.

On the assumption that economic opening would increase the demand for skilled workers and modify the skill profile, the human resource development strategy included improving the basic skills imparted by the education system. Bearing in mind the deficiencies in training in general, the starting point for reform was the quantitative and qualitative improvement of basic and secondary education. Due to budget constraints, the improvement plan aimed to raise the efficiency of educational services and at the same time to target spending to students facing the greatest financial hardship. The first objective was to ensure equality of opportunity, in order that all children might receive at least nine years of quality education. With that aim in mind, curricula were redesigned, the examination system overhauled and the necessary measures taken to group the six lower secondary education tracks into one integrated general school system. These steps were all designed to eliminate the differences in quality, prestige and spending per student implied by a highly differentiated education system.

In 1991, a reform of upper secondary education was begun. The most important aspects of the reform were the introduction of a common curriculum, along with the required complementary training of teachers and principals, the preparation of textbooks and educational material and the rebuilding and equipping of some schools. The strategy adopted was to implement the reform gradually over a period of 15 years.

The educational reforms receive funding from the World Bank, but since this is insufficient, efforts are being made to tap new resources by means of several schemes to share costs with the private sector. The adoption of schools by private firms and the granting of student loans are the most frequently used mechanisms at present. In respect of secondary education, one proposal under examination calls for the distribution of costs in such a way that the State pays the salaries of all school staff, while the students (or their families) cover all other expenses. The students' contribution —registration and monthly tuition— would go into a fund to be administered by the State.

Like Bolivia, Paraguay is a bilingual country. Hence the reform envisages a readaptation of the education system in this area. Bilingual education is to be introduced, and the national programme for mother tongue instruction (in most rural areas, Guaraní) is to be strengthened.

In Peru, the thrust of education policy is on increasing social equity, and this entails reducing educational disparities between the public and private systems and between rural and urban areas. As part of efforts to assist the most vulnerable groups, activities are being coordinated with the National Institute for Education and Health Infrastructure (INFES) and the Ministry for Women's Affairs and Human Development (PROMUDEH).

As in Paraguay and Bolivia, the transfer of responsibilities is not to the municipalities, but rather to the schools, and this requires training school principals in educational service management. The aim is to reach the goal of total coverage by combining centralized administration of public education, greater autonomy for schools in curriculum development and training of teachers and principals in administration and management.

Enhancing the quality of education has also come in for special attention. During 1995, early education centres and single-teacher establishments received almost 800,000 textbooks and exercise books, 200,000 teachers' manuals and 15,000 educational kits. In an effort to improve the quality of teaching and learning, nearby 20,000 primary teachers have undergone a training programme, and basic curricula are being designed that will be adopted gradually.

The Ministry of Education is starting to implement a national quality-measurement system, involving both scholastic achievement tests and participation by the education community. Two pilot tests have already been given to 50,000 students in primary grade four, in 1,667 schools and accompanied by surveys of principals, teachers and parents. The goal for 1997 is to extend the assessment to pupils in the sixth year of primary education.

In **Uruguay,** the four basic objectives of reform are to consolidate social equity; raise the status of the teaching profession; upgrade education quality; and strengthen institutional management in order to facilitate attainment of the first three objectives.

The initiatives for promoting social equity seek to benefit the 40% of children of pre-school age who live in households in the lowest income quintile. The benefits include, *inter alia*, expanded coverage of early, basic and secondary education; expanded full-day schooling; and providing lunch to students who live in households with unmet basic needs.

Another major strategy of the reform is to provide teachers with refresher training. In view of the low level of qualifications held by teachers in general and the marked disparities in their training, a number of initiatives have been started to encourage enrolment in academic centres and training activities for teachers without a degree. The goal for 1999 is to double the number of university graduates who each year enter the teaching profession and to triple the number of teachers who graduate each year.

Class hours in high schools were increased from 648 to 810 hours of instruction annually, so that students are required to be at school for 972 or 1,170 hours, if make-up hours are included.

Future efforts will focus on strengthening basic education in English, addition of computer facilities, provision of textbooks and teaching libraries, distribution of teaching materials and funding of quality improvement projects.

The project to modernize secondary education and teacher training aims at expanding infrastructure in secondary schools; supplying textbooks, books, materials and equipment; and promoting the development of a new curriculum. One aspect of the programme to improve the quality of primary education is the introduction of a regular learning assessment system covering two components: skills actually acquired by students and the institutional and socio-cultural context in which teaching and learning take place.

3. Health system reforms

a) Contrasting health conditions in the region[35]

The region is in the throes of a polarized epidemiological transition (Bobadilla, Frenk and Lozano, 1990) that exhibits two simultaneous trends: communicable and degenerative diseases are on the increase, on the one hand, and, on the other, the distribution of well-being in terms of health is weighted against the very poor. In order to eliminate or reduce this inequality, greater investments need to be made in the poorest segments of the population.

The health system reforms being undertaken by a majority of the countries of the region should be viewed within the context of their specific health needs and the resources allocated to meet those needs. There are great differences between the countries as regards population size and distribution, income and health expenditure, disease burden, human resources available to the health sector and the population's access to health care. It is not surprising, then, that the health situation varies enormously between and within the countries (see box V.8). The following sections provide an overview of some of the indicators that demonstrate the existence of this wide range of situations within the region.

i) Access to health services[36]

A remarkably large number of countries report high percentages of the population with access to health services: fully one third of the countries of the region have coverage rates of over 90% and in most of these cases, rates exceed 95%. This group is mainly comprised of small countries in the Caribbean subregion and include the Bahamas, with a rate of 98%, followed by Barbados, Trinidad and Tobago, Uruguay, Costa Rica and Cuba. In three quarters of the countries of the region, 60% of the population or more have access to health services.

In a number of countries, however, health services are inadequate; for example, coverage amounts to only 34% in Bolivia, 44% in Peru, 46% in Honduras and 50% in Haiti (see table V.9).

Health service coverage is only a very basic, crude measure of actual health care delivery, however. It is also necessary to consider the quality of the services provided, their efficiency and their cost. For example, under the public health system in Chile, a simple mammogram requires four separate trips: one to the doctor to get the order, a second to pay for the examination and obtain a receipt, a third for the actual mammogram and a return visit to the doctor to be informed of the results. Not only is this expensive and time-consuming, but it is also undoubtedly a deterrent, since many women, particularly poor women, will simply not make the necessary effort.

---

[35] ECLAC, on the basis of official data.
[36] Unfortunately, the latest available comparative data are for 1990. Efforts should be made to update these figures in order to ascertain how far health care reform is in fact extending coverage.

> **Box V.8**
>
> **THE POPULATION'S HEALTH PROFILE**
>
> In its latest health report, the World Health Organization notes that the countries of the region are experiencing changes in the profiles of their population and the health problems they confront. Almost all have shown declines in infant and childhood mortality and increases in life expectancy at birth, primarily as a result of the control of infectious diseases in the early years of life. As populations have aged and become concentrated in large urban areas, chronic and degenerative diseases, particularly cardiovascular disease and cancer, have become more important as causes of morbidity and mortality. The countries that have reduced early mortality the most and have achieved the lowest birth rates have the highest incidence of chronic diseases. At the other end of the spectrum are those countries that still have high infant and child mortality, primarily from diarrhoea and acute respiratory illness.
>
> Poverty, as an expression of social inequity, is the underlying cause of most of the morbidity and mortality in the region. Poverty levels in most countries are still higher than they were in the 1970s. Throughout the 1990s, there has been a growing understanding of the interdependence of the factors that contribute to human well-being and of the power of integrated approaches to improve the health status of the population. The Governments of the region increasingly acknowledge that the health sector's boundaries must stretch if countries are to effectively address conditions such as poverty, inequality, marginalization and gender-based discrimination, which lead to gross inequities in health and health care.
>
> **Source:** World Health Organization (WHO), *World Health Report, 1996. Fighting disease, fostering development*, Geneva, 1996.

ii) Births attended by trained health staff

Important inferences can be made about national health practices and priorities by reviewing the proportion of births that are attended by trained health staff. Striking differences exist among the countries of the region as regards this essential and life-saving public health practice. In the majority of the countries, this is a high-priority objective, and in nearly 40% of them between 95% and 99% of births are professionally attended. Elsewhere, however, coverage is very low: in Ecuador the rate is 23%, in Paraguay 27% and in Guatemala 28%.

Large differentials exist between the overall rate of access to health services and the rate of professionally attended births. In Ecuador, 61% of the population has access to health services, but only 23% of births are attended. In El Salvador, the ratio is 59% to 31%; in Guatemala, 50% to 28%; in Paraguay, 54% to 27%; and in Nicaragua, 69% to 40%. Even in Colombia and Jamaica, where access to health services is quite extensive, the gap is significant.

Table V.9
HEALTH ACCESS
(In percentages)

	Percentage of population with access to health services (1990)	Births attended by trained health staff (1991)	Immunization coverage (average 6 antigens) (1995)
Antigua and Barbuda			97
Argentina	92	95	77
Bahamas	98	95	90
Barbados	97	98	95
Belize	86	87	86
Bolivia	34	40	84
Brazil	72	70	83
Chile	93	99	92
Colombia	75	80	90
Costa Rica	96	96	91
Cuba	98	90	99
Dominica			92
Dominican Republic	71	85	94
Ecuador	61	23	88
El Salvador	59	31	97
Grenada			87
Guatemala	50	28	81
Guyana	84	93	89
Haiti	50	40	33
Honduras	46	46	95
Jamaica	89	73	92
Mexico	77	95	93
Nicaragua	69	40	91
Panama	79	85	89
Paraguay	54	27	80
Peru	44	46	95
St. Kitts and Nevis			100
Saint Lucia			96
Saint Vincent and the Grenadines			100
Suriname	88	91	71
Trinidad and Tobago	97	99	82
Uruguay	96	99	88
Venezuela	76	99	81

Source: World Health Organization (WHO), *The World Health Report 1996. Fighting Disease; Fostering Development*, Geneva, 1996.

There is another group of countries, however, where greater priority is being given to ensuring professional childbirth care. In the Dominican Republic, for example, where the rate of access to health care is 71%, 85% of births are attended; in Mexico, the ratio is 77% to 95%; and in Venezuela, where 76% of the population at large has access to health care, fully 99% of births are professionally attended. These figures represent major achievements and attest to the high priority that is being given to minimizing infant and maternal mortality and ensuring healthy birth outcomes, and thus illustrate the possibilities that are open to other countries (see table V.9).

iii) Immunization coverage

The majority of the countries in Latin America and the Caribbean report encouraging figures on the immunization of children in the first year of life, and all have reliable information available for 1995. Haiti, where only 33% of children receive all the necessary immunizations every year, is the only country that is lagging far behind in this respect. In nearly every other country, irrespective of the other characteristics of the health system, immunization coverage is high (between 80% and 90%) or very high (over 90%). There are two countries —Saint Kitts and Nevis and Saint Vincent and the Grenadines— with 100% coverage. The performance of some countries, however, such as Argentina (77%), Suriname (71%) and Venezuela (81%) could be much better than it is (see table V.9).

iv) Access to safe drinking water and adequate sanitation

Information for 1994-1995 on access to safe drinking water and adequate sanitation reveals significant differences within the region and points up the limited access to sanitation that is available in a number of countries which are considered well-off in other respects.

Costa Rica, where 100% of the population has access to safe water, leads the region. In last place are Haiti and Paraguay, where a mere 28% and 35% of the population, respectively, have safe water. The remainder of the countries fall into a middle range, with between 58% and 96% of the population having access to drinking water.

In public health terms, the limited nature of the regional population's access to adequate sanitation services has a great impact on childhood morbidity and mortality and on the demand for health services. Only two countries have achieved 90% coverage. Costa Rica leads with 99%, followed by Guyana with 90%, while Haiti, where barely 24% of the population has access to adequate sanitation, lags far behind. A number of countries that are economically well-off seriously neglect this fundamental human right: only 68% of Argentine citizens, for example, have adequate sanitation; in Chile the rate is 71%; in Uruguay, 61%; and in Venezuela, 59% (see table V.9).

v) Urban-rural disparities in health, water and sanitation

Only one country in the region, Trinidad and Tobago, can claim that its rural and urban populations have equal access to health, water and sanitation services. In Uruguay and the Dominican Republic, sanitation conditions are actually better in rural areas than in urban areas. In such an advanced country as Chile, on the other hand, water and sanitation conditions are such that the proportion of the inhabitants in rural areas who have access to safe drinking water is less than half that in urban areas. In the remaining countries, the majority of the rural population has much less access to these health safeguards and preventive factors and to favourable environmental conditions (see table V.9).

b) Problems with health systems

Numerous exogenous factors —ranging from geographical barriers and the quality of communications systems to cultural or ethnic differences or similarities within the population— facilitate or hinder the population's access to health services and demonstrate just how important intersectoral policies are. Other factors may have to do with the level of social development (for example, illiteracy indexes) or trends in economic development (as manifested, for example, in income structure and concentration and the percentage of wage earners in the labour force). Health-related demands voiced by politically-influential organizations also have a great effect. Endogenous factors, too, can be crucial to access; examples include whether coverage mechanisms are voluntary or compulsory, what proportion of social expenditure is allocated to health and to what extent the sector is integrated.

Obstacles that block poor people's access to health services also vary depending on the provider. Clearly the poor can hardly afford private medicine, yet the aggregate health resources available to society are further depleted when resource allocations to private health care, from which the poor derive no benefit, are high and inefficient.

Where universal coverage is not a goal, social security serves a clientele drawn only from specific employment or occupational categories. Where universal insurance coverage does exist, as in Costa Rica, subsidies end up being directed to the poor and are thus progressive in nature; government policies that broaden health coverage to encompass the whole population —including vulnerable groups such as own-account workers, the elderly and the poor— smooth out the inequalities inherent in multi-tiered funding systems and make it possible to expand the universal service package. For this to happen, however, the bulk of the labour force needs to be employed, and it is thus a viable option for middle-income countries with both the financial resources and the necessary political resolve and administrative capability (World Bank, 1993, p. 166). In cases where the health insurance system is unified and strives for universal coverage, limitations on access may be due to financial or geographical constraints.

A low budget or a badly organized health sector can also prevent the poor from gaining access to health services. Moreover, even when services are free of charge, they generally involve implicit costs for the user, such as the time spent travelling to the health centre or waiting for long periods or when a patient is turned away, the cost of transportation or lodging, etc. Any inefficiencies in the services themselves may also have a high opportunity cost.

There is thus an urgent need to speed up the rate of health coverage extension, improve the quality of care and raise productivity in order to overcome the sector's myriad microeconomic inefficiencies and increase its effectiveness. There is something of a paradox in the way the countries' different baseline situations affect the size of the task that faces them, since, where coverage is lower and health disparities greater, administrative costs are actually higher; meanwhile, the more integrated or coordinated health systems, unlike stratified health schemes, have tended to reduce inequalities in terms of health facilities and standards.

To illustrate this point, on the basis of the annual average increase in the percentage of the economically active population (EAP) with social insurance coverage between 1960 and 1985/1988, it has been calculated that it would take Mexico and Nicaragua between 45 and 64 years to achieve universal social insurance coverage, including the poor; Peru and Ecuador would need between 80 and 98 years; Honduras, Bolivia, Paraguay, Guatemala and El Salvador would take between 176 and 272 years; and the Dominican Republic would need 530 years (Mesa-Lago, 1992, p. 24).

Health system organization is greatly affected by the phenomenon of demographic transition, which has to do with the ratio between crude birth rates and mortality rates. This process has reached different stages in the various countries of the region: incipient transition, moderate transition, transition in progress, or advanced transition (see figure V.8). Countries at the incipient or moderate stages exhibit the greatest inequalities in terms of health.[37] The stage reached in the demographic transition determines the population's age structure and thus influences its specific health-risk profile. Accordingly, it is an important consideration in defining health priorities and the cost structure of services.

It is essential to control the escalation of costs that may result from treatment of non-communicable diseases and other health disorders associated with given life styles and other social factors, such as accidents. Unjustified cost increases may also arise from technological changes that do not have a proportional impact on health status and encourage the overprovision of services.

The current trend is to give preference to market instruments for the allocation of resources and regulation of economic activity in the health sector, even in those countries of the region where health service coverage is very low. The fact of the matter, however, is that the market has serious difficulties in this respect. If the challenges involved in achieving greater social equity are to be met effectively and resources are to be used efficiently, the health sector will need to adopt fresh approaches that take account of the existence of imperfect competition, the limits of consumer sovereignty, asymmetric information and the various exclusion mechanisms at work in the sector, all of which calls for an adequate regulatory system for health markets in the public and private spheres, embracing both funding agencies and health service providers (see box V.9).

---

[37] Inequalities in terms of health are any unnecessary, avoidable or unfair differences in the population's health conditions that affect the very poor and groups with health risks or specific illnesses or whose access to services is restricted by geographical barriers (Whitehead, 1990).

Reforms cannot be restricted to the public sector but must include the private sector as well, since what the private sector does may generate social costs as a result of overprovision of services, adverse selection by beneficiaries, high intermediation costs, disproportionate increases in health plans, inadequate protection against catastrophic and age-related illnesses, and cross-subsidies from the public to the private sector. A lack of transparency in the various health-service markets hampers competition and reduces the social efficacy of the services. Under such circumstances, joint public/private schemes are not usually able to generate the required relations of synergy and competition either (see box V.10).

Figure V.8
THE DEMOGRAPHIC TRANSITION IN LATIN AMERICA AND THE CARIBBEAN
(1990-1995)

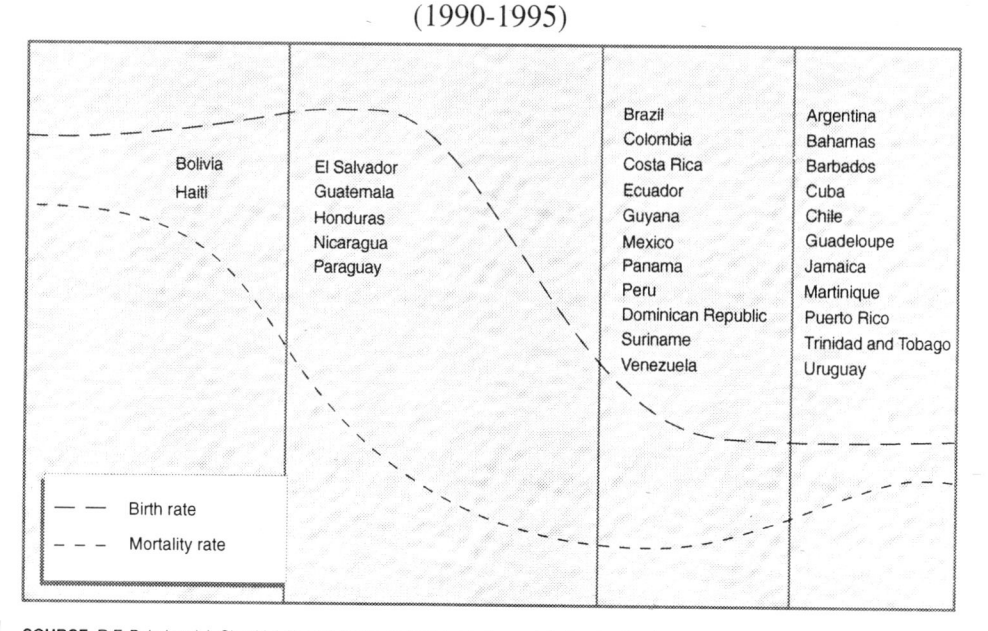

Bolivia Haiti	El Salvador Guatemala Honduras Nicaragua Paraguay	Brazil Colombia Costa Rica Ecuador Guyana Mexico Panama Peru Dominican Republic Suriname Venezuela	Argentina Bahamas Barbados Cuba Chile Guadeloupe Jamaica Martinique Puerto Rico Trinidad and Tobago Uruguay

— — Birth rate
- - - Mortality rate

SOURCE: R.F. Bajraj and J. Chackiel, "La población en América Latina y el Caribe: tendencias y percepciones", *Población y desarrollo: tendencias y nuevos desafíos*, Pensamiento Iberoamericano, No 28, and Notas de Población, No. 62, Madrid, June 1996.

Box V.9
ALTRUISM AND EFFICIENCY IN HEALTH INSURANCE

In order to safeguard the public from health-care costs, health systems are funded on the basis of different forms of pooled savings arrangements, which may consist of a combination of private insurance, public-sector insurance and national health services. Whether the insurance is individual or collective in nature is crucial to its operation as a funding mechanism.

In private insurance schemes, people pay an individual or group risk premium and obtain benefits in the form of payments for services used. In public-sector insurance schemes, people pay taxes or compulsory contributions irrespective of individual risk, and they, too, receive benefits in the form of payment for services. National health services are financed out of the treasury and provide in-kind benefits in the form of direct medical care.

Changes favouring market mechanisms as a resource-allocation instrument figure prominently among the health system reforms being undertaken in the region. Some countries, such as Chile and Colombia, have incorporated market elements into their insurance structures and have sought to change the rules on health insurance contributions; the specific forms taken by these changes are described below in the discussion on individual countries.

Nevertheless, the introduction of market mechanisms is not in itself a guarantee of greater economic efficiency. For various reasons, the market faces serious difficulties as a resource-allocation mechanism and regulator of economic activity in the field of health care. Regulatory and supervisory instruments and institutions need to be created that will promote socially acceptable levels of distributive equity and resource-allocation efficiency within the economic system. There are at least four basic lines of reasoning in this regard, of which three have to do with the efficiency of insurance mechanisms and the fourth with equity objectives.

Private insurance raises two fundamental problems. The first, "moral hazard", arises when the insured person is able to manipulate the probability of certain events occurring or the size of the loss being insured against. The second, "adverse selection", has two facets: it occurs either when the insured is in a position to conceal information from the insurer, who is thus unable to distribute risk efficiently; or when not all risks are equally profitable and there is no redistributive "pooled risk premium" insurance scheme that will guarantee the insured suitable coverage for given risks. In public-sector insurance, there is the problem of "free-riders", i.e., individuals who obtain insurance benefits without contributing, or while contributing as little as possible, even though they have a level of income or private insurance that makes such action unjustifiable. This problem may also arise in pooled risk insurance schemes.

The second consideration concerns the user's difficulty in taking rational and informed decisions (constraints on consumer sovereignty) due to an inadequate grasp of the relevant information and to conditions of asymmetric information between providers and users. This results in a loss of efficiency in unregulated markets owing to the supplier's "quasi-monopoly" on information and brings a variant of Say's law into play, whereby supply creates its own demand.

The third argument refers to the externalities generated by virtue of the fact that health is a public good. Thus, an unregulated market solution will lead to under-production of socially desirable elements such as preventive care or information.

Finally, from the standpoint of social equity, a health system reform must address three fundamental aspects: i) horizontal coverage —who to include; ii) vertical coverage —what types of medical services to provide; and iii) funding arrangements —how to obtain funding and the size and financing of subsidies. Redistributive equity will be adversely affected if the market's operational difficulties lead to the exclusion of people on grounds of income level, age or cost of treatment (catastrophic illnesses).

Source: K. Arrow, "Uncertainty and the welfare economics of medical care", *The American Economic Review*, vol. 53, No. 5, December 1963; Joseph White, *Competing Solutions: American Health Care Proposals and International Experiences*, Washington, D.C. The Brookings Institution, 1995; and Jorge Katz and Alberto Muñoz, Organización del sector salud: puja distributiva y equidad (LC/G.102), Buenos Aires, ECLAC office in Buenos Aires, 1988.

Box V.10

THE CHALLENGES OF PUBLIC/PRIVATE PARTNERSHIPS

Given health markets' characteristics, market forces and competition need to be backed up by efficient public administration of regulatory and oversight functions, service delivery and funding. The experience of industrialized countries, and certainly of Latin American and Caribbean countries, indicates that the share of public expenditure on health services has remained constant over time. Among members of the Organization for Economic Cooperation and Development (OECD), public health expenditure as a percentage of total health expenditure falls, on average, within a range of 70% to 75%. In the United States, which is probably one of the countries where the private sector plays the most active role in the health industry, public expenditure accounts for around 42% of total spending on health care. In Chile, where major health sector reforms were implemented in 1983 in order to allow private-sector participation, public spending on health in 1995 equalled 56% of the total.

In the region as a whole, the challenge for health-sector reform is not merely to improve the productivity of the public sector's service delivery and to find incentives for the private sector to take part in health-service funding and delivery; the crucial task is to combine public- and private-sector participation in such a way as to boost the efficiency of the sector as a whole and help increase the coverage of the population and of medical services and in this way lead to greater equity within the health system.

The dynamic of a public-private mix should be judged in the light of health reform objectives and tasks, which themselves determine the nature of the system's regulation. The following are some of a health system's social objectives:

1. **Universality:** Ensuring the greatest possible coverage for all age groups. The chief task of regulation here is to prevent private insurance schemes from excluding older age groups by raising their premiums at the stage in their life cycle when they are least able to pay.

2. **Comprehensiveness:** Broadening the range of services classified as medically necessary. The principal aim of regulation here is to prevent private insurance schemes from excluding persons suffering from catastrophic or chronic illnesses; this is an important consideration given the region's stage in the epidemiological transition.

3. **Structure of funding:** Ensuring that funding sources uphold equity objectives as well as the goals of efficacy and efficiency in health service provision. The main task for regulation here is to incorporate redistributive mechanisms into funding, which involves setting means-tested premiums, while providing benefits according to need.

The aims of a health system's economic administration include the following:

1. **Cost control:** Limiting cost increases by building cost-containment mechanisms into both funding and service delivery. The chief task in this connection is to ensure the presence of competition as a cost-control mechanism in a heterogeneous, segmented market.

2. **Demographic transition:** The ageing of the population is inevitable, and private funding schemes therefore need to make allowance for this phenomenon by actuarial means and alternative funding mechanisms need to be established to deal with its effects. The chief task here is to adapt funding schemes and service delivery to the needs of an ageing population.

3. **Technological development:** The health-service delivery apparatus must adapt to the latest technological advances by instituting cost-control mechanisms that prevent an overprovision of services and the installation of new technologies without a prior evaluation of their benefits.

4. **Improvements in the efficiency and quality of health service delivery:** Ending the oligopolistic nature of the supply of medical services by incorporating features that will stimulate competition in health service provision. The main challenge here is to introduce incentives to boost productivity.

c) A regional overview of health reforms

Health system reform is clearly now a part of the regional agenda, and some countries have already embarked upon the reform process, although the majority are still at the point of considering proposals or engaging in political negotiations to this end. While there are a variety of national orientations and strategies, generally speaking the reforms aim to make benefits more equitable and to introduce a greater element of altruism and equity into funding schemes; to improve the efficiency and efficacy of care; to raise public-sector productivity through administrative changes; to regulate the private sector in order to increase the social impact of its services; to contain escalating costs; and to foster synergy between the public and private sectors.

Some of the reforms are intended to be comprehensive in nature and thus address such aspects as funding, intersectoral competition, regulation, or public-sector administration. Others are partial reforms, affecting only one of these aspects. All, however, involve changing the configuration of the sector.

Despite these differences, reform efforts have tended to converge around such ideas as launching sanitation campaigns and reinforcing primary care; articulating a national health system; strengthening decentralization and local health systems; dealing with inequality of access by providing basic universal services or undertaking specific activities that target vulnerable groups or groups at risk, or through demand subsidies. Renewed emphasis has been placed on outpatient care and self-care, and new forms of hospital administration are being sought.

The prevailing trend is towards the separation of funding from service delivery in the public sector and towards the definition of specialized financial, regulatory, evaluative and provider functions. In a number of cases the emergence of quasi-markets is being encouraged. However, precisely because of this separation and specialization of functions in the public sector, together with the changes being made to the public-private mix, ministries of health are being endowed with powers —for example in the area of regulation— that overreach their traditionally weak institutional capabilities. Hence the urgent need to reinforce these ministries' financial and technical capacities if the reforms are not to founder.

The path of reform is of course not a smooth one; every aspect of the process not only raises technical problems or demands funding, but also requires the political agreement of a broad spectrum of actors who stand to gain or lose from the suggested changes. Moreover, the priority given to different measures and the setbacks and progress experienced in each country depend to a large extent on its initial situation in terms of the institutional structure of the public health system and of its particular mix of public and private actors.

Table V.10 summarizes the main instruments of reform in a number of countries of the region and assesses their progress; as may be seen, implementation of the most comprehensive changes is concentrated in a few countries. The special situation of the English-speaking Caribbean countries is examined in box V.11.

Table V.10
INSTRUMENTS OF HEALTH SECTOR REFORM, 1995

Rationale and emphasis of reform measures	Arg	Bol	Bra	Col	CR	Ch	Ecu	ES	Gua	Hon	Mex	Nic	Pan	Par	Pe	DR	Ven
Sector morphology management																	
Articulation of national health system	X		E	X	E	X	y	y	y	y	y	X	y	y	y		y
Reinforcement of oversight function of Health Ministry	X	y	X	X	X	E	X	y	y	y	y	X	X	y	y/E	y	y
Promotion of local health systems	E				E		y	y	y	y		E	y	y			
Reinforcement of sub-national, decentralized organizations	E	y	X	E	E	E	y	y	y			X	y	y	E	y	y
Modification of public-private mix	E		y	E	E	E		y	y	y	y	E	y	y	y		
Regulation of private health markets; regulation of social security	E		y	E		E		y						y	y		y
Management																	
Restructuring of hospital management	E		E	X	X	E	y	y				y	y		y		y
Separation into specialized functions of financing, insurance, regulation, evaluation and service delivery. Promotion of quasi-markets	E		X	E	X	E	y				y	y		y	y	y	y
Performance contracts with public health service providers			E		X	E	y					y			y		
Incentives and sanctions based on individual and institutional performance	X		E	X	E	E	y		X			y	y		y	y	y
Improvement of human resources management												y			y		
Funding																	
Use of capitation payments	E			E		E									y		
Use of advance payments by diagnostic or treatment groups	E		E	E		E					y				y		
Increase in solidarity and social equity of funding	E		E	E	E	E	y	y	y	y	X	y	y	y	y	y	y
Social Equity																	
Basic universal benefits; unification of benefits	X		y	E	E	E	E	y	y	y	X	E	y	y	y	y	y
Expansion of coverage through universal and targeted programmes	X	y	E	E	E	E	E	y	y	y	y	E	y	y	y	y	y

Source: Based on country reports presented at the Special Meeting on Health Sector Reform organized by IDB, IBRD, ECLAC, OAS, WHO/PAHO, UNFPA, UNICEF and USAID, Washington, D.C., September 1995, and additional information.

E = implementation begun; X = measure in initial phase of implementation; Y = measure announced but not yet implemented.

> **Box V.11**
>
> **HEALTH SYSTEM REFORM IN THE CARIBBEAN**
>
> Health indexes in the English-speaking countries of the Caribbean are very high. These countries have reached an advanced stage in the epidemiological transition and all have sound public health systems designed along the lines of the British system which are remarkable for their degree of integration.
>
> The reforms currently under way do not presume to alter the basic characteristics of the system but instead aim to deal with the problem of rising costs and to improve the use of resources. The emphasis varies from country to country, but the measures proposed to accomplish these tasks include cost recovery through means-tested co-payments (user fees); improving the quality of care; measuring the cost-structure of services; introducing cost-containment mechanisms; preparing indicators on service delivery and resource utilization; introducing national health insurance that will allow access to services not provided by the public health system; and improving the referral system. In some cases, greater private-sector participation is also being encouraged.
>
> Naturally, there are distinctive features in each country's health-sector reforms. **Jamaica**, for instance, emphasizes decentralization of the different areas of competence. **Trinidad and Tobago** has separated the relevant functions within the system: the regional health authorities, who are responsible for providing services, are accountable to the Ministry of Health in its capacity as a purchaser, through annual service agreements covering not only the volume of services, but also their quality and appropriateness. These authorities may contract services from suppliers in either the public or the private sector who meet the established performance standards. Improvements in private-sector regulation are also in the pipeline. **Barbados** plans to encourage private-sector participation and promote joint public and private funding and service delivery systems while at the same time regulating the activities of private agents and stimulating competition between the two sectors.
>
> This group of countries have either introduced or plan to introduce some form of co-payment or user fee as a means of containing and rationalizing public expenditure. Existing user-fee mechanisms need to be improved, since the criteria for exemption are unclear and overly flexible. It is therefore essential to set up transparent procedures for identifying beneficiaries in order to ensure that the user-fee system operates efficiently and has its intended redistributive impact.
>
> In addition, in light of the above-mentioned characteristics of health markets, a fundamental task for those countries that propose to do away with the public-sector monopoly on service provision will be to tighten up the regulation of the private sector and press on with administrative reforms that will strengthen public-sector competitiveness within this new framework.
>
> **Source:** Based on country reports presented at the Special Meeting on Health Sector Reform organized by ECLAC, IBRD, IDB, OAS, PAHO/WHO, UNFPA, UNICEF and USAID, Washington D.C., September 1995.

d) Lessons to be learned from selected health system reforms

In order to illustrate the challenges facing the region's reform effort, a number of reform initiatives are outlined below.

The emphasis in **Argentina** (Arce, 1996; Flood, 1996; Montoya, 1996; Tafani, 1996) has been on changing the structure of the country's social insurance health programmes, which, since they are administered by trade unions and thus are attached to specific employment sectors, allow little choice of health service provider. The reforms have fostered freedom of choice for users; the automatic subsidies from the redistribution fund (Fondo Solidario de Redistribución) are now targeted and means-tested separately for each programme; the economically inactive population can choose among a variety of service providers; procedures have been set in motion to make the social insurance health programmes' scale of operations more economically viable; responsibility for enrolment in and contributions to the National Health Insurance System has been vested in a single agent; and a membership register has been compiled to increase transparency and cut down on evasion.

There is still work to be done on optimizing competition between the public and private sectors, possibly owing to the fact that thus far the emphasis has been on funding and little attention has been paid to certain characteristics of the health services market. Prepaid health benefit administrators have extremely high costs and provide a very low level of services. Intermediation has hypertrophied, although the glut on the market has led the agencies themselves to introduce a number of rationalization measures. These developments call for a complementary agenda, inasmuch as administrative bodies and private service providers are not subject to regulation, and the changes made in the funding arrangements for social insurance health programmes have triggered oligopolistic or oligopsonic tendencies.

In addition, the self-management of hospitals was introduced as an instrument for achieving a health care system that is integrated, efficient, effective and of high quality, as well as for guaranteeing free services. It consists of decentralized hospitals under jurisdictional guidelines, with strategic, delegated administration; this should generate changes in the organizational culture. According to official figures, 85% of public health providers are already operating under this system. Collection for services performed in public hospitals but covered under other plans should increase the financial resources of the hospitals.

In **Brazil** (Brazil, 1995; Medici, 1994), one hallmark of the 1990s has been the effort to consolidate the Unified Health System (SUS), which represents a very ambitious attempt, considering the country's size and complexity, to combine the public health and social security services. Because of the controversy surrounding the definition of its various institutional functions and powers, the SUS has not yet taken final shape, and its regulatory, evaluative and oversight functions remain relatively vague.

The question of funding, which has been affected by the fiscal adjustment process, has been critical. Since, at the federal level, health services are financed through the social security budget and are therefore related to the pensions budget, their funding will be influenced by the social insurance reforms that are currently under discussion. It is essential to ensure regular funding for the states and municipalities so that they can raise the quality of their health services, and it is equally important to ensure that a coherent fiscal basis is established for decentralized expenditure. Specific allocations for subsidized health care have yet to be made, as to date these services are still being funded out of the revenues from general payroll taxes.

With the aim of boosting the management capacity of SUS, it has been recommended that funding should be linked to the performance of the various functions for which decentralized units are responsible; another important step in this connection would be to make greater use of such incentives as performance evaluation indicators. Consideration has also been given to regulating the private health industry —a major objective in view of the significant role it plays in the sector (it accounts for 72% of all hospital beds)— and to the need to achieve a synergistic, competitive relationship between the public and private subsystems in order to ensure better resource utilization. It is essential that efficient mechanisms be set up for controlling costs and payments to private providers in order to solve the problems involved in fee-for-service arrangements.

Colombia (Colombia, 1995; Morales, 1996; Plaza, 1996) has begun decentralizing expenditure and has introduced structured competition among insurers and health care providers within the framework of a comprehensive social security system containing a redistributive component. The system includes a contributory scheme, jointly funded by employees and employers, and a subsidized scheme for the neediest; in both schemes, benefits are regulated under a compulsory health plan.

The central element of the contributory scheme, which is much like an integrated insurance system, is the Solidarity and Guarantee Fund: the Fund ensures an even spread of resources and equal treatment based on a capitation premium adjusted for each age group in order to forestall risk selection and to allow for age-related cost differences. Each contributing worker pays 12% of his or her basic wage.

The subsidized scheme is targeted mechanism funded by central government transfers to the departments and municipalities and by the Solidarity and Guarantee Fund, whose own financing comes from contributions equivalent to one per cent of each payment into the contributory scheme and from other inputs from the family allowance system and central government.

The bodies that perform both the funding and the insurance functions for this system are known as health promotion agencies (EPS). These agencies form the backbone of the benefits system and thus play an integrating role. They are private institutions to which the Fund delegates responsibility for enrolling members and collecting payments, as well as for arranging and guaranteeing health services covered by the compulsory health plan for their members, to whom they are required to offer a choice of providers. The health plan itself is administered by public and private health care providers (IPS). A variety of cost-control mechanisms exist; there is a fee of 150 pesos per person, payment is based on a system of diagnostic groups, and there is a list of generic medicaments that must be used.

While Colombia has no plans to replace supply-side subsidies entirely with demand-side subsidies, the final ratio of one to the other (i.e., whether demand subsidies should, for example, comprise 60% or 80% of total subsidies) has not yet been determined.

Most EPS contracts with providers are still on a fee-for-service basis, with all the perverse incentives this entails. Capitation payments have come into wide use mainly at the first level of care, partly because the lower financial risk existing at this level makes such an arrangement more acceptable to providers. There has been a significant expansion of what are known as "third sector" health providers (cooperatives or independently-run community organizations) offering care under the subsidized scheme.

Clearly, the aim of this reform is to use financial mechanisms and an integrated structure to improve efficiency. The emphasis is on administrative changes that will increase microeconomic efficiency and the efficacy of action in the health sector. Given the altruistic aspect of this system and the need to expand its coverage, it is vital that efficient fiscal mechanisms be set up to limit evasion and avoidance of payment obligations. Such hindrances as the persistence of traditional management styles and the poor vertical and horizontal integration of different levels of care also need to be removed to allow the system to shift towards demand subsidies. Finally, it is necessary to find efficient ways of financing the externalities that demand subsidies will not cover, such as teaching and research activities in public hospitals.

Costa Rica (Costa Rica, 1995 and 1996; Salas, 1996) has one of the region's least stratified health systems. Even so, it suffers from such flaws as fragmentation and a lack of continuity of care, a deterioration of outpatient care and reductions in the coverage of preventive programmes, as well as geographical constraints on access, problems with doctor-patient ratios and long waiting periods for appointments —particularly with specialists— or medicaments. This is a centralized system that suffers from weak management development mechanisms, administrative rigidities, a lack of incentives for efficiency, rising costs and, according to recent estimates, declining productivity. Payment collection is inefficient, resource distribution and allocation poor, and evasion and avoidance of contributions widespread.

As a result of the reforms, there is now a clearer separation of functions: the Ministry of Health has been made responsible for regulation and promotion; while the Costa Rican Social Security Fund (CCSS) is in charge of the operational side of promotion, preventive care, recovery and rehabilitation. An innovative aspect of the reform programme which contributes to the system's articulation is the effort made to promote the development of what are known as basic integrated health care teams. By the end of 1995, 229 of these teams were working in the system's 31 health districts; this figure represents 28% of the target of 800 set for 1998, by which time half of Costa Rica's regional hospitals' admissions are supposed to be health-team referrals.

A great deal of emphasis has also been placed on the question of management. Administrative changes currently under consideration include ways of modifying the personnel recruitment system, introducing performance-based hospital budget allocation scheme and individual staff performance incentives, and strengthening hospital management. In 1996, under the newly-created national evaluation system, the CCSS signed a "results agreement". Towards the end of the same year, seven hospitals in their turn signed agreements with the Fund regarding specific aspects of their internal organization, quality of care and service provision. If successful, this pilot scheme may be extended throughout the hospital system beginning in the second half of 1997.

Chile (Chile, 1995; Sojo, 1996a) has a dual health system whose public and private subsystems are structured differently and do not compete with one another. The aim of administrative reform in the public subsystem is to consolidate its cost advantage over the private sector, improve efficiency and attain greater social equity through a capitation mechanism and a payment scheme based on diagnostic groups.

The reform programme has clarified the division of functions among the Ministry of Public Health, the National Health Fund (FONASA) and the country's health services, and has established an instrument known as a "management agreement", which makes concrete results the basis for allocating funding. In order to raise human resource productivity, there are plans to modify existing public-sector recruitment and remuneration modalities and to give health care facilities a more flexible, less centralized structure. In addition, career development mechanisms now takes greater account of performance, merit and efficiency. Steps are being taken to promote the assignment of individual responsibilities, to forge a link between the performance of individual staff members and of the institution itself, and to ensure that staff members' continued employment within the system is based on the results of competitive examinations.

The impact of these administrative improvements is severely limited, however, by the sector's dual structure and centralized budgeting system. In order to ensure that the effectiveness of services can be assessed as well as their microeconomic efficiency, performance measures and standards need to be introduced to allow evaluation of the quality of service.

As regards the private sector, FONASA has helped to limit the public-sector's cross-subsidization of private health insurers (ISAPRES) and, since the powers of the Superintendency of Health Insurance Institutions were extended in 1990, important changes have been made. The insured's right to any surplus generated in excess of the value of the health plan and the mandatory contribution of 7% of the insured's income has been recognized. The system has also been made more transparent by the requirement that not only fees for medical care but also coverage percentages and limits should be expressed in Development Units (UFs). It has been made easier for people to switch insurers, and a large number of exclusions have been eliminated.[38] A ceiling was set on age-related increases in the cost of a health plan, whereby the amount of any rate hike must not exceed the difference in cost for a young person and an older person at the time of enrolment.

However, in order to arrive at lasting, reliable solutions for the problems raised by the system's lack of social equity —particularly in relation to old age and catastrophic illness— and to correct the lack of competition between the two subsectors, changes in the basic structure of the system are now being considered. The idea has been raised of introducing a compulsory, universal, integrated health plan under which the insured would have a free choice of provider but insurers would not have a right of refusal; additional benefits would be negotiable. A reform of this nature would require a social consensus as to the degree of solidarity and social equity to be built into the system.

The advances described in this section have been coupled with attempts on the part of the Governments to increase funding for the health sector. As shown in table V.11, per capita public expenditure on health has gone up in 10 out of 13 countries.

---

[38] The only exclusions now remaining concern cosmetic plastic surgery, private nursing care, and hospitalization for the purposes of bed rest. Undisclosed pre-existing conditions are also excluded, but with a cut-off date of five years.

Table V.11
TRENDS IN PER CAPITA EXPENDITURE ON HEALTH

Country	Real per capita social expenditure (1987 dollars)		Absolute variation (1987 dollars)	Percentage variation
	1990-1991	1994-1995		
Sectoral average [a]	51.5	62.9		
Argentina	141.4	176.8	35.3	25.0
Brazil [b]	54.3	57.1 [c]	2.8	5.2
Chile	41.2	58.8 [c]	17.7	43.0
Colombia	15.5	48.8	33.3	214.6
Costa Rica	105.2	113.5 [c]	8.3	7.9
Ecuador	17.6	22.7	5.2	29.6
El Salvador	14.4	15.2 [c]	0.8	5.5
Guatemala	7.8	6.9	(0.9)	(11.2)
Honduras	23.6	26.3	2.7	11.2
Nicaragua	41.5	34.5	(7.0)	(16.8)
Panama	123.5	143.6 [c]	20.0	16.2
Paraguay [d]	3.9	11.2	7.4	188.9
Peru	5.2	...	...	...
Dominican Republic	8.2 [e]	...	...	...
Uruguay	79.2	102.4	23.2	29.3
Venezuela	38.1 [e]	...	...	...

Source: ECLAC, *Social Panorama of Latin America. 1996 Edition* (LC/G.1946-P), Santiago, Chile, 1997, table IV.2. United Nations publication, Sales No. E.97.II.G.4.
[a] Owing to lack of information, averages for the sector do not include Dominican Republic, Peru or Venezuela.
[b] Central government expenditure only.
[c] Includes 1994 only.
[d] Central government budget expenditure only.
[e] Includes 1990 only.

4. Housing

a) An overview of housing conditions in the region

i) Urbanization and the demand for housing

Following the intense urbanization process observed in the region during the last few decades, 350 million people in Latin America and the Caribbean, or 74% of the total population of the region, now live in urban areas. However, the 1990s have seen a deceleration of the process as population growth in the region slows, mainly as a consequence of the lower fertility rates associated with urban lifestyles. This phenomenon is particularly marked in large cities, which are not growing as rapidly as previously; a more balanced pattern of settlement has thus developed which, at the least, is not adding further to the acute concentration of the population in sprawling urban conglomerations previously observed in most Latin American countries.

The reduction in population pressure during this period has not, however, diminished the great need for new dwellings, which continues to increase unabated. A comparison of census figures shows that despite the slower pace of population growth, the formation of new households is still on the rise at a rate of around 3% per year. This increase is related to the progressive reduction in the average size of households in the region as the process of demographic transition progresses and a growing number of families throughout the region adopt an urban lifestyle.

An analysis of a group of eight countries which have gathered comparable census information for the last two decades reveals an acceleration in the rate of increase in household units in three countries: Panama (from 2.8% to 3.6%), Paraguay (from 3% to 3.9%) and Peru (from 1.8% to 3.2%). In the other five cases (Brazil, Chile, Ecuador, Mexico and Venezuela), the rate of increase in household units has slowed but not as much as population growth has. For example, in Brazil, the decrease in the population growth index (from 2.5% to 1.9%) was sharper than the drop in the rate of increase in the number of households (from 3.1% to 2.9%) in the same period.

The region now also has more highly diversified family structures which have given rise to new requirements in terms of housing standards and locations in keeping with the growth patterns of the countries' urban centres. For example, in countries, such as those of the Southern Cone, where the process of urbanization occurred the earliest, the relative ageing of the population brought about by the decline in fertility and the increase in life expectancy has raised the number of single- and two-person households, many of which consist of elderly persons. In countries where the process of urbanization is still under way, a substantial number of young persons and couples now approaching adulthood are forming a dynamic sector of demand with very specific housing and other urban requirements. Meanwhile, in countries at the incipient and moderate stages of the demographic transition, where population growth rates are still between approximately 2.5% and 3% and where large, often multi-generational or extended families are still the norm, the nuclearization of the family has yet to take place.

One characteristic of changing family structures in Latin America and the Caribbean which affects the composition of the demand for housing is the high number of female-headed households. Of the 13 countries for which information is available, only Peru and Paraguay recorded a slight decline in the percentage of female-headed households between the 1980s and 1990s. With few exceptions, female-headed families (whether extended, composite or nuclear) have a higher poverty index than those headed by men and thus constitute at-risk groups that deserve special attention in the formulation of housing policies.

ii) Urban poverty and housing shortages

Given the scale of urbanization in the region, poverty is now a primarily urban phenomenon and the city is the backdrop for a good deal of the social inequity and exclusion affecting Latin American and Caribbean societies. Concern about the spread of urban poverty, which excludes a substantial part of the population from access to housing, urban services and job opportunities, has led the countries to treat the improvement of living conditions for the lowest-income households as a priority objective of their human settlements policies (ECLAC, 1996c). Furthermore, Governments recognize income distribution —which is now more concentrated and inequitable than at the end of the 1970s— as a serious obstacle to progress in reducing housing shortages and other unmet urban needs in the region.

As shown in table V.12, only two out of every three existing dwellings in the region provide adequate accommodations, and the serious problems posed by makeshift housing are concentrated among the lowest-income group. Significant differences may be observed among the countries in this regard, ranging from those with a higher proportion of adequate housing (Argentina, Chile, Cuba, Uruguay and Venezuela) to those with more limited housing stocks (Bolivia, El Salvador, Guatemala, Nicaragua and Peru).

As indicated in table V.13, the countries face a considerable housing shortage in both quantitative and qualitative terms, which, in most cases, greatly outstrips the efforts being made within the framework of housing policies to generate sufficient new housing units to accommodate at least the new households that are being established and so avoid adding further to the cumulative deficit in this respect. Out of every 100 households, only 60 have adequate accommodations, while 22 need to improve their existing housing unit and 18 need to add a new room or rebuild the dwelling they currently occupy.

So far, however, practically nothing has been done to improve the existing housing stock, and the rates of deterioration and obsolescence therefore remain high. This inaction makes the housing deficit more acute.

The current quantitative deficit in the region, i.e., the shortfall in the number of dwellings, is estimated at approximately 18 million units, and the formation of new households is thought to be increasing this figure by a further 2.68 million per year. Therefore, the region would need to attain a construction rate of between 2.3 and 3.2 million units per year in order to prevent the cumulative deficit from growing. According to another estimate, the total shortfall for 1995, in terms of the need for both new construction and upgrades, was approximately 50 million units (ECLAC, 1996d).

Table V.12
HOUSEHOLDS AND AVAILABLE HOUSING

Country	Year	Estimated households	Adequate dwellings	%	Dwellings beyond repair	%	Repairable dwellings	%
Argentina	91	9 380 204	6 434 209	75.2	624 274	7.3	1 496 212	17.5
Bolivia	92	1 614 995	880 172	54.5	406 979	25.2	327 844	20.3
Brazil	91	35 517 542	19 490 609	56.1	5 098 394	14.7	10 145 712	29.2
Chile	92	3 365 462	2 394 995	76.7	364 760	11.6	361 212	11.5
Colombia	85	5 824 857	3 303 051	62.9	525 127	10.0	1 423 095	27.1
Costa Rica	84	527 299	339 840	67.9	43 804	8.8	116 386	23.2
Cuba	81	2 350 221	1 698 649	74.1	335 427	14.6	256 100	11.1
Ecuador	90	2 136 889	1 375 212	68.4	296 609	14.7	336 834	16.7
El Salvador	92	1 091 728	508 858	48.5	359 873	34.3	180 461	17.2
Guatemala	89	1 610 994	874 111	54.9	283 225	17.8	433 952	27.2
Honduras	88	808 222	481 658	63.2	90 921	11.9	189 767	24.9
Mexico	90	17 394 368	11 382 906	71.0	1 964 712	12.3	2 687 615	16.7
Nicaragua	91	...	128 545	20.1	289 994	45.3	220 992	34.5
Panama	90	541 704	365 650	69.7	86 268	16.5	72 366	13.8
Paraguay	92	873 694	517 578	60.5	143 080	16.7	194 889	22.7
Peru	93	4 762 779	2 231 469	50.4	872 221	19.7	1 323 828	29.8
Dominican Republic	81	1 140 798	676 791	59.3	126 238	11.0	337 769	29.6
Uruguay	85	902 300	685 934	83.3	40 998	4.9	104 553	12.7
Venezuela	90	3 750 940	2 672 168	76.0	529 702	15.1	315 359	9.0
Region			Average	63.1		14.0		23.0

Source: ECLAC, Human settlements: the shelter of development (LC/L.906(CONF.85/3)/Rev.1), Santiago, Chile, 23 January 1996, table 8.

Table V.13
CURRENT HOUSING STOCK DEFICIT AND HOUSING NEEDS OF NEW HOUSEHOLDS

Country	Quantitative deficit		Qualitative deficit		Total deficit (100%)	Annual increase in households
	No.	%	No.	%		
Argentina	1 449 783	49.2	1 496 212	50.8	2 945 995	152 378
Bolivia	406 979	55.4	327 844	44.6	734 823	44 400
Brazil	5 881 221	36.7	10 145 712	63.3	16 026 933	909 000
Chile	609 255	62.8	361 212	37.2	970 467	72 000
Colombia	1 098 711	43.6	1 423 095	56.4	2 521 806	200 000
Costa Rica	71 073	37.9	116 386	62.1	187 459	25 000
Cuba	395 472	60.7	256 100	39.3	651 572	42 000
Ecuador	424 843	55.8	336 834	44.2	761 677	69 000
El Salvador	402 410	69.0	180 461	31.0	582 870	31 000
Guatemala	302 931	41.2	433 952	58.8	736 883	69 000
Honduras	136 797	41.9	189 767	58.1	326 564	42 000
Mexico	3 323 847	55.3	2 687 615	44.7	6 011 462	535 000
Nicaragua	289 994	56.8	220 992	43.2	510 986	29 000
Panama	103 688	58.9	72 366	41.1	176 054	16 000
Paraguay	161 227	45.3	194 889	54.7	356 116	30 000
Peru	1 207 483	47.7	1 323 828	52.3	2 531 310	105 000
Dominican Republic	126 238	27.2	337 769	72.8	464 007	49 000
Uruguay	111 812	51.7	104 553	48.3	216 366	8 400
Venezuela	763 413	70.77	315 359	29.2	1 078 772	148 000
Average		45.7		54.3	100%	2 581 000

Percentage coverage of the Latin American and Caribbean population in 1990: 96.15%

Source: ECLAC, Human settlements: the shelter of development (LC/L.906(CONF.85/3)/Rev.1), Santiago, Chile, 23 January 1996, table 9.

> **Box V.12**
>
> **HOUSING: AVAILABILITY AND NEEDS**
>
> Each country in Latin America and the Caribbean presents a different picture in terms of the current availability of housing units and the rate of formation of new households. On the one hand, in countries such as Paraguay and Peru, which during their most recent intercensal periods saw a sharp increase in the number of households and at present have a very limited stock of adequate housing relative to current demand, enormous construction efforts are needed to deal with the cumulative housing shortage and accommodate the new households being formed each year. Under such circumstances, housing production is a priority area that requires support from the various sectors and actors involved in construction at the national and supra-national levels. In other countries, such as Mexico and Panama, the rate of growth in housing demand has also been high but, according to the most recent census, the housing stock has also expanded. Ensuring an adequate housing supply to at least keep pace with the formation of new households is a major challenge that must be met in order to maintain a satisfactory ratio between households and housing. A third group of countries has displayed a lower rate of household growth during the last decade (less than 3% per year on average). This group includes Argentina, Brazil and Chile, which, compared with other countries, have a more satisfactory stock of acceptable dwellings (over 130 satisfactory units per 1,000 inhabitants) and are therefore under less pressure to build new houses as long as they maintain sufficient production to keep up with the increase in households.
>
> **Source:** ECLAC, Human settlements: the shelter of development (LC/L.906(CONF.85/3)Rev.1), Santiago, Chile, 23 January 1996, p. 65.

Given the extent of the housing shortage, which includes a major qualitative component, and the fact that in the 1990s existing systems have demonstrated a very limited capacity for alleviating this deficit solely through the construction of new units, increasing attention is being given to the possibility of placing more emphasis on the improvement and maintenance of existing dwellings as a means of dealing with this problem. Such an approach thus far been used very little in the region.

iii) Access to sanitation

In most countries, a major objective with respect to sanitation continues to be to provide all households with access to clean water and waste disposal systems to ensure that minimal sanitary conditions will prevail. Raising basic sanitation standards is one aspect of the effort to achieve social equity and human capital development, and significant financial, technological and institutional resources are being mobilized for this purpose in most countries. In some cases, these innovations involve offering the private sector the opportunity to invest in and operate these utilities.

In some countries, in order to extend the coverage of drinking water distribution there is an urgent need to upgrade catchment and treatment facilities. In the Caribbean, for example, in order to overcome the shortage of water resources, the vast number of leaks will have to be repaired and pollution of available sources will need to be controlled.

Improvements in the coverage of sanitation services have been reflected in a decline in infant mortality in the region. Furthermore, the experiences of countries with large-scale sanitation programmes show that the provision of potable water and sanitation has motivated families to improve and enlarge their dwellings and enhance their surroundings. In rural areas, major challenges are still to be faced with respect to sanitation.

With the extension of water supply services and the improvement of consumption patterns, one issue that most countries clearly view with concern is the treatment of waste water properly before discharge. At the beginning of the decade, ECLAC reported that few sewerage systems were treating waste water properly before discharging it into the nearest waterway (ECLAC, 1990a). Progress in this regard has fallen short of what is demanded by the environmental problems faced in the countries of the region.

iv) Social expenditure on housing

After declining in the 1980s in real per capita terms and as a percentage of GDP, government expenditure on housing improved significantly but in the early 1990s had not yet regained the levels recorded in the early 1980s in most of the countries. Hence, in order to expand the coverage and quality of their housing policies, the countries are seeking, on the one hand, to bring in fresh funds, primarily from the private sector, and, on the other, to adjust their programmes in such a way as to focus their available resources more effectively on priority groups, especially the poor, and to achieve efficiency levels whereby production of housing goods and services may be expanded and improved within the available budget.

Mention should be made of the performance of the construction sector during this period following the sharp decline in this sector's importance within the economy in the 1980s. Between 1990 and 1994, construction expanded by an average annual rate of 3.6%, thus exceeding the rate of GDP growth (2.9%) during the period. The sector's contribution to GDP thus rose from 3.8% to 5.3%, a percentage which, although lower than in the 1980s, creates a favourable climate for strong construction activity in the coming years (ECLAC, 1996d).

In view of the above-mentioned figures on the cumulative housing shortfall and the acute need for new housing generated by the rapid pace of new household formation, countries are striving to steer this construction drive towards the production of middle- and low-cost housing. Bearing in mind that simply in order to hold the cumulative quantitative shortfall at its 1995 level, it would be necessary to more than double the funds currently earmarked for this purpose (ECLAC, 1996d), combining the State's contributions with those of the private sector and those of the beneficiaries themselves has become an essential component of any housing system that seeks to expand access to housing.

b) Changes in housing systems

i) Developing adequate finance systems

In order to attract new resources and investments to the housing sector, many countries have replaced their traditional resource management systems, which operated separately from the rest of the financial system through specialized mortgage banks, with open financial systems, which have generally proven to be more efficient and transparent. The growth of the construction sector is largely due to the confidence which institutional investors have shown in these new housing finance systems. Although so far private-sector participation in the housing industry has been concentrated in the most profitable market segments, there have been a number of interesting national experiments involving the extension of its participation to include the provision of housing to middle- and lower-middle-income groups, thereby relieving some of the pressure on the Government's budget in this area. In Chile, for example, which introduced finance improvements at an early stage, it was possible to cut back public-sector investment in housing from 72% of the total in 1972 to just 19% in 1994 without any reduction in the proportion of housing units registered under State support programmes.

On another front, the trend has been to widen the coverage of low-cost housing programmes by encouraging the beneficiaries themselves (even those with the least resources) to save under joint financing programmes. The concept of highly subsidized programmes, which have been difficult to replicate and at times regressive as well, has given way to one in which the amount of savings effort to be demanded is determined more precisely and the beneficiary's financial commitment prior to and after obtaining the housing unit is crucial.

ii) Targeting and accessibility

For most of the countries of the region, targeting housing expenditure has been established as a major challenge for this period, in view of the limited availability of State resources to tackle the housing problem. In order to make housing accessible to families who need it, a series of financial, regulatory and institutional instruments have been established which include highly selective application and allocation systems and different types of subsidies.

Although some countries still maintain and prefer a supply-side subsidy, which takes the form of tax exemptions or preferential credits for housing production, this approach is being replaced in a large number of cases by demand-side subsidies. This may be because direct subsidies to families in need of housing have proven to be more conducive to the establishment of fair and objective systems for providing access to this asset, since they allow for more accurate targeting of those in need and moderate the regressive tendency of housing policies of the 1980s.

Efforts are being made to apply clear, objective and transparent rules to application procedures for low-cost housing to encourage needy families to opt for established systems of housing allocation instead of setting up squatter settlements or pressuring the authorities. In countries such as Costa Rica, social statistics systems have favoured better targeting of low-income families, as well as permitting the establishment of objective criteria for the allocation of housing benefits.

iii) Diversifying housing stocks

The preference for allocation systems with objective and transparent rules has not prevented Governments from carrying out interesting experiments during this period involving the targeting of specific groups or housing situations requiring priority attention, such as urban renewal, high-density housing or group applications and facilities for female heads of household. Significant efforts are being made to use low-cost housing to rehabilitate or renovate degraded downtown areas in Argentina, Chile, Uruguay, Colombia, Mexico and many other countries of the region.

The consolidation of predominantly urban societies in most countries of the region and the wide diversity of housing needs have obliged the Governments to take a different view of the rigid mass-produced low-cost housing projects typical of the 1970s and to diversify the supply to cater to the demands of specific groups, including young people, female heads of households, senior citizens, inner-city slum dwellers and the disabled. The sharp increase in housing-related expectations associated with improvements in living standards in many countries, and above all in large cities, has placed the issue of urban housing quality at the centre of housing policies.

Countries that still have a large rural population are also acutely aware of the seriousness of the rural housing shortage and of the importance of addressing it through programmes appropriate to the geographical, economic and cultural realities of the sector. In view of the cost of providing rural dwellings and infrastructure for a widely scattered population, efforts are being made to promote the formation of tighter clusters of peasant families so as to achieve economies of scale and at the same time facilitate the rural population's access to social services and job opportunities.

Lastly, since more than 50% of the regional construction and investment deficit in urban and rural residential areas of Latin America and the Caribbean is qualitative in nature, increased attention is likely to be paid in coming years to the market for housing upgrades and maintenance; such a tendency would have definite benefits in terms of the housing situation in the region.

iv) Housing and urban policies

Given the high degree of urbanization in the region, housing problems in Latin America and the Caribbean are inevitably linked to urban problems. On the one hand, policy makers are finding it increasingly difficult to satisfy housing programmes' enormous demand for land and infrastructure while holding costs to acceptable levels. On the other hand the practice of locating low-cost housing on cheaper land on the outskirts of cities has heightened the problems of urban sprawl and segregation, with their attendent problems of exclusion and loss of human capital.

Conscious of the fact that low-cost housing standards and designs have contributed in no small way to the problem of urban sprawl in the past, creating huge low-density zones that swallow up agricultural land and even spill over into disaster-prone areas, housing agencies have become more sensitive to urban issues. They have begun to advocate land-use densification in the cities and the siting of housing complexes on the basis not only of land costs but also of the urban and social implications of their placement. These include the accessibility for low-cost families of education and health facilities, which are considered fundamental for improving the quality of life and opportunities for advancement of the urban poor, above and beyond the advantages of obtaining a dwelling.

In Colombia, among other countries, the regulatory and legal framework governing urban real estate ownership and markets are being revised, and consideration is being given to reforms whose general thrust is to improve land management in urban and outlying areas and to include an assessment of operating and user costs for city facilities in the decision-making process relating to housing placement. The concrete gains made in this field are small, since they require sensitive political agreements that are not always easy to obtain.

The restoration, maintenance and modernization of a country's housing stock provides definite advantages for urban centres: not only are they a means of responding to housing needs without necessarily resorting to an expansion of the city, but at the same time, they ward off the social, functional and physical obsolescence of neighbourhoods. These programmes, together with sanitation and upgrade programmes for makeshift settlements, constitute some of the unconventional courses of action included in the spectrum of sectoral responses to housing needs.

v) Decentralization of housing management

Although in some countries there has been a degree of participation at the subnational and local levels in policy-making on housing for some time now, in the vast majority of cases this area of policy-making is highly centralized and is administered by a ministerial body or specialized national institute. Nevertheless, in recent years, the countries have demonstrated a growing interest in the introduction of greater decentralization in the formulation and management of housing policy and have handed over some areas to the municipalities. Despite the difficulties encountered thus far in decentralizing national housing policies, especially as regards institutional arrangements, transfer of funds and the creation of management capacity at the subnational level, bringing housing programmes within the scope of local authorities should help to correct the negative effects that many of them have had on urban development.

One of the crucial factors in this process has been the work carried out by the national preparatory committees in the different countries prior to the United Nations Conference on Human Settlements (Habitat II), held in Istanbul in June 1996, which was attended not only by national Governments but also by local authorities, non-governmental organizations, members of the private sector and community representatives. At the fifth Regional Meeting of Ministers and High-level Authorities of the Housing and Urban Development Sector in Latin America and the Caribbean, held in Kingston in November 1996, the countries agreed to reactivate or maintain these multisectoral groups to carry forward the development of urban and housing policies, thus paving the way for cooperation between national bodies and local governments.[39]

5. Social security reform

The design of social security systems affects the well-being of the population, since it has a bearing on the prospects for protection against loss of income and the costs associated with the contingencies of sickness, old age, disability and survivorship.

---

[39] Agreements of the fifth Regional Meeting of Ministers and High-level Authorities of the Housing and Urban Development Sector in Latin America and the Caribbean, Jamaica, November 1996.

a) The situation in Latin America

In Latin America, pension systems are generally characterized by a lack of social equity. Their development has not been uniform, and coverage extends only to a small percentage of the population, living in urban areas and employed in the formal sector. There are marked and unjustified disparities between groups and geographical areas as regards coverage. In addition, in many cases, pension systems are excessively expensive, because of high administrative costs, growing deficits, widespread evasion and payment delays, a sizeable State debt and a low real return on investment.

The countries can be divided into three clusters —pioneer countries, intermediate countries, and latecomer countries— based on the year their social security systems were set up and their subsequent development (Mesa-Lago, 1978). Systems differ according to the age of their programmes, population coverage, wage and economic burdens, financial balance and demographic aspects. The most significant aspects of these systems from the standpoint of social equity are their coverage limitations (see table V.14) and the obstacles that may stand in the way of expanded coverage.

b) Recent changes in financing

During the first half of the 1990s, the largest increases in resources allocated to social security pensions were recorded in Argentina, Ecuador, Panama, Paraguay and Uruguay.

In Argentina, the significant rise in current expenditure in the sector was attributable largely to the pension readjustment made in order to meet budgetary targets set out under the Pensions Act, combined with recognition of obligations of social security institutes towards pensioners. In Ecuador and Paraguay, the increase in spending on social security also reflected a considerable expansion in current expenditure, as a result of larger benefit payments over the period. Uruguay conducted four-monthly adjustments of retirement and other pensions, as stipulated by the Constitutional amendment approved in the late 1980s. This explains the substantial increase in absolute terms in per capita expenditure on the sector between 1990 and 1995.

In Colombia, a large volume of resources was allocated to expanding social security coverage to indigent segments of the population, under the "Revivir" programme begun in 1994. This expansion of coverage benefited some of the working population not previously covered by the system, thanks to the creation of the Pension Solidarity Fund in 1995.

As a consequence of the reforms under way, one of the main features of which is the assumption of future liabilities with a progressive reduction in revenues, the financing requirement for this sector should be expected to increase, though this does not necessarily imply greater expenditure.

c) The reforms in progress

Major changes are being made to pension systems in Latin America. These reforms have the following objectives: i) to differentiate between risks, in such a way that financial management is adapted to the probability of certain events occurring; ii) to administer the

Table V.14
TOTAL POPULATION AND ECONOMICALLY ACTIVE POPULATION WITH SOCIAL SECURITY COVERAGE, 1970-1995
(Percentages)

Country	Economically active population (EAP)				Total population		
	1970	1980	1985-1988	1990-1995	1980	1985-1988	1990-1995
Argentina	68.0	69.1	79.1	81.4[a]	78.9	74.3	100.0[a]
Bahamas	85.3	85.9	-	-	-	-	-
Barbados	75.3	79.8	96.9	-	-	-	-
Bolivia	9.0	18.5	16.9	-	25.4	21.4	21.3
Brazil	27.0	87.0	-	-	96.3	-	-
Chile	75.6	62.8[b]	81.1[b]	100.0[b]	67.3	100.0[a]	100.0[a]
Colombia	22.2	30.4	30.2	-	15.2	16.0	-
Costa Rica	38.4	68.3	68.7	77.3	84.4[c]	83.1[c]	86.2[c]
Cuba	88.7[b]	93.0[a]	-	-	100.0[a]	100.0[a]	100.0[a]
Ecuador	16.3	25.9	27.4	28.0	9.8	15.8	17.2
El Salvador	9.6	19.7	19.4	22.6	8.8	11.0	14.2
Guatemala	27.0	33.1	27.1	29.0	15.2	13.1	16.4
Honduras	4.2	14.4	12.8	-	7.3	10.3[b]	13.0
Jamaica	58.8	80.9	93.2	-	-	-	-
Mexico	28.1	42.0	40.2	43.7	53.4	53.7	58.4
Nicaragua	14.8	16.8	29.0	14.3	9.1	22.0	13.0
Panama	33.4	52.3	59.8	64.0	49.9	57.4	-
Paraguay	10.7	8.1	8.1	8.7	18.2	18.5	22.3
Peru	35.5	37.4	32.0	-	15.7	22.2	23.8
Dominican Republic	8.9	11.6	10.2	12.7	-	4.2	5.6
Uruguay	95.4	81.2	73.0	-	86.1[d]	87.7[d]	-
Venezuela	24.4	49.8	54.3	-	45.2	49.9	-

Source: Prepared by Carmelo Mesa-Lago, on the basis of official figures.
[a] Based on legal coverage. In Argentina, counting only the employed required to contribute to the national system (without taking into account participants in provincial systems), the figure for 1995 is 71.4%. In Chile, the figure includes the indigent and the uninsured who receive assistance.
[b] The figures refer to participants over the period 1980-1994, but there is considerable duplication (an insured person may be enrolled in two or more private pension funds); if active contributors are considered, coverage drops to 61.5% for 1994.
[c] Includes assistance to the indigent; if social services provided by the Ministry of Health are included, coverage is 100%.
[d] Includes coverage provided by the Ministry of Health, the Social Insurance Bank (BPS), mutual-aid societies and the armed forces.

Table V.15
TRENDS IN PER CAPITA SOCIAL SECURITY EXPENDITURE[a]

Sector	Real per capita social expenditure (1987 dollars)		Absolute variation (1987 dollars)	Percentage variation
	1990-1991	1994-1995		
Social security [b]	82.9	124.3		
Argentina	128.1	331.9	203.8	159.2
Bolivia	...	...	...	...
Brazil [c]	119.2	128.8	9.6	8.1
Chile	123.6	137.2	13.6	11.0
Colombia	40.9	51.1	10.2	25.1
Costa Rica	104.5	126.0	21.5	20.6
Ecuador	22.3	39.0	16.7	75.3
El Salvador	13.1	20.3	7.2	54.8
Guatemala	6.4	5.9	(0.5)	(7.1)
Honduras	4.6	3.4	(1.2)	(26.5)
Mexico	...	...	...	...
Nicaragua	...	...	...	...
Panama	117.2	177.3	60.1	51.3
Paraguay [d]	10.8	23.0	12.1	112.3
Peru	...	...	...	...
Dominican Republic	3.3 [e]	...	...	...
Uruguay	304.1	447.8	143.7	47.3
Venezuela	63.4 [e]	...	...	...

Source: ECLAC, *Social Panorama of Latin America. 1996 Edition* (LC/G.1946-P), Santiago, Chile, 1997, table IV.2. United Nations publication, Sales No. E.97.II.G.4.
[a] Average data for 1990-1991 for all countries except Bolivia, Brazil, Chile, Costa Rica, El Salvador and Panama, figures for which correspond to 1994 only.
[b] Owing to lack of information, averages for the sector do not include Bolivia, Mexico, Nicaragua, Peru, Dominican Republic and Venezuela.
[c] Includes central government expenditure only.
[d] Includes central government budgetary expenditure only.
[e] Includes 1990 only.

resources of programmes efficiently, maintaining basic macroeconomic equilibria (e.g., in public finances, social security, and efficiency of labour and financial markets); and iii) to enhance the role of the private sector, both in the administration of resources and provision of benefits.

The proposal that contributions should become the main source of financing and the basis for determining benefits represents a radical departure from traditional systems. This new approach has two implications with a direct impact on social equity: i) it may prove to run counter to the principle of solidarity by excluding those who are unable to contribute, but are still subject to the risks the social security systems protects against; the inclusion of an altruistic component in the new systems is vital if the current reforms are to contribute to social equity,[40] ii) if the link between contributions and benefits is established on the individual level, no redistribution will take place among contributors; in contrast, the establishment of a collective link makes redistribution possible.

It should be emphasized that the effects in terms of social equity do not depend on whether the system is a public or private one, but rather on whether the benefit and contribution mechanisms are individual or collective.

In the case of social security pensions the transition from a pay-as-you-go (transfer) system to one based on defined contributions, with benefits dependent on individual capitalization, may have an impact on equity, both directly, owing to the transfer component, and indirectly, owing to the impact on the economy's dynamic efficiency.

The contribution to solidarity and the attainment of dynamic efficiency are two of the objectives of social security that have an impact on social equity. In fact, pension systems are commonly credited with the following two functions:

i) a social function, which is to provide an old-age, disability or survivors' pension;[41] it is important to distinguish between benefits based solely on contributions, which go to people who have contributed to the system, and benefits not related to contributions, made to those who do not have the ability to save and financed out of the contributions of others or general taxes;

ii) an economic and financial function, which is to make a contribution to basic macroeconomic equilibria and enhance national saving without replacing other voluntary forms of saving, as well as complementing the growth of the financial sector through instruments that facilitate the intermediation of the funds accumulated and the development of regulatory agencies.

Hypothetically, a worker in possession of full information would opt for a particular system on the basis of two criteria: the amount of the pension to be received on retirement versus contributions made during his or her working life, and the utility to be obtained from the contributions in relation to the average for all workers, which depends on the manner in which a given system fulfils its social function.

---

[40] There is currently a debate as to whether benefits not met by contributions should be covered by subsidized social security systems or by the public sector, through budget allocations.

[41] The concept of a "good pension" is relative. A good pension is one which, in real terms and in the event of disability, old age or survivorship, provides a significant proportion of the average income on the basis of which the participant made contributions during his or her working life.

Until a few years ago, social security pension plans in Latin America were based on pay-as-you-go systems entailing transfers from those currently in the workforce to pensioners, along with an implicit commitment by the State that contributors, once they had reached retirement age, would benefit from the contributions paid in by the new generations of workers. Such a system reaches its point of equilibrium[42] under ideal conditions: constant population growth and financial stability. Where this occurs, each retiree will receive on average a rate of return on his/her contributions equal to the growth in total real wages of contributors. Returns will diverge from the average if an altruistic component is included that provides for the transfer of resources.

The other financing method is that incorrectly[43] presented as the result of the privatization of pension systems, but which should actually be called an "individual capitalization system". Under this system, benefits are paid for entirely out of funds accumulated through the capitalization of each participant's contributions. Pension contributions are transformed into individual savings funds. Contributions correspond to a portion of each contributor's earnings over every stage of the individual's working life. Under this scheme, each contributor receives on average a rate of return on his or her contributions equal to the rate of return in the capital markets. Since such a system in its pure form contains no altruistic component, the rate of return will diverge from the average only as a consequence of differences in the way individual funds are managed.

Given these alternatives, there are two factors that influence a retired worker's well-being: i) the rate of growth in real total wages of contributors versus the rate of return on capital during the individuals' working life;[44] ii) the effects on individual rates of return of the average rate of return for all workers enrolled in the system, as a result of components unrelated to contributions that serve to redistribute income among participants.

---

[42] Pay-as-you-go systems require actuarial adjustment; as young systems they show surpluses which should be invested as reserve funds, to be used to pay pensions when the system faces financial imbalance during its mature phase. Those actuarial calculations require monitoring the economic and age dependency ratios between those of retirement age and contributors, since losses occur as the ratio increases and contributions and benefits are not adjusted in response to the rise in demographic dependency.

[43] Since the Chilean reform, the introduction of such a system has been termed "privatization of the pension system". However, in practice, even though the system is financed by worker contributions and the funds are managed by private firms, the State is involved at four levels: i) it regulates demand by making it mandatory for workers to make contributions; ii) it regulates certain aspects of supply through its supervision of private pension funds; iii) it finances welfare and supplementary pensions; and iv) it administers and finances the old system until it is phased out.

[44] This rate is usually greater in the dynamically efficient economies. In its annual preliminary overview of the economies of Latin America and the Caribbean, ECLAC provides data for 15 countries of the region with respect to interest rates on deposits and on loans (as indicators of the return on savings invested in the banking system) and the rate of GDP growth, which, absent changes in income distribution, should correspond to the growth rate of total wages and salaries. Between 1990 and 1992, in 11 countries the interest rate on deposits was lower than the rate of GDP growth, which would tend to favour the adoption of pay-as-you-go systems in those countries. However, in nine cases, the interest rate on loans was higher than the rate of GDP growth, which would tend to favour the establishment of capitalization systems. Of course, the bank interest rate is an imperfect and incomplete indicator of returns on investment in capital markets.

d) Types of pension reforms

The countries that have reformed or are in the process of reforming their pension schemes have incorporated a capitalization component into those schemes (ECLAC, 1996a). The argument in support of such schemes is that they overcome at least three weaknesses of the pay-as-you-go system by: i) setting out explicitly the Government's obligation to contributors to the former system who are still working; ii) strengthening the relationship between the contributions of each worker, the financial management of the contributions and the benefits to be received from the accumulated fund; and iii) dispensing with the redistributive function of the pension plan, which is now handled through the government budget.

Since, however, at the time reforms are introduced, there is already a system in operation, the reforms differ in the way in which the fiscal costs are distributed between the participants and the rest of the population.[45]

Generally speaking, four generations of reforms may be distinguished. The first, which has served as a model, is the reform implemented in Chile, where one scheme was entirely replaced by the other. This was followed by two other types of reform, those that established parallel and competing schemes (Colombia) and those that established mixed or integrated schemes (Argentina, Uruguay). Lastly, some countries are now introducing sequential reforms in which the old system is first made uniform and streamlined and is then replaced by the other (Costa Rica).

Table V.16 establishes a typology of pension reforms (Mesa-Lago, 1996) using seven specific national examples classified on the basis of the three pillars distinguished by the World Bank: i) a mandatory pillar, with a State-administered system for redistribution and insurance purposes, which guarantees a minimum or standard benefit and is financed by taxes (pay-as-you-go system); ii) a mandatory pillar, with a privately-administered system for savings and insurance purposes, which operates either through an individual savings plan, to which only the insured contribute, or a State-regulated company-sponsored fully-funded individual capitalization plan, to which both the insured and the employer contribute; and iii) a voluntary pillar, similar in every other respect to the second.

The alternative methods of financing the altruistic components come under the first pillar. The various reform schemes may or may not give priori recognition to the principle of non-contribution-based (welfare) pensions and the need to guarantee a minimum pension to those who qualify. The schemes also differ with respect to the sources of funding of the altruistic components of the pensions, either drawing upon the contributions of other participants or upon other sources such as the government budget.

Table V.17 presents a classification of national redistributive systems. The extreme case is once again the Chilean model, in which funding of the altruistic component (welfare pension and supplement required to reach a minimum pension) comes from general taxation, which means that there is no redistributive element in the social insurance scheme as such.

---

[45] The fiscal costs result from: i) the need to continue paying pensions to the retired segment of the population without being able to rely on contributions from the segment still working; ii) the need to recognize the past contributions of those now joining the capitalization system; and iii) the need to finance welfare and minimum pensions guaranteed by law.

Table V.16
PILLARS OF PENSION REFORM IN SEVEN COUNTRIES OF LATIN AMERICA

Country	Mandatory pillar		Voluntary pillar [a]
	Administered by the public sector	Administered by the private sector	
Argentina	Yes, standard basic pension, both in new public scheme and in public component of mixed scheme (but not in private pension funds (AFJPs)); or welfare pension	Yes, in AFJPs for those who opt for mixed system, but AFJPs may also be public or of another kind	Yes, in AFJPs for those who opt for the mixed system
Colombia	Yes, minimum pension for those who opt for the public system (and another based on earnings and contributions); or minimum guaranteed pension in private pension fund (SAFP)	Yes, but only for those who opt for SAFPs; SAFPs may also be public or of another kind	Yes, in SAFPs for those who opt for this system
Costa Rica	Yes, minimum pension in unified public system (and another based on earnings and contributions), or means-tested welfare pension	No, but voluntary supplementary pension schemes may exist within or outside the public system	No
Chile	Yes, minimum pension guaranteed by State (in private pension fund (AFP)); or means-tested welfare pension	Yes, throughout the new AFP system	Yes, throughout the new AFP system
Mexico	Yes, minimum pension within public system (and another based on earnings and contributions), but no minimum pension in Retirement Savings System (SAR) or welfare pension	The basic pillar is public and the SAR is a purely complementary scheme (partially administered by banks but funds controlled by the State)	Yes, in SAR
Peru	Yes, minimum pension for those who opt for the public system (and another based on earnings and contributions); and minimum pension in private pension fund (AFP), but no welfare pension	Yes, but only for those who opt for AFPs	Yes, in AFPs for those who opt for this system
Uruguay	Yes, basic pension in public system; or means-tested welfare pension, but no minimum pension in retirement savings funds (AFAP)	Yes, in AFAPs for those who opt for the mixed system, but AFAPs may also be public	Yes, in AFAPs for those who opt for the mixed system, but only above a high wage level

Source: C. Mesa-Lago, "Pension system reform in Latin America: the position of the international organizations", *CEPAL Review*, No. 60 (LC/G.1943-P), December 1996, table 3.
[a] Insured's contributions only.

The other systems, whether mixed or parallel, include a redistributive financing component, so that the yield on the funds of the contributors is affected not only by the ratio between the return on capital and the increase in real wages, but also by the way in which the redistributive component affects the relative yield.

Table V.17
CLASSIFICATION OF REDISTRIBUTIVE SYSTEMS

	Basic minimum pension	Welfare pension
Public pay-as-you-go system based on contributions	Argentina Uruguay	
Public scaled premium system based on contributions	Colombia (optional) Costa Rica Mexico Peru (optional)	
Public system and taxes		Argentina Costa Rica Chile Uruguay
Capitalization system and taxes	Chile (partly, plus capitalization) Peru Colombia	

Source: C. Mesa-Lago, "Pension system reforms in Latin America: the position of the international organizations", *CEPAL Review*, No. 60 (LC/G.1943-P), December 1996.

PART THREE: GUIDELINES FOR AN INTEGRATED APPROACH

VI.   Economic policies

VII.   Social policies

VI. ECONOMIC POLICIES

1. The challenge of changing production patterns with social equity

ECLAC has been developing various issues connected with its proposal for changing production patterns with social equity in a series of documents published in recent years (ECLAC 1990b, 1992a and 1996a). This time, emphasis has been placed on the potential contribution that public policies can make to the achievement of vigorous and stable growth that will help to generate productive employment and make it possible to overcome the shortcomings in terms of equity. This is the meaning of the expression "quality of growth".

Growth calls for a certain degree of socio-political stability, and this, in turn, means complying with certain minimum requirements as regards equity. This mutual dependence between growth and equity means that it is necessary to advance towards both objectives simultaneously rather than sequentially. In Latin America and the Caribbean this issue has been the subject of constant concern which has been reflected in ECLAC's studies.

According to this point of view, changing production patterns with social equity makes it possible for countries to set themselves and subsequently fulfill the objective of simultaneously achieving growth and equity. Such an achievement, however, is not an automatic result of growth itself, since no matter how high growth rates may be they do not necessarily lead to equity, just as social policies alone cannot offset all the factors causing inequity. This is why the areas of complementation between the two objectives are so important: maintenance of the basic macroeconomic balances, including stimulation of saving and investment and proper resource allocation; rapid spread of technology; investment in human resources and the generation of jobs of growing productivity; the adoption of efficiently managed social policies which have an effective impact, and reform of the State on the basis of a modern concept of public policies.

Growth and equity are the result of both economic and social policy. In this respect, we must get away from the idea that the sole purpose of economic policy is to promote growth, while social policy should confine itself to the question of distribution. Neither of these is neutral in terms of distribution, while both of them affect the capacity for growth. For this reason, an integrated approach is needed in which public policy as a whole furthers both changing production patterns and social equity.

In order to make any noticeable headway in social tasks it is necessary to take a unified approach to economic and social policy, so as to support all forms of competitiveness which further social cohesion, and vice versa. Such an approach does not ignore the conflicts between growth and equity which practical considerations sometimes make unavoidable, but it seeks to minimize them. Above all, however, it focusses attention on the many areas of complementarity which may exist between the two dimensions. This is reflected in macroeconomic management, production development policies, social policies and the way all these factors interact. At the same time, it should basically translate into institutions which make the objectives of growth, stability, equity and competitiveness more credible for society.

The fact that the processes of adjustment, macroeconomic stabilization and structural reform which have taken place in Latin America and the Caribbean have occurred at the same time represents a fundamental change in the region's development process. The simultaneous occurrence of macroeconomic stabilization and modernization of production —including structural, institutional and organizational aspects— has not been an easy matter, however, and it has followed very different paths not only as between the various countries but also within them.

Likewise, it is clear that not so much progress has been made in various aspects relating to the implementation and actual application of the economic and social guidelines, after adapting them to the particular structural, organizational, legal and institutional features of each country.

Thus, almost all the economies of the region suffer, to a greater or lesser degree, from structural and institutional problems which make it hard to achieve a steady increase in growth solely on the basis of market signals. The most obvious requisite for making the economy function well is the existence of competitive markets or of institutions which help to promote or simulate them. When markets are segmented or incomplete, this reduces the possibilities of multiplying linkages within production systems and ensuring the spread of demand and technical progress from the leading modern sectors to the rest of the economy.

The marked differences in institutional development between and within countries go a long way towards explaining why the results obtained vary so much, in spite of the relative similarity of the guidelines followed. Taking account of these differences leads to the assignment of higher priority not only to the links between economic and social policies but also to those between territorial aspects and competitiveness: that is to say, between economic policy, technological change and the regional base, including the social actors.

Public policies which seek to relieve the most serious forms of deprivation and marginality have so far suffered from insufficient capacity and limited effectiveness; social expenditure has been severely limited by the efforts to observe fiscal discipline, and the management of social policies has not been renovated fast enough or thoroughly enough. This goes to make up a gloomy social picture with latent problems that may make it difficult to sustain the development process.

The distributive dimension of development depends to a crucial extent on the adoption of policies deliberately aiming to promote better social dissemination of the fruits of growth.

Among the economic factors to be taken into account in this respect, the most fundamental are: i) economic growth conditions the demand for labour, so that recovery of the levels of activity that characterized the region in the past could potentially permit improvements in distribution, and ii) the type of growth needed calls for the adoption of patterns of production specialization in line with the resource and factor availabilities of each country.

In this respect, a development strategy must be adopted which maintains a constantly growing demand for labour, which ensures that that demand is in line with the supply of skills, and which makes it possible to do away with the obstacles faced by the low-income sectors in gaining access to the labour market and to productive jobs.

The level of the income obtained from labour depends to a considerable extent on the human capital of the workers, which in turn depends on the extent and quality of the education and training received. This gives rise to two further policy guidelines: i) the need to design retraining programmes for the labour force if the adoption of new patterns of technology renders their existing skills obsolete, and ii) the need to formulate an educational policy which ensures broad coverage, avoids dropping-out and pays attention to the quality of teaching so as to increase the likelihood that students will find a place in the labour market when they are adults.

In lower-income households, the low rate of labour participation (total number of employed and unemployed persons, divided by the population of working age) means that a high proportion of their working-age members —especially spouses— are not economically active, because very often the large number of under-age dependents forces them to stay at home without being able to enter the labour market. It is worth noting here, as a policy suggestion, that it would be desirable, both in firms and in residential areas, to set up public or subsidized systems to enable parents to leave their children in the care of responsible establishments (crèches, kindergartens and day care centres, for example) so as to facilitate the incorporation of mothers in the labour market.

In the short term, greater equity can be achieved through compensation policies, focussed especially on extremely poor sectors, and social "safety nets" in order to reduce the negative effects of fluctuations in the level of economic activity. Such policies also play an important role in giving coherence and legitimacy to the long-term guidelines.

The advance towards the institutionalization of market economies makes it necessary to accompany the economic reforms with others of a political nature, including the institutional adjustments mentioned earlier. In some societies, basic political reforms are still under way, such as making electoral systems clearer and more trustworthy, tackling obvious cases of inequality, and ensuring a modicum of governance in the political system, while in others the challenge is rather to proceed with the establishment of institutional machinery and build up the consensuses needed to face the challenges of growth, equity and competitiveness in the context of open economies.

2. Public policies and the quality of growth

Gaining access to higher levels of productivity and employment imposes certain requirements at the macroeconomic level. ECLAC considers that the most important of them is to achieve stable GDP growth of the order of 6% per year. This cannot be obtained without a significant increase in investment —bringing the regional average to around 27% of GDP— or without a suitable combination of national and external saving which will enable such an increase to be financed in a manner compatible with macroeconomic stability (ECLAC, 1996a). Growth alone is not enough, however. It is also necessary to fulfill microeconomic and systemic requirements in order to generate positive forces and externalities which will help the production units and workers currently located in backward segments of the system to participate effectively in the process of change, so as to improve the situation and income of the poorest groups.

a) A growth-oriented macroeconomic structure

Proper macroeconomic balances are an essential condition for achieving faster growth with greater equity. The way these balances are attained is of decisive importance for the achievement of such objectives, however. In this respect, the macroeconomic balances which make the greatest contribution are those which are most sustainable and integral.

The fact that emphasis is placed on the stability of the desired growth means that the sought-for macroeconomic balances must be sustainable in time. Another way of securing the same objective is to pay careful attention to the impact of macroeconomic factors on efficient resource allocation: that is to say, to avoid distortions which hold the economy back from the expanding production frontier.

Stability on the macroeconomic front is a necessary condition both for stimulating saving and investment and for raising growth rates. If it is desired to achieve some degree of congruence between effective demand and the production frontier, as well as to be able to reduce the effect of sharp changes in outside conditions, it is necessary —with different degrees of emphasis and intensity, depending on the particular national situations— to adopt consistent monetary, credit, fiscal and trade policies and suitable wage or income policies, together with measures to promote saving, investment and productive development.

Programmes which concentrate on a single variable as the leading factor in the stabilization process usually give rise to procyclical effects which jeopardize the sustainability of the programme or of the expansion of production capacity. Approaches of this nature may lead to stabilization accompanied by stagnation, or short-lived stabilization followed by a return to instability.

The ebb and flow of capital movements in the 1990s has been a special source of external impacts. This situation demands systematic efforts to ensure, on the one hand, that inflows of funds are absorbed in an efficient manner, and on the other that these resources really are connected with the process of productive investment and that a suitable proportion of such investment goes to the production of tradeable goods. All this calls for the application of active foreign exchange policies, a strict system for the prudential supervision of the financial system and, sometimes, measures to discourage capital movements, especially of a short-term nature.

In order to avoid the destructive multiplier effect of automatic adjustments, coherent and appropriate monetary, credit, fiscal, trade and wage or income policies are required, together with explicit production development policies, all applied with a degree of emphasis and intensity in keeping with the situation in question. In the case of production development policies, it is basically a question of coordinating the development programme with short-term policies so as to promote a change in the structures of expenditure and production which will make it possible to maintain a higher rate of utilization of local production capacity and strengthen capital formation rather than weakening it.

In order to achieve these objectives, direct and indirect public policies can be applied to regulate the global level of aggregate demand and influence the composition of expenditure and production through selective instruments designed to reallocate resources and develop markets when they are incomplete or non-existent.

The efficiency of macroeconomic policy is reflected in the extent to which it succeeds in: i) securing a sustainable increase in the rate of utilization of production capacity, labour and capital; ii) stimulating capital formation, and iii) raising productivity by promoting improvements in factor quality and greater efficiency in their allocation. When viewed from this angle, the macroeconomic policy followed in a number of countries of the region displays some shortcomings, although it has proved possible to reduce inflationary pressures and improve the fiscal situation (ECLAC, 1996a).

The idea is that economic policy should seek primarily to take an overall view of the macroeconomic balances so as to avoid a situation where rapid progress is made in respect of some of them (such as reducing inflation), at the cost of unsatisfactory results in other areas (such as a heavy current account deficit, exchange-rate lags or high levels of unemployment). As well as the maintenance of low inflation and fiscal stability, the necessary balances also include avoidance of non-sustainable current account deficits, maintenance of a rate of domestic saving in keeping with the investment process, preservation of a suitable real exchange rate, and measures to bring aggregate demand as close as possible to full utilization of the existing production capacity (Rosales, 1996a).

If such balances are to be feasible, progress towards one objective must not affect others to such a point as to cause temporary inconsistencies in economic policy. Thus, achieving growth with stability by giving priority to the ongoing good performance of the macroeconomic variables is an effective way of establishing suitable links between economic policy management and the decisions on saving, investment, productivity and the spread of technology involved in the effort to change production patterns.

Securing proper relationships between levels of aggregate demand and supply and between their tradeable and non-tradeable components depends to a crucial extent on the evolution of key relative prices such as interest rates, wages and the exchange rate. These not only affect macroeconomic management but also condition the quality of the evaluation and subsequent profitability of investment projects.

b)   Growth and informal-sector employment

Increasing the number of good-quality jobs depends on the rate and sustainability of economic growth and, ultimately, on the saving and investment effort, while an improvement in real wages depends fundamentally on increased productivity and the equitable distribution of its results. Labour policies do of course play an important role as regards facilitating the adaptation of firms to the new context of competitiveness and translating economic growth into new good-quality jobs, but they are no substitute for a climate of growth and promotion of investment.

When macroeconomic policies react passively to sudden external changes —variations in international interest rates, in the terms of trade, or in the availability of capital— or to changes at the domestic level —fluctuations in construction activities or in the consumption of durable goods— this leads to erratic or "stop-and-go" progress. In such cases, the inevitable result is a decline in the average net utilization of production capacity, followed by a negative impact on employment, which reacts with a certain degree of delay to fluctuations in the level of activity.

The size of the disparity between effective demand and production capacity has important immediate (static) and longer-term (dynamic) effects. For a start, greater use of installed capacity increases the effective productivity of resources, thus also increasing the yield on capital and/or the remuneration of labour. From the dynamic standpoint, higher rates of utilization and the consequent increase in effective productivity tend to stimulate investment in new production capacity and, hence, the generation of better-quality jobs.

One of the fundamental macroeconomic balances is connected with the rate of utilization of production capacity. If there are marked fluctuations in the latter, they will adversely affect investment and employment. Furthermore, they have a negative effect on equity, since the lower-income sectors, which have less human capital, as well as small and medium-sized enterprises, have a more limited capacity to react to continual changes and imbalances. Instability thus becomes a source of considerable inequity and encourages speculation rather than production.

The way anti-inflation programmes are approached can significantly affect the rate of utilization of the available resources, and this, in turn, affects rates of return and the formation of new production capacity. When such programmes are based exclusively or excessively on a single monetary variable, they usually give rise to a pronounced increase in real interest rates. This excessively favours the financial dimension over productive activities and tends to keep the economy back from the production frontier.

A context of high interest rates and exchange-rate lag is not the most suitable environment for boosting the generation of productive employment. Moreover, in a situation of low growth, with relative prices biased against employment, not much can be gained from reforms to improve the functioning of the labour market. Efficient economic policy uses instruments that act on the market where distortions are generated, and not on the market affected by them. The adaptation of the financial and foreign exchange markets to high and sustained growth rates is probably a more effective means of creating employment than the use of labour policies to try to solve problems deriving from economic policy.

c) **Competitiveness and labour costs**

Increasing competitiveness is an essential condition for growth and, hence, for generating employment. The driving force behind current growth is greater competitiveness, which is connected mainly with increased productivity and maintenance of the macroeconomic balances, rather than with labour costs.

The fact that such costs have risen more slowly than productivity in the industrial sector has favoured an increase in the margin of competitiveness. However, exchange-rate lag and changes in relative prices eat away firms' profitability levels and shift most of the burden of the adjustment to the labour force. As a result, enterprises —especially in the industrial sector— reduce employment levels as a means of increasing productivity and recovering their profit margins. In many countries this type of adjustment has led to facilitation of the dismissal of workers, more flexible hiring arrangements, and reduction of labour costs in general, including wages. Thus, while the macroeconomic balance and the competitiveness of enterprises is maintained in the short term, this is achieved at the cost of a decline in employment levels and an increase in the instability and vulnerability of the workers.

Despite the fact that the labour markets of the region lag behind noticeably in terms of wage levels, emphasis is placed on the need to reduce labour costs in order to become more competitive. Actually, however, labour costs only partially affect competitiveness. Comparison of the Latin American countries with those of Asia and the United States shows that the lower competitiveness of the region would appear to be due to lower labour productivity rather than to higher labour and wage costs.[46]

The fact that labour and wage costs are lower in the countries of the region goes along with lower productivity per employee, and the competitiveness of the Latin American and Caribbean economies is more affected by the low levels of productivity than by the incidence of labour costs.[47]

In most of the countries, real wages rise more slowly than the product per employee, at constant prices. This means that competitiveness is being gained in this way. In many cases, however, despite this increased productivity and the slower wage increases, competitiveness is going down or stagnating as a result of the exchange-rate lags which reduce the returns in dollars and increase national-currency labour costs.

The pressures to reduce inflation and increase competitiveness, in a context of vulnerability with regard to external finance and insufficient domestic saving, affect the rate and sustainability of growth and, hence, the possibilities of improving labour performance.

Advances in competitiveness call for macroeconomic balances which give priority to saving, investment and increases in productivity. This approach must be complemented, however, with suitable policies on human resources training, dissemination of technology, development of the infrastructure and internationalization of production. This, it would appear, is the integrated view of the promotion of competitiveness which is gaining ground in the region (Rosales, 1996b).

d) Production development policies

The sectors exporting primary commodities have become the segment of production with the most dynamic effects on growth, although their direct impact on employment is only slight. In later stages, however, they have been joined by subsectors which generate more added value, both in industry and services, thus increasing the number of good-quality jobs and the level of employment in the highest-productivity segments of the informal sector.

Earlier export promotion policies paid little attention to the branches based on the use of natural resources. Recent advances in such fields as microelectronics, informatics, telecommunications and satellite technology have made it possible to significantly improve the information on the quality and volume of economically available natural resources, however. This provides a renewed argument for the acquisition and strengthening of

---

[46] According to ILO, the labour costs in Latin American manufacturing are low (US$ 2.70 on average) compared with those of the Asian countries (US$ 3.80) and the United States (US$ 16.1) (ILO, 1994).
[47] For example, the highest labour costs in the region are only half those of the Republic of Korea, but this comparative advantage is practically wiped out by Latin America's lower productivity.

comparative advantages based on non-traditional natural resources, which offer appreciable economic rents.

Full utilization of the natural resources potential of the region should be reflected in a strengthening of the linkages between such exports and the other sectors of production, since such linkages bring with them intermediate demands for goods, services and labour, improvements in quality, and the dissemination of technical progress. There are no very clear signs that this is happening in the region, however. Instead, the tendency is towards precarious types of linkages between companies engaged in the exploitation of natural resources and their economic and social environment (universities, technological and training centres, public institutions and other firms).

The proposal on changing production patterns with social equity calls upon countries not to under-utilize their natural resources base, but at the same time to redirect industry towards international markets and to give growing priority to forward and backward links with natural-resource-based sectors (Stumpo, 1996).

The advances made in the design of development strategies based on clusters established around natural resources make certain demands in respect of production development policies. Firstly, research and prospection activities must be carried out in order to define the size of the gap in terms of technology and know-how among the sectors which are potential candidates for entering the respective natural resource branch. Secondly, export development and promotion policies must be adapted to the aim of establishing such potential linkages.

In this latter field, mention may be made of the promotion of quality standards, the establishment of technical training institutes, the execution of training activities, and the establishment of production development incentives in general. Likewise, environment policy may be a factor that facilitates production linkages among natural-resource-based activities and other secondary and services activities. As experience shows, what begins as an "environmental restriction" quickly becomes a factor that promotes innovation by raising the quality of a product, or giving rise to a totally new one, and improving efficiency in the use of energy and water, the disposal of wastes, and the organization of the production process (Stumpo, 1996).

Another key element at this level is the territorial context where a natural resource is located. In other words, production development policies aimed at promoting linkages around a natural resource should also seek closer linkages with decentralization and territorial development policies.[48]

e) Technological modernization

The generation, dissemination and adoption of technical progress, like the quest for increased competitiveness, is a process of a systemic nature, because the competitive performance of an economy depends not only on enterprises themselves but also on their environment and the externalities and synergic relations that are generated. This is why it is necessary to take action not only at the enterprise level but throughout the whole extent of

---

[48] The territorial component of production development is analysed later on in this chapter.

the "national innovative system", especially with regard to the production system, the technological infrastructure and the linkages between the two (ECLAC, 1996a).

The State therefore needs to take direct action as the promoter and indirect action as the (usually partial) financial backer of firms, organizations and networks in which know-how is accumulated and disseminated on forms of organization, technological advances, and other relevant topics. In seeking to speed up the process of adaptation, generation and dissemination of technology, it is not enough merely to increase expenditure on the supply of technology, especially as regards the resources allocated to public sector technology institutes. On the contrary, as the experience of both more industrialized and developing economies shows, in many fields it is vitally necessary to try to ensure that the supply of technology meets the needs of the production system.

Practical experience suggests that relatively modest increases in the allocation of resources could be enough to promote the formation or improvement of networks of academic, technological and business bodies so as to make possible a generalized increase in productivity not based exclusively on fixed capital investment. Such increases in resources should go preferably to strengthen effective interaction among the various institutional actors concerned, and should be increasingly based on the resources that the private sector devotes to innovation. Action to strengthen such systems should include support for information networks, the strengthening of inter-firm cooperation mechanisms, the protection of intellectual property, the promotion of sectoral research and technological extension centres, the adoption of international quality standards and regulations, and professional training.

In this sense, the transition from the present almost guaranteed financing of the public supply of technology to a system where there is greater competition for funds on the basis of assessable projects that reflect the special features of the various phases of technological research —basic, pre-competitive and competitive— should be reflected in an increase both in the social return on these resources and in the dynamism and contacts of the institutes in question with the production base. Similarly, giving bonus points in the evaluation to projects which are co-financed by private firms could help promote closer links with companies' actual production and technological needs.

f) Investment in human resources

In addition to the implementation of credit and marketing programmes, raising the productivity of the more backward sectors will call for heavy investments in training and upgrading of skills, as well as concern to ensure that there is some degree of correspondence between increases in productivity and wages.

The speed with which the rapid dissemination of technology is effectively reflected in a systematic rise in total factor productivity and greater international competitiveness depends on it being supplemented with equally heavy investments in the creation of human capital of a quality commensurate with the technical progress achieved. This means, in the long term, improving the quality and appropriateness of education, as well as increasing its duration and coverage and effective access to it, while in the short term it means redoubling training and retraining efforts, especially for young people and the unemployed.

It is noteworthy that although all studies stress the high rate of return on training activities (normally over 20% per year), an average worker in the region currently receives only the equivalent of one or two weeks of training in the whole of his 40 - 50 years of working life.

This is due to three factors. First, because of fiscal limitations the public sector is not in a position to significantly increase its expenditure on training, so that this can reach reasonable levels (six months' training, or 2% of a worker's working life). Second, generally speaking employers are mainly interested in financing training in skills that will raise a worker's productivity within their own firms (specific training), and not in other types of skills (general training), because in that case a worker's wages have to be raised in line with his increased productivity. Unfortunately, general training is what is most needed at present in the region. Third, the main interested party —the worker who will benefit from general training— does not usually have resources to finance it, and there is no private market that provides loans for such an investment, because of the lack of real guarantees for this type of credit.

The lack of private institutions that will advance loans for investments in human capital results in faulty allocation of capital within the economy: there is over-investment in physical capital goods and under-investment in human capital and organizational improvements, so that the national product and total factor productivity are reduced and there is a negative impact on productivity and the demand for labour. This is one of the main causes of underemployment and unemployment in the region, and is a clear example of a market flaw which adversely affects both efficiency and equity (see box VI.1).

Box VI.1
TRAINING POLICIES

The training market is usually "incomplete". Completing it involves furthering the linkages between the supply of training and the demand for it, regulating the content, quality and relevance of training activities, and improving the incentives for the training of employers and workers and the formation of training enterprises. The public sector should also improve the arrangements for identifying training needs by sectors, regions and size of enterprises and subsequently process and disseminate this information.

At the same time, in order to tackle the issues of the coverage, quality and efficiency of the system, it is necessary to improve the capacity for the design and evaluation of public training policies, strengthen their operation through demand incentives, secure closer coordination with supply, and strengthen the links between the training system and enterprises. In order to gain the best possible knowledge of business firms' training needs and thus ensure the suitability of the services offered, the design and financing of training courses could be linked to commitments by specific firms as regards on-the-job practice or steady jobs for suitable students.

Inter-agency coordination is also important, for improving the coherence of the various training policies, programmes and actions and for linking training more closely with policies for the development of production and technology and with unemployment insurance. In all these areas it is essential to promote the participation of employers and workers in order to strengthen the certification of skills, the timely identification of needs, and the ongoing evaluation of public training policies.

Source: O. Rosales, "Industrial policy and promotion of competitiveness", *CEPAL Review*, No. 53, (LC/G.1832-P), Santiago, Chile, August 1994.

In order to overcome this problem, it is proposed that pension funds (both those that the debtor is expected to accumulate in the future and those that his guarantor actually possesses) should be used as a guarantee for such loans. Once the debtor has completed his studies, the money owed would be automatically deducted from his pay (or, if he fell behind in his payments, from his guarantor's pay) in the form of higher than normal social security deductions until the debt and interest was paid off. This combination of adequate collateral and guaranteed payment would encourage the private sector to grant loans for investments in human capital.

The problem of training lies not only in its insufficient amount but also in the fact that it is often unsuited to the real needs of the country. Consequently, as well as increasing the amount of training it is necessary to improve the quality of its supply, make its institutions more flexible, and link it up much more closely with companies' real needs.

g) Territorial aspects and production development

The pressing needs of the present phase of technological transition raise the challenge of making innovations in production and organization throughout the entrepreneurial structure. This can hardly be achieved merely by entering the dynamic production linkages of the world economy, which are in any case restricted to a small segment of the entrepreneurial and production sector.

There is no guarantee that these external linkages will ensure sufficient spread of technical progress among the whole set of companies located in the different regions and local economic systems within a country. These latter systems are mainly made up of companies which are quite small, although they play a decisive role in the generation of employment and income. They play a vital part in securing a more balanced distribution of economic growth throughout the country, but they do not usually have an adequate local supply of basic infrastructure and advanced business services to facilitate their modernization process.

This is why it is so important to make the necessary institutional reforms to ensure that the incipient decentralization process under way in much of the region includes substantial elements of economic development and promotion of strategic consensuses among the different social actors (Alburquerque, 1997).

The generation and distribution of wealth at the national and sub-national levels depend to a great extent on specific territorial policies and institutions to promote the endogenous economic development, agreed upon among the different social actors on the basis of local initiatives, with a view to the attainment of suitable levels of production efficiency and competitiveness. Thus, the demands of globalization do not only affect activities linked with international markets, but also have a decisive impact at the **microeconomic** level, in connection with changes in forms of production and business management, and at the **mesoeconomic** level, where it is necessary to create a set of intermediate-level institutions and organizations to give rise to innovative territorial environments and thus redesign public management in consensus with the various other actors of society and reach decisive agreements to promote economic growth and the generation of productive employment (Vásquez and Garofoli, 1995).

Economic policies aiming to change the real variables of the economy with a view to changing production patterns (at the microeconomic level of productive and business activities) consequently call for a decentralized and territorial-based approach in order to adapt them to the actual circumstances of each local production base and entrepreneurial structure. This is even more evident in the present phase of economic development, in which the de-localization and segmentation of the different phases of production activity, as well as the practice of subcontracting by companies, have made it clear that flexible forms of organization and production are more efficient and capable of functioning within networks.

Consequently, it is only in those territories (whether they be regions, micro-regions or confederations of municipalities) whose various public and private actors are capable of building innovative environments, on the basis of their own resources and specific circumstances, to meet the technological and organizational challenges posed by the new forms of production and management and the growing internationalization of economies and consumption patterns, that those actors will be in a position to act as efficient leading agents of technological and socio-economic change at the sub-national levels.

The wide range of different territorial environments is only apparently at variance with the advance of globalization, as the latter can take place precisely by taking advantage of such territorial differences: the only condition is that the micro and mesoeconomic policies must be compatible with macroeconomic adjustment policies so as to stimulate the creation of territorial forms of behaviour, environments and institutions and thus increase the production efficiency and competitiveness of the different local production and entrepreneurial structures in the countries of Latin America and the Caribbean (see box VI.2).

3. Promotion of micro-enterprises

As the economies of the region have gradually achieved greater stability, thanks to economic reforms, there has also been a gradual resurgence of interest in medium-term issues: that is to say, in the design of development strategies. It is therefore hardly surprising that micro-enterprise (ME) promotion strategies are increasingly common in the regional debate on options for development with equity, in view of their importance for creating employment and income opportunities for broad sectors of the Latin American and Caribbean labour force.

In order for such strategies to be effective, however, the promotional instruments and programmes must be adapted to the characteristics of the various types of MEs, since these enterprises display considerable heterogeneity. A good way of identifying their differences is to classify them according to their accumulation potential. According to this criterion, there are three types of ME: i) those with enhanced accumulation, which generate surpluses and can gradually expand their scale of production; ii) those with break-even levels of accumulation, which are only capable of reproducing the original production process, and iii) subsistence-level MEs, which suffer from an ongoing process of decapitalization which serves to remunerate the activities of "micro-businesses".

This classification has important implications for the formulation of promotional policies. Subsistence MEs absorb major segments of the economically active population when structural and cyclical imbalances occur in the modern sectors of the economy. This category

> **Box VI.2**
>
> **PUBLIC-PRIVATE ASSOCIATION AND COOPERATION
> IN ENTERPRISE CLUSTERS IN PERU**
>
> Despite the difficulties that have to be faced in Peru, groups of firms from various subsectors of the economy have carried forward an important initiative which has resulted in the successful formation of local enterprise clusters.
>
> Within the context of the Programme for the Promotion of Small-scale and Micro-enterprises of the Ministry of Industry of Peru, a national survey has been carried out which reveals that there are more than 100 local clusters of small-scale and micro-enterprises which were established in recent decades.
>
> A feature of these initiatives is that in most of them there has been a substantial improvement in productivity, since although the enterprises started almost from subsistence levels they have now attained the national average levels; although in many cases they have not yet reached international levels of productivity, the advances they have made indicate a significant capacity for improvement.
>
> The explanation for this phenomenon does not appear to lie in official centralist-type policies, but rather in the process of local social mobilization with the participation of public and private agents in favour of the productive development of these groups of enterprises.
>
> One of the leading examples of these clusters is the Gamarra textile and clothing manufacturing and trading complex, located in the La Victoria district of Lima.
>
> **Source:** Ramón Ponce, "The new role of business associations in the development of production", paper presented at the International Seminar on the New Role of Business Associations in the Development of Production, organized by ECLAC/Friedrich Ebert Foundation/Fundación Sercal, Santiago, Chile, 25-26 October 1995.

includes most of the MEs in Latin America and the Caribbean, which act as a social and occupational "buffer". Enhanced-accumulation MEs, for their part, attain considerable levels of specialization and integration through their subcontracting activities with larger firms, and if the promotional policies are appropriate they can even successfully enter external markets. Finally, the potential of break-even MEs will depend on the markets they occupy and the appropriateness of the existing promotional policies.

Analysis of experience in the region reveals that policies for promoting this subsector use an approach based on active collaboration. This means that the main role assigned to the State is to create a suitable environment for facilitating the work of private bodies, without the adoption of integral government intervention programmes. The Colombian experience is an exception to this trend, since that country has adopted a National Micro-enterprise Development Plan which executes programmes and applies instruments in keeping with the differing characteristics of the enterprises, differentiating between social and production objectives. In this sense, the Colombian system is closer to one of guided collaboration.

Within the active collaboration system, two sub-levels may be distinguished, according to the level of maturity reached by the approaches used and the diversity of the instruments applied. In the first sub-level are Chile and Ecuador, where there is active and growing participation by the State in the definition of programmes and broad instruments. The difference in the case of the second sub-level is that while the State is sensitive to the issue, the progress made in terms of instruments and programmes is of more recent date (see table VI.1).

With regard to the implementation of instruments and programmes, there appears to be greater attention to the questions of access to credit and training, but activity is less intensive in the areas of technical assistance and organizational development.

4. Policies against rural poverty

a) National experiences and policy options

In recent years, various proposals have been put forward for policies to replace the now financially precarious systems of subsidies, protection and extension services which were for many decades part of the environment in which poor rural dwellers lived and worked in some countries of the region. These schemes, although excessively centralized and technocratic, did allow a good deal to be learned about the dynamics of rural poverty and the potential of the rural poor for rising out of it. Generally speaking, the current proposals incorporate and combine both elements taken from approaches already applied in the past and updated theoretical elements, giving rise to some promising hybrid proposals. Most of them are aimed at strengthening poor agricultural producers so that they can form more competitive family micro-enterprises or associative ventures. At the same time, however, we must not overlook other types of programmes which, although they do not help to improve the income of the rural poor directly or immediately, do so in the medium term (educational services) or relieve poverty by raising the quality of life through the provision of services (drinking water, electricity, housing and communications).

Faced by the dual challenge presented by the reduction of the presence of the Welfare State in rural areas, at the same time that trade is being liberalized, with all that that demands in terms of competitiveness, governments and specialized agencies have analysed previous efforts to support the rural poor with a view to formulating innovative proposals. The World Bank has reassessed and redesigned the integrated rural development programmes which gave mixed results in the 1970s. UNDP, for its part, has incorporated various practical experiences and a conceptual framework in which participation is given special emphasis, in its proposal on sustainable human development at the local level, with special reference to rural areas. What is emerging is an integrated, holistic rural development proposal, based on a systemic approach in a local or micro-regional setting.

Despite the heterogeneity of the various rural social groups, the successful results achieved by a large number of programmes provide grounds for recommending that priority should be given to projects that favour the development of production at the peasant level in the areas of agricultural, agro-industrial and non-agricultural rural activities. In the last two years, the evaluations made of regional and micro-regional projects supported by the International Fund for Agricultural Development (IFAD), the European Union and various bilateral programmes indicate that these initiatives can bring about a sustainable increase in the income of poor rural families if they include effective arrangements for participative planning and community-level management. It would appear that the proportion of peasant

Table VI.1
STRATEGIES FOR THE DEVELOPMENT OF MICRO-ENTERPRISES (MEs) IN THE 1990s

Nature and country	Objective	Programmes	Responsible institution	Beneficiary sector
Guided collaboration Colombia (1993)	To integrate MEs into national development in economic terms To implement specific and integrated programmes with regard to production potential	Training and advisory assistance; technological development; credit; marketing; organizational development; social security	The National Planning Department of the Ministry of Economic Development is responsible for the administration and coordination of the National Plan for the Development of Micro-Enterprises (PNDM)	The PNDM draws a distinction between enhanced-reproduction, break-even and subsistence-level MEs. The first-named are given integral attention in order to increase their linkages with the national economy; the second type of MEs are given support in accordance with their viability in the market, and the third class of MEs are given strong social aid in order to keep up employment and incomes
Active collaboration Sub-level 1 Chile (1996)	To support the development and consolidation of MEs and small-scale producers in order to improve the income levels of the poorest groups	Training and credit; on a secondary level, technical assistance	The Solidarity and Social Investment Fund (FOSIS), which comes under the Ministry of Planning and Cooperation	Break-even, subsistence and, to a lesser extent, enhanced-reproduction MEs employing up to nine persons in the manufacturing and services sectors and up to five persons in the commerce subsector
Ecuador (1992)	To improve the productivity of workers in the sector and their families	Credit, training, technical assistance and organizational development	National Corporation for Assistance to Small-scale Productive Units (CONAUPE) coming under the Ministry of Social Welfare	Informal subsistence-level MEs employing between 1 and 10 persons, in all sectors of the economy
Sub-level 2 Guatemala (1992)	To generate and consolidate employment in the informal sector by improving the linkages of MEs with the economy	Credit and training	Micro-enterprises Replication System, 1988 (SIMME), coming under the National Commission for the Development of Micro- and Small-scale Enterprises	Informal subsistence-level MEs employing up to eight persons, in all sectors of the economy
Mexico (1993)	To support production projects that will generate employment and raise the standard of living	Credit, training and appropriate changes in the legal system	National Solidarity Programme (PRONASOL), of the Ministry of Social Development	Subsistence-level and break-even MEs employing between 1 and 14 persons, in all sectors of the economy
Peru (1993)	To generate a favourable environment for the development of MEs by making the financial system and legal framework more flexible	Credit and appropriate changes in the legal system	National Social Compensation and Development Fund (FONCODES)	Priority is given to informal break-even and subsistence-level MEs employing between 1 and 10 persons, in all sectors of the economy

Table VI.1 (concl.)

Nature and country	Objective	Programmes	Responsible institution	Beneficiary sector
Bolivia (1992)	To simplify rules, promote training and generate mechanisms for improving linkages with non-governmental organizations	Credit and modification of the legal framework	The Ministry of Planning and Coordination coordinates networks of executing agencies	Subsistence-level and break-even MEs employing between 1 and 14 persons, in all sectors of the economy
Uruguay (1991)	To coordinate programmes aimed at MEs	Credit and training	There are various responsible State institutions, including the National Directorate of Handicraft Workers and Small- and Medium-scale Enterprises, coming under the Ministry of Industry and Energy	Subsistence-level, break-even and enhanced-reproduction MEs employing up to 10 persons
Brazil (1992)	To implement support policies for micro- and small-scale enterprises through programmes for their modernization and improvement of their productivity, among other aims	Training	The Brazilian Assistance Service for Small and Micro-enterprises (SEBRAE), an autonomous social organization independent of the public administration	Mainly subsistence-level MEs in the informal sector
Venezuela (1992)	To support and promote the development of MEs in order to improve the income of the sectors most vulnerable to the effects of the economic crisis To support and promote grass-roots consumer organizations	Training, technical assistance and credit	The Support Programme for the Popular-level Economy, coming under the Ministry of the Family. There is also the Venezuelan Social Investment Fund (FONVIS), which comes under the Ministry of Planning and Coordination	Subsistence-level MEs in all sectors of the economy
Argentina (1996)	To facilitate the access of MEs to credit	Credit programmes for micro- and small-scale enterprises	The Ministry of Economic Affairs and Public Works and Services, through the Under-Secretary for Industry	Micro- and small-scale enterprises employing up to 20 persons, in all sectors of the economy

Source: L. Tapia and Van Hemelryck, "Planes y políticas de fomento a la microempresa en América Latina", Documento de trabajo, No. 154, Santiago, Chile, Sur, June 1996.

enterprises (both family and associative) capable of incorporating appropriate know-how and competing successfully is higher than was generally expected. On the one hand, their experience with multiple crops seems to make them more receptive to new varieties and practices than larger-scale traditional single-crop farmers, and on the other the abandonment of the attitude of technocratic superiority sometimes displayed by the old unilateral "transfer of technology" appears to have liberated and strengthened know-how and analytical and organizational capacities which were previously not used.

Although it is true that many poor rural dwellers do not have the necessary land and education to take advantage of the opportunities offered by expanding markets, they are nevertheless benefitted by the creation of jobs and the new need for associative service enterprises generated by the growth of peasant enterprises as the main driving force of rural development. Young people with reasonable levels of education, in particular, are finding new rural opportunities which offer a decent standard of living, in such areas as management, education, training and, above all, the associative marketing of agricultural products, which is a key component of all peasant production development strategies designed to improve competitiveness.

b) New bases for community participation

Within the context of this emerging consensus, it is proposed in particular that the new programmes in support of small rural producers should be *participative* and *community-based* (World Bank Group, 1996; Banuri and others, 1996). Although this general principle is not new (it goes back to the rural community development programmes of the 1960s), these proposals are innovative in that they form part of a more general trend towards decentralization of the **comprehensive and sustainable** management of local resource **systems**, with the participation of all the interested parties ("stakeholders"). Above all, the concept of "participation" is taking on a new meaning which is at once more complex and more concrete than the optimistic definitions of other eras. The more recent proposals usually incorporate the concepts of the assumption and exercise of power ("empowerment") and accountability to the beneficiaries, as well as the idea of creating negotiating spaces and skills. This is a novel approach because it means that the programmes are essentially client-driven rather than being run by the central government or technicians (Ashby and Sperling, 1992).

In short, what is needed is, on the one hand, to change the local and regional environment so as to make possible the democratization of development and the strengthening of the previously excluded groups as social actors, and on the other to train planners and extension workers in the essential socio-cultural dynamics of peasant society. The new roles which it is proposed to assign to the leading rural actors stress in particular the need to understand peasant social organization, priorities and strategies, which may be very different from the schemes proposed from the standpoint of developed, "modern" urban societies.

The new proposals for peasant-level production development also stress the need for **an integral approach** in programmes that seek to change complex existing situations. As well as tackling the challenge of competitiveness, the aim is to strengthen food security at the household level and raise the status of rural life as a socio-cultural system which can play a valuable role in terms of protecting the environment and sustaining cultural diversity. With the incorporation of young people in rural development programmes, there is also beginning to be an awareness of the value of a human resource which is rarely the subject of specific policies (ECLAC, 1996a).

The main policies and programmes for combatting rural poverty seek to strengthen family and community agricultural enterprises. Agricultural labourers and non-agricultural manual workers usually come from peasant families, and they too are often interested in becoming agricultural micro-entrepreneurs. At the same time, however, it has been noted that it would be wrong to propose only a single solution for rural poverty, with an excessively sectoral approach (SUR, 1996). Likewise, greater support needs to be given to the non-agricultural activities of peasant families and the possible unionization and legal protection of seasonal workers and non-agricultural workers, together with the provision of more opportunities for training in fast-growing activities such as tourism.

c) **Specific instruments**

As well as supporting the generation of better incomes, public policies must combat rural poverty through direct improvements in the quality of rural life by promoting the redistribution of consumption by means of fiscal expenditure on infrastructure and services. As already noted, in contrast with the old State systems for the development of roads, electrification, housing, etc., various **funds** have now been set up to enable the poor to satisfy these needs more flexibly and rapidly through community-level projects designed for each specific situation. Some of the social investment funds (SIFs), which often concentrate their efforts on rural areas, have been particularly successful in the construction of social infrastructure such as schools, health centres, drinking water systems and the like. However, SIFs also support production development in the poorest rural areas through small-scale irrigation projects, collection and storage centres, and other initiatives. In addition, some SIFs finance social services such as the hiring and training of rural schoolteachers, the fitting-out of primary and pre-primary schools, health centres and community pharmacies, and the supply of supplementary food aid for children. In recent years, the innovative efforts of the SIFs have been focussed on speeding-up and simplifying the process of approval of the projects submitted and training members of poor communities to formulate project proposals, as the technical inability of potential beneficiaries to draft written projects is a serious stumbling-block in this process.

The studies made of the evolution of rural income support the hypothesis that **education** is a key element for breaking, in the medium term, the vicious circle of the inter-generational transmission of rural poverty. However, it is also well known that there is a close relationship between the educational attainments and the economic and social origins of students, both in Latin America and the Caribbean and in other regions. Nevertheless, this apparent determinism, which potentially militates against any hope of achieving greater equity through education, is beginning to yield in the light of the encouraging news being received on new educational processes, especially in the poorest rural areas, which incorporate parental and community participation as an integral element of their strategies.[49]

This approach based on the participative management of rural education appears to enhance the most beneficial effects of a set of measures designed to improve the learning process, since it recognizes the fact that the risk of failure is due not only to shortcomings in the student himself and his environment, but also to the fact that in the traditional approach to education it is assumed that a child automatically brings with him from his home and family the accepted codes of the prevailing culture. However, children from lower-class backgrounds —especially peasant children and those from families of peasant origin— and their parents often have codes and stores of knowledge different from those assumed by the standard form of traditional education. Consequently, there will be an improvement in performance if two-way bridges are built between teachers and parents, so that both can understand each other in the two silent languages represented by the cultures of the school and of the home environment. Such a change is resisted by many teachers because of the ideology of the Enlightenment which has marked education for the past two centuries, and also because of the feeling of insecurity of rural teachers regarding their position, which leads them to keep their distance from the "low-class" environment of the peasant culture and community.

At the same time, the participation of parents and the community is vital for achieving an improvement in the impoverished and inefficient socio-cultural system characteristic of typical traditional rural schools. The full system centered around "the school" includes —or should include— parents and the environment with which the children interact. As individuals with unique capacities, they can be co-participants in the necessary transition of the school system to a state of greater efficiency and efficacy. A system of this type cannot be designed in advance: instead, its forms of interaction and the new culture of the school emerge from the contact among the actors involved, especially the teachers and parents.

With regard to access to education, except in a few countries of the region only one-third or less of rural young people complete more than the six grades of basic schooling considered to be the minimum for mastering the operations demanded by the proper application of the new agricultural technology.[50] The situation is even worse in the case of older persons. This represents a serious impediment not only to efforts to modernize agriculture but also to the development of non-agricultural activities in rural areas and rural dwellers' possibilities of successfully entering the urban environment.

It is important not only to expand the coverage of school enrolment, improve the quality of the education provided and seek to increase the number of years of schooling of rural children, but also to bear in mind, when designing the curricula for basic rural schools, that only about half the students will be engaged in agricultural work proper when they are adults, either because they migrate or because they take up non-agricultural rural work.

---

[49] Among the examples of such strategies are those applied in Mexico (PARE); El Salvador, Programme for Education with Community Participation (EDUCO); Colombia, Escuela Nueva; and Brazil (Competitive Selection of Directors and Other Management Officials by the School Councils of the State of Minas Gerais).

[50] In 1994, according to rural household surveys, the percentages of young people of both sexes between 20 and 24 years of age who had completed seven years or more of formal education were as follows: Chile, 72%; Colombia, 35%; Costa Rica, 32%; Honduras, 16%; Mexico, 41%, and Panama, 48%.

In short, public policies on education, creation of infrastructure and improvement of productivity, as well as those designed to reduce rural poverty, combine the lessons learned from decades of programmes and projects with promising experiments involving different ways of giving greater decision-making power to beneficiaries. These efforts deserve a leading place in national strategies for overcoming poverty, unemployment and underemployment and social marginalization, not only in view of the key position that rural poverty occupies in the vicious circle of transmission of inequality in society, but also because the studies show that rural poverty can indeed be reduced.

5. Agricultural modernization policies

a) Access to land

In many Latin American countries, the lack of social equity is connected with the land tenure system. This justifies governments' concern to change the polarized structure of land tenure and thus reduce the accompanying rural poverty. It should be borne in mind, however, that the solution to such poverty does not lie just in improving the access to land, for when such access is made easier, it should be complemented with the availability of credit, inputs, irrigation, technology, information, insurance and markets.

In programmes for providing access to land there are three main options: agrarian reform programmes; land tenure reforms assisted by market mechanisms, and tax mechanisms.

Quite apart from a possible dichotomy between efficiency and equity, it may be noted that in the past practically all agrarian reform programmes have suffered from numerous intrinsic problems. To mention only a few of these: i) land is a special good with big differences in terms of quality and/or geophysical characteristics, so that it is difficult to compare two units of land, even when they are the same size, or to determine their economic or production value; ii) in the reformed sector, beneficiaries sometimes display very different management capacities, and this is made worse by lack of support for gaining access to the necessary inputs, such as capital and technology; iii) the administrative capacity of the bodies responsible for agrarian reform programmes has often been inadequate, and iv) it must be borne in mind that agrarian reform can have negative effects on the non-reformed sector, such as disinvestment because of the fear of expropriation.

In order to promote a land market, a clear definition of title and ownership is required, as well as the establishment of private property rights so that they can be traded. It is also necessary to deliver title deeds to landowners, and this is not feasible without modern and efficient land registration systems. In practically all the countries of the region, the land information systems are in need of significant improvement as regards the reliability of the data and the efficiency of the procedures used. If it is desired to impose redistributive reforms by law or to change the rural land ownership structure on the basis of the market forces, then a clear definition of ownership rights is crucial for achieving the sought-for results.

The idea is to use land taxes for non-budgetary purposes, such as increasing the productive use of land, discouraging land speculation, or redistributing the resource for the benefit of small producers or environmental objectives. The problem is that such taxes are hard to manage, which is why past experiences in this regard have not been very promising. In practice, there are three ways of applying a land tax: i) the tax can be *in rem* (i.e., on the basis of the area of the property); ii) it can be based on the net income generated by the land, or its commercial value; or iii) it can be based on objective measurements such as soil quality.

An *in rem* tax is the easiest to apply in administrative terms. Its disadvantage is that it does not take any account of the productivity of the land. If small farmers own land with less production potential, then such a tax becomes regressive. All these indicators are hard to establish in rural areas, where land registers and soil quality maps tend to be faulty and land markets are few in number and far from perfect.

The difficulty raised by a tax based on the commercial value of land is precisely the problem of appraising that value. In most Latin American and Caribbean countries, the quality of the information provided by land registers is insufficient, so that the authorities have to resort to surveys in order to determine land prices. In the past, there have been many cases which show that such a system involves serious moral hazards (that is to say, distortions in the behaviour of the actors in order to get round the regulations, especially when it is desired to apply a progressive tax). Consequently, if this system is to be effective the appraisals must be carried out by third parties, on the basis of the effective purchase prices of equivalent land in the same area. This is not an easy problem to solve. Nevertheless, the very low level of the taxes on agricultural land in the region suggest that tax reforms could help both to improve the land market and to raise land productivity by penalizing inefficient use.

Formal credit institutions do not usually have adequate information on crops, yields, production risks and marketing, so that they tend to demand very high guarantees. The costs of the local infrastructure and staff needed to supervise the credits on the spot are prohibitive, the repayments are insufficient, and there are serious problems with the guarantees. This is why there do not appear to have been any cases in the region where the formal financial sector has stepped in to make up for the elimination of preferential terms for agriculture. The informal financial sector continues to be important for small producers, although its loans are usually only small and are for the purpose of consumption or for making up working capital, while between 30% and 50% of all agricultural producers have no access to credit at all.

Various recent projects for the delivery and clearing of land title deeds are aimed precisely at reducing the obstacles represented by the lack of collateral. Programmes of this type have been carried out in Chile, Colombia, Honduras, Mexico, Nicaragua and Peru, with financing from the World Bank, the IDB and bilateral sources such as the German Technical Cooperation Agency (GTZ), to name only a few.

b) **Agricultural credit policy aspects**

There are also a number of examples of successful initiatives outside the region, and increasingly within it too, in which responsibility for selecting and supervising borrowers and guaranteeing the loans made has been handed over to groups made up of loan beneficiaries themselves or members of the local community.

In quite a number of the case studies carried out in 1995,[51] the **intermediation of agro-industry** was described as being similar to that of a lender or supplier of credit for the producers with which agro-industrial enterprises had purchase contracts. The advantages of this arrangement are that the credit is negotiated locally, bureaucratic formalities are reduced to a minimum (generally to a single additional clause in the contract), disbursements are made as needed, the technical assistance staff is also responsible for supervising the credits, repayments are simply deducted from the produce sale price, and transaction costs are therefore reduced. However, these linked transactions (purchase contract linked with the provision of credit and/or inputs) make it possible to use obscure bookkeeping practices, to transfer costs from one item to another, and even to make it difficult for many producers to calculate the implicit interest charged by the agro-industry on the credits in question, the costs of which sometimes come close to usury. Consequently, institutional measures to regulate such contracts and a system (such as arbitration, for example) to ensure that they are properly fulfilled would be useful precautions in the continuing growth of this segment of the financial market.

c) Research and technology transfer in agriculture

Various studies have shown the high social return (over 20%) of research and technology transfer in agriculture (ECLAC, 1995c). However, the private sector's investments and efforts in this field are less than optimal, partly because the areas involved are largely "public goods".

Agricultural research has all the features of an "imperfect market" in which small producers clearly face greater difficulties in benefitting from the research, participating in it and gaining access to the resulting information, especially in the case of private research, as much of this is concerned with inputs (seeds, fertilizers, pesticides, veterinary products and machinery) which small producers do not use very intensively, especially when they are faced with credit restrictions. There are a number of areas of agricultural research in which the private sector simply does not invest, such as self-pollinated crops, farm management, and matters relating to the environment and health.

Generally speaking, it is easier to make improvements in crops that are already grown in the peasant economy than in new crops which, furthermore, require inputs (water, capital, investment lead time) that peasants do not possess and practices (single-crop farming, know-how, rapid adaptability, overcoming the risk threshold) that they do not know or are not willing to adopt. A number of successful initiatives (in Guatemala, El Salvador and Colombia, for example) show, however, that small producers have considerable learning capacity, provided the technology transfer is in keeping with their situation and is accompanied by sufficient efforts to overcome other obstacles such as access to credit (Dirven, 1996).

---

[51] As part of the ECLAC/FAO/GTZ project "Promotion of the economic and social integration of small and medium-sized producers with agroindustry".

The case studies carried out by ECLAC have shown that **agro-industry can be an efficient agent for the transmission of new technologies**. Even though the growing demands of consumers and legal requirements are impelling agro-industry to enter into more and more subcontracting agreements with farmers, however, the universe of small producers with which it has purchase agreements is still relatively small.

d) Other challenges for rural policies

Finally, shortcomings in terms of infrastructure (roads, electricity, drinking water, irrigation, communications,[52] storage) restrict the area of operations and influence of the various agents acting in the rural environment, thus **limiting competition and excluding potential producers and markets**. The statistics clearly show that it is in the areas with the most acute infrastructural shortcomings that small producers are most numerous. Consequently, opening a line of investment in public works specially aimed at making up for these disadvantages would be an example of investment with a high economic and social return.

A basic problem faced by credit institutions, transport firms, agro-industry and intermediaries in general is that they have to deal with a host of small producers who are geographically scattered and often far from road and telecommunications systems, thus giving rise to extra costs. Transaction costs are high and represent a significant barrier to the modernization of small producers. These costs can be substantially reduced, however, if producers form associations among themselves, because this makes it possible to obtain economies of scale and establish a focal point for negotiations. Changes in the law (on property ownership and contracts, for example), improvement of the infrastructure (roads and telecommunications), and an increase in the ready understanding and availability of information (on prices and contract conditions), among other measures, can also help reduce transaction costs. Action by the State or by non-governmental organizations to take measures to reduce such costs or take over part of them could be the decisive factor in motivating economic agents to do business with small producers.

Since many government credit, technical assistance or marketing agencies have been restructured, or their operations have been cut down, there are now new gaps in markets that were already highly imperfect. In these circumstances, there is no inducement to modernize or to engage in competitive production, or else producers do not take these initiatives to the full extent of their potential, especially in the case of small and medium-sized production units.

Governments —together with trade associations and other non-governmental organizations— have a new and important role to play as facilitators of vertical coordination agreements, primarily aimed at **doing away with market flaws and reducing transaction costs** (by promoting producers' organizations, changing the law on contracts and strengthening the institutions responsible for ensuring their fulfillment, improving systems

---

[52] In Chile, for example, the National Confederation of Regional Federations of Peasant Cooperatives (CAMPOCOOP) is seeking finance to install a computer network and connect up to the Internet in order, among other things, to receive daily information on prices in the various markets where the varieties its members produce are being sold, so as to have a better basis for negotiations.

> **Box VI.3**
>
> **EL SALVADOR: INTEGRATION OF SMALL PRODUCERS OF BASIC CROPS INTO INTERNATIONAL HORTICULTURAL MARKETING CHAINS**
>
> Traditionally, the small-scale producers now associated with the Del Tropic Foods corporation were engaged in the production of basic grains. As a result of the promotional action taken by that firm after they had signed a contract with it, however, they began to produce okra and *vigna sinensis* beans, which Del Tropic Foods exports frozen to the United States (95%) and Europe (5%) in the amount of 5,000 metric tons per year. Out of the total area growing produce for the firm, 30% corresponds to medium-sized and small producers.
>
> The small producers linked with this firm are mostly cooperative individual smallholders: i.e., members of a cooperative formed after the 1980 agrarian reform. The average area cultivated by each of these producers is between 1.0 and 1.5 hectares.
>
> This contractual linkage has given the following results:
>
> 1. The peasants have diversified their production. As the new crops supplement the basic ones, the producers have increased the degree of utilization of their holdings and their incomes, as well as the level of employment of both family members and the surrounding population.
>
> 2. Innovations have been made, since the producers have been obliged to adapt to a strict working schedule with staggered dates of sowing and the technified use of fertilizers and pesticides in accordance with the conditions laid down in the contract with the agroindustry. They have also gained a scientific knowledge of how to combat pests and diseases which they can now apply to their traditional crops, while the knowledge gained in growing this particular type of bean has been used in the cultivation of other traditional pulses.
>
> The following advantages have kept the producers interested in keeping up their contractual relationship:
>
> 1. The stability of the price they will receive, which the agroindustry fixes in advance in the contract on the basis of the prices prevailing in world markets.
>
> 2. The provision of fertilizers by the firm at prices lower than those of the local market.
>
> 3. The provision of constant readily-available technical assistance.
>
> **Source:** ECLAC, *Quince años de desempeño económico. America Latina y el Caribe, 1980-1995* (LC/G.1925/Rev.1-P), Santiago, Chile, July 1996, box III.3, p. 109. United Nations publication, Sales No. S.96.II.G.3.

for collecting and disseminating information on markets and prices, promoting the establishment of quality standards, etc.).

Agro-industry (or agribusiness) can fill some of these voids (in the areas of credit, specialized inputs, technical assistance, information and transport), and it can also act as an intermediary between agricultural producers, markets and technology sources (ECLAC, 1995d).

If agro-industry fills the voids in imperfect markets in this way, this will increase its costs. In compensation, however, this makes an association with it more attractive to agricultural producers, who would often be willing to accept prices somewhat below those of the market in the light of these considerations. However, linked transactions (purchase contracts involving the provision of technical assistance, credit or inputs, for example) suffer from a number of potential problems such as their lack of clarity with regard to the absorption of costs and the transfer of risks. Finding a solution to these problems could boost the modernization drive among small and medium-sized agricultural producers.

VII. SOCIAL POLICIES

This chapter presents a set of proposals for designing social policies that take account of the economic and social changes faced by the Latin American countries in order to progress in the achievement of social development, as expressed at the Copenhagen World Summit for Social Development.

1. Traditional features of social policies

When we look at the evolution of the Latin American and Caribbean countries over the last 50 years, we see that substantial progress has been made in terms of the living conditions of the population, as exemplified by the reduction in infant mortality rates, the increase in life expectancy at birth, extension of the duration of formal education and a reduction in illiteracy rates, and expansion of the coverage of basic sanitation and drinking water services. At the same time, however, other indicators reveal that little progress has been made in terms of equity. These indicators include in particular the persistence of structural poverty, resort to informal solutions for finding employment and generating income, and phenomena of social exclusion and lack of social cohesion.

Both the advances and the shortcomings are due partly to the way social policies have been carried out, which, as noted in Part One of this document, has been characterized by such features as segmented access; a quest for universality which has not been realized in practice; the provision of social services through fragmented systems frequently marked by duplication of functions and services, which leads to waste of resources and inter-agency competition; bureaucratic inertia, which keeps ineffective programmes in operation, or the discontinuation of programmes whose aims are not achieved in the short term.

Social programmes do not reach the neediest. The poor do not have access to them because of cultural barriers, illiteracy, lack of information about the programmes, or the fact of living in isolated places, because the services are usually designed to meet the needs of other social groups and require the presentation of certificates, etc. Likewise, the services are not really free but involve transaction costs (transport, time, etc.) which are generally not taken into account when the programmes are designed, so that eventually they prove to be beyond the reach of those who have the least resources.

In view of this state of affairs, criticisms have been made and new approaches suggested regarding the design and implementation of social policies. These criticisms and suggestions are increasingly widespread in the region and have inspired some of the proposals and guidelines put forward below, which are presented in the broader context of the assertion that social development is only viable when there is sustained economic growth accompanied by a real concern for equity.

Although growth is naturally important, since, among other things, it generates the jobs that allow people to earn an income with which to satisfy their needs and those of their families, it must be emphasized that social policies have a positive influence on the reduction of poverty and the possibility that people can get productive jobs and feel part of the society they live in, while at the same time they can help both directly and indirectly (through their influence on economic growth) to improve the living conditions of the population.

2. The role of social policies in achieving the objectives of the World Summit for Social Development

a) Types of social policies

Three types of social policies may be distinguished:

i) **Compensatory social** policies, which are aimed at the groups affected by economic changes or any type of crisis;

ii) Policies based on **investment in human capital**, which seek to provide the population with the qualifications they need to work better. This is particularly important nowadays, when, for example, an increasing number of years of schooling are demanded for entry into the labour market, and these qualifications are also essential for emerging from a situation of poverty, for the persons who succeed in achieving this in the upward phase of an economic cycle are precisely those who are qualified to occupy the jobs generated by growth. It is the responsibility of social policy to provide the population —and especially its poorest members— with human capital so that they will be in a position to take advantage of such opportunities.

iii) **Social integration** policies aimed at overcoming the marginality of various social groups who are affected by forms of exclusion based on ethnic origin, gender, etc. (ECLAC, 1994b).

b) Financing

Social policies have to compete with a variety of other uses for public and private resources, because the availability of the latter is always limited by the multitude of needs that exist: as soon as one need is satisfied, another one will arise which will very likely require even greater resources. Thus, for example, once more or less complete quantitative coverage of primary education is attained, the problem of the **quality** of the education will arise. It is therefore necessary to establish reasonable priorities and strike a balance between social investment and investment in production. It is not always valid to advocate an automatic increase in resources for social purposes, because the solution of problems such as poverty also depends on the creation of more jobs, which requires investment in production activities. What is important is not so much to spend more on social activities, but to spend the resources better.

The Latin American countries can be classified in three groups according to the percentage of GDP and amount of resources per capita that they allocate to social expenditure: those with a **low** level of social expenditure (less than 8% of GDP or US$ 70 per capita); those with a **moderate** level (between 8% and 11% of GDP and between US$ 70 and US$ 200 per capita), and those with a **high** level (over 11% of GDP and over US$ 200 per capita) (see chapter V.1).

In view of the already mentioned importance of social policies, even for the promotion of economic growth, it is worth emphasizing the need to increase the amount of resources allocated for this purpose. Countries which spend only a small amount must redouble their efforts and, above all, allocate the resources efficiently, while those that are already spending more must review their priorities and increase the efficiency of their resource use and the efficacy of their programmes.

The sources of funds are primarily domestic efforts and greater efficiency in the use of resources for social purposes, and international cooperation, which is particularly important in the case of countries that devote only small proportions of their GDP to social policies and have unsatisfactory social indicators.

When more resources are required for social purposes, consideration should be given to the **restructuring of public expenditure** in order to draw off funds from such items as military expenditure, the financing of inefficient public enterprises, non-essential expenditure and regressive subsidies. According to some studies, "the potential is enormous for restructuring national budgets and international aid in favour of human development" (UNDP, 1991, p. 17).[53]

---

[53] There are a number of arguments for considering that reallocation is viable. First, democratic procedures involve the obligation to take care of the needs of the poor, as they form a substantial proportion of the voters in every election; second, the new development model demands investment in human resources, and third, in recent years poverty has become predominantly urban, and hence more visible, disturbing and dangerous, in most of the countries of the region.

c) Social expenditure and the level of well-being

The level of social expenditure is not a good indicator either of social development —which is also related with the economic performance of the country— or of investment in human capital, because it does not really make it possible to gauge if results are being obtained in this respect. There can be a high level of social expenditure, without this necessarily meaning an improvement in the living conditions of the population or an increase in its supply of human capital and, on the other hand, there may be a low level of social expenditure, but if the resources are used efficiently and are devoted to programmes with a high social impact, they may make a positive contribution in both respects.

It is therefore absolutely essential to rationalize the use of resources for social purposes, since "data for Latin America show that the pattern of social expenditure is regressive in most countries", so that greater public expenditure is not always the answer when trying to increase the well-being of the poor. It is often more important to seek better allocation of expenditure within the sector and more efficient use of the available funds. Extra spending on social services in general will not automatically aid the poor. The existing structure for the provision of such services must be reoriented in their favour, in terms of both quantity and quality (World Bank, 1990, p. 42).

d) Efficiency and efficacy of social expenditure

In order to rationalize resource utilization, they must be used as efficiently as possible and greater efficacy must be obtained in achieving the objectives of the projects financed with them.

In order to increase the efficiency of social expenditure, some recurrent problems must be eliminated or overcome, especially errors in programme design and implementation, lack of monitoring and evaluation, and dishonest diversion or appropriation of funds or benefits.

In order to increase the efficacy of social programmes, they must really have an impact on the target population, for which programme evaluation is required (see box VII.1).

i) **Improving social policy management**. For this purpose, a suitable information base is required. Routine indicators (on poverty, public social expenditure, etc.) are useful for diagnostic purposes, but they are not much use for evaluating the results of specific policies and programmes.

ii) **Changing the institutional structure**. The role of the State is changing. Depending on its own traditions, each country is placing greater or lesser emphasis on State participation in some areas and varying its fields of action. The dominant tendency, however, is to combine the State's presence with that of other actors and with a substantial role for the market. In line with this trend, the State continues to have considerable responsibilities in the social field, where it finances, promotes and executes programmes, either directly or through other actors (the charitable, commercial and informal subsectors, for example), as appropriate.

> **Box VII.1**
>
> **WHAT IS IMPACT?**
>
> 1. **Coverage is not impact.** For example, coverage is the number of people receiving food aid under a given programme, whereas impact is the reduction in the rate of malnutrition achieved through that programme. Increasing the number of beneficiaries (the coverage) may be a mistaken objective if the target population is not properly identified: for example, if food aid is given to those who do not have unsatisfied needs in terms of their intake of calories or proteins.
> 2. **Investment in social infrastructure is not impact.** For example, constructing or improving school buildings is investment, whereas the impact of educational programmes is what the children learn.
> 3. **Current expenditure is not impact.** Resources used to pay wages or purchase inputs for operating a service are current expenditure. The impact, however, is the degree of satisfaction that the beneficiaries receive from the benefits provided.
>
> In reality, the foregoing are means for achieving the ends of social policies. The impact is a measure of whether those ends have been achieved or not.
>
> The **impact** is the magnitude of the benefit received by the beneficiaries of programmes, in line with the sought-for objectives.
>
> **Cost-impact analysis (CIA)** methods make it possible to analyse both the efficiency and efficacy and the impact of programmes and projects. **Efficiency** is the ratio of the cost of the inputs to the value of the products (goods or services) obtained. **Efficacy** is the extent to which the objectives of a programme or project are achieved within a given period of time, without reference to the cost. When the contextual effects are eliminated and only the net effects of the project are considered, this is the **impact**.
>
> The evaluation of impacts requires an initial measurement called the "baseline", after which one or more comparison lines of results are established. The differences between the two make it possible to determine the magnitude of the changes attributable to the project. These measurements are made during the implementation of the programme, at the end of it, or even sometimes after it has finished and sufficient time has elapsed for all its effects to make themselves felt.
>
> a) In *ex ante* evaluations, **CIA makes it possible to select the best project option** or to select a project out of several different ones that all have the same objectives. Both the costs and the products and impact are estimated. Within the margins of uncertainty that apply to any estimate, there is a much higher level of knowledge and standardization in the case of costs than with regard to the impact, which must be estimated on the basis of the existing *ex post* evaluations of similar projects and expert judgements.
>
> b) In *ex post* evaluations, **CIA makes it possible to determine the alternative with the best cost/impact ratio, and the reasons for this**, learning from the experience gained in the project's implementation.
>
> **Source:** E. Cohen and R. Franco, *Evaluación de proyectos sociales*, Mexico City, Siglo Veintiuno, 1992.

iii) **Social reforms need to be carried out**. The organizational structure of the State social services must be modified to eliminate the fragmentation of institutions, duplication of effort, and the dispersal of resources. Up to a few years ago, it was asserted that in view of the state of the traditional social services it would be preferable to seek parallel ways of doing things, rather than to try to change the institutions. It was because of this that the idea of setting up social investment funds (SIFs) gained currency. Today, however, it is clear that such funds cannot have the objective of solving the general problems of social policy themselves, but only of helping to solve those problems by carrying out specific tasks and showing that it is possible to be both efficient and efficacious in social matters. This is all the more evident in view of the fact that the resources at the disposal of these funds are very limited compared with those of the public social budget. For this reason, it is urgently necessary to set about reforming the social sectors.

iv) **The need for a social authority**. Every government has an economic authority. In the social area, in contrast, it is common for there to be fragmentation of institutions and lack of coordination among programmes. In the light of this situation, various measures have been tried, such as making the Vice-President of the Republic, a particular minister or a committee of ministers responsible for coordination. Generally speaking, these solutions have not proved to be effective, mainly because each Minister has his own budgetary resources, whereas the coordinator does not have any special funds at his disposal. A social authority must have resources if its coordinating function is to be accepted.

A unique coordination initiative which is worthy of careful study is that of the Bolivian Ministry of Human Development, which subsumes all the social ministries and institutions.

v) **Decentralization**. The central government must establish guidelines, allocate resources, and regulate and control the execution of projects and the proper use of resources, but it could probably withdraw from the task of project execution.

vi) **Adjusting the allocation of human resources in the social sector**. As in other areas of State activity, the social sector suffers from an excess of functionaries and a shortage of properly trained staff. It is of fundamental importance to restore a suitable balance between the needs in terms of staff and the actual supply of staff members, as well as to train those staff members who will be kept on and to improve both future recruitment and wages.

vii) **State social policy**. The results of social policies and programmes can only be achieved in the medium and long term. There should be a basic consensus to ensure that social policies will be maintained longer than the term of office of a particular government, so as to eliminate lack of continuity and sudden changes of course. This calls for the establishment of basic agreements on social reform, not only among the political parties but also with those engaged in the production sector and with society at large.

e) Criteria for the design and execution of social programmes

Increasingly, initiatives are being taken in the region which put into effect approaches differing from the traditional view of social policies. Targeting, decentralization, demand-side subsidies, tendering-out of the execution of programmes and projects among public, private or charitable bodies, etc. are new ways of implementing social policies in part or in full so as to ensure that they reach the beneficiary groups more efficiently.

Targeting is a way of securing broader satisfaction of the needs of those outside the scope of traditional social programmes. Targeting means identifying the target population (the potential beneficiaries) as accurately as possible and designing the programme or project in the light of that population's characteristics, thereby concentrating the available resources on a limited number of persons in order to increase the per capita impact. This approach seeks to improve on the system which provides a homogeneous supply of services: i.e., a supply which is the same for the whole population and does not take due account of the differences between beneficiaries. In short, it takes account of the heterogeneous nature of poverty.

It is generally agreed that a targeted approach is appropriate in special circumstances, when resources are scarce and needs grow more numerous. Some experts believe, however, that in the long run greater benefits are provided by broad but well-designed policies which are subjected to modifications in the course of the growth process (UNDP, 1990, p. 103).

Arguments have also been put forward, however, in favour of the use of targeting on a permanent basis. The more precise is the identification of the problem (the needs to be satisfied) and the persons affected by it (the target population), the easier it will be to design **differentiated and specific** measures for its solution. Moreover, the scarcity of resources for the execution of social programmes is not something that is restricted to periods of crisis. When a decision is taken to spend more on education or health, this means taking away resources from an alternative use. Resources are always scarce and there are never enough of them to cover all needs.

"The distribution of social services is not neutral with respect to income groups" (UNDP, 1990, p. 182). Indeed, it is asserted that "If substantial benefits accrue to non-deserving groups or do not accrue to deserving groups, the intervention is poorly designed" (UNDP, 1990, p. 102). Both these statements highlight the need for targeting.

Targeted policies avoid dispersal of resources and ensure that they are concentrated on the group that needs them most. It is worth stressing, then, that "targeting increases the impact per unit of resources invested and reduces the final costs" (Schejtman, 1989, pp. 118-119).

Targeting is based on a criterion of inclusion, but also of exclusion. This avoids giving treatment to those who do not need it, thereby sometimes even obviating damage. Thus, for example, in school meal programmes which deliver meals indiscriminately, children who are already sufficiently well fed at home end up suffering from obesity problems (Cohen and Franco, 1992).

The full or partial execution of some activities by private agents may also be considered when appropriate, taking due account of past experience in this field.

Demand-side subsidies give beneficiaries freedom to choose what other better-off sectors of society already enjoy. This is achieved by giving beneficiaries vouchers or paying a subsidy for every child enrolled in public or private schools, as is already done in some countries of the region. If this is accompanied by a system for the evaluation of school results (along the lines of the Chilean system for measuring the quality of education (SIMCE)) and wide dissemination of the results of the evaluation, parents will have the necessary material for making an informed choice of their children's school. It may be assumed that a system of this type will give rise to competition among educational establishments and thus improve the quality of education.

f) Conclusions

Technical proposals are not enough to secure meaningful changes in social policy. Political will (and strength) is also required, and this will undoubtedly call for the support of social movements and political parties which are interested in changing the status quo. The remainder of this century will probably be favourable in terms of the emergence of agreements and coalitions that will help to install a new form of social policy.

This forecast is based on various reasons. On the one hand, the attainment of favourable conditions of governance demands that the population should have a decent standard of living. Social policy thus becomes a fundamental mechanism for the renewed legitimation of the State. On the other hand, social policy is taking on special importance because it is necessary to have suitably qualified and flexible human resources in order to keep up with the rapid incorporation of technical progress in production processes.

Social policy is thus seen to be an instrument which contributes to the proper functioning of the economy and the political dimension.

3. Social integration: action guidelines

From the point of view of opportunities, social integration may be achieved by improving the conditions of employment, income, housing and education of those sectors labouring under the heavy burden of exclusion. These are the best basic defences.

There are also other fields of action worth mentioning, however, aimed specifically at strengthening **social support mechanisms** (based on mutual support, the collaboration of non-governmental organizations and quasi-autonomous government bodies, and public sectoral policies for the social area).

a) **Job training programmes** for poor urban young people with low educational attainments, in the absence of social support facilities for embarking on their working life.

b) **Support programmes for the self-development efforts of indigenous communities**, that is to say, autochthonous communities and peoples which are seeking to define their own improvement goals, as social actors within the national community, which usually include in particular the strengthening of their own culture, the recovery of their language and historical memories, and their own independent management of their material development.

c) **Support programmes for families at risk**, such as those headed by poor women, those with substandard educational resources, or those living in shanty towns.

d) **Programmes for the protection of children, young people and mothers who are exposed to family violence and abandonment.**

e) **Programmes to strengthen community life** in depressed areas by promoting dialogue, mutual cooperation and the collective management of ventures to satisfy the community's basic needs.

f) **Cultural and recreational development programmes** for children and young people in depressed areas with little access to cultural goods.

SOCIAL POLICIES Chapter VII - 193

g) **Programmes to combat the consumption of drugs**, with emphasis on patterns of consumption which undermine general standards of social coexistence and aggravate the vicious circle of reproduction of marginality, and **policies to combat drug trafficking**.

h) **Low-cost housing programmes** in makeshift settlements.

i) Strengthening of citizens' security and access to justice by providing **more police protection in high-risk areas** (areas controlled by gangs, parallel authorities and organized crime), **more effective operation of the penal system** in order to neutralize everyday violence, and **legal aid services** for those who need them.

4. Suggestions and recommendations on sectoral policies

a) Educational policies

i)   Demand for education and community participation

Optimizing the conditions for access to the educational system and graduation from it calls for the revitalization of the demand for education and participation by the community. This will make it possible to improve the relevance of the supply of education (especially that aimed at the less-privileged sectors) and promote greater continuity within the system, obviating premature abandonment of studies and offering better subsequent employment opportunities.

How can we ensure that educational reforms and increased expenditure on education make a real contribution to equity and quality? This does not depend solely on the amount and mix of the inputs in the education process, but also on the use that is made of them. It is not just a simple question of resource allocation; the way schools and families capitalize on such resources to generate dynamics that steadily improve educational performance and the favourable impact on living conditions is also very important. Consequently, equity also depends on how the enhancement potential of the inputs in the education process is distributed.

Traditionally, efforts to improve the efficacy of education have been focused on variables directly linked with educational supply: material inputs, teaching methods, schoolbooks, etc. These efforts are important, but it must not be forgotten that nearly 60% of the performance differential is due to out-of-school factors (World Bank, 1995). Thus, "the educational climate of the home (the number of years of schooling possessed by the adult family members) is the factor that most seriously affects children's educational performance, accounting for between 40% and 50% of the total impact of the socio-economic and family context ... Economic capacity (per capita income levels of households) accounts for between 25% and 30%; the physical infrastructure of a child's dwelling (whether the home is overcrowded or not) comes in third place, and finally comes the level of family organization, the extremes of which are represented by single-parent households headed by a woman and households where both married parents are present" (Gerstenfeld and others, 1995) (see box VII.2).

> **Box VII.2**
>
> **INFLUENCE OF EDUCATIONAL CLIMATE AND INCOME LEVEL OF THE HOME ON EDUCATIONAL PERFORMANCE**
>
> (*Simple average of Latin American countries around 1990*)
>
> | | Quartile 1 | Quartile 2 | Quartile 4 |
> |---|---|---|---|
> | Educational climate of home 0 - 5.99 | a/ 42 | a/ 37 | |
> | | b/ 6.1 | b/ 6.9 | |
> | Educational climate of home 6 - 9.99 | a/ 23 | a/ 17 | a/ 12 |
> | | b/ 7.8 | b/ 8.4 | b/ 9.7 |
> | Educational climate of home 10 or more | | a/ 9 | a/ 7 |
> | | | b/ 10.1 | b/ 10.9 |
>
> **Source:** P. Gerstenfeld, "Comparación regional del impacto de las características del hogar en el logro escolar", in *Variables extrapedagógicas y equidad en la educación media: hogar, subjetividad y cultura escolar*, Pascual Gerstenfeld and others, Políticas sociales series, No. 9 (LC/L.924), Santiago, Chile, ECLAC, December 1995, diagram 2.
>
> **Notes:** a/ = Percentage of children aged 7 to 14 who are behind in their studies.
> b/ = Average number of years of schooling of non-independent young people between 15 and 24 years of age.

Thus, the results in education depend not only on the quality of the educational supply, but also on the demand conditions. The poorest students usually study in an educational climate which is less favourable to the continuity of their studies and their educational attainments, and educational performance is linked to the socio-cultural context prevailing in the schools (see tables VII.1.a and VII.1.b).

Improving the demand conditions involves a change in policy approaches and the criteria for resource utilization. In the past, demand has been considered to be a "black box" in which cultural and territorial factors, socialization and availability of material resources all interact.

In order for the most vulnerable groups to be able to take proper advantage of the supply of education, coordinated measures must be taken concerning children's homes, the local community and the schools themselves. In order to raise the levels of quality and equity, then, it is necessary also to take account of the demand for education (homes and communities), as the unavoidable complement to supply-side educational policies. It will be necessary to mobilize parents' centres, community leaders, social workers, non-governmental

Table VII.1.a
URUGUAY: RESULTS IN MATHEMATICS, BY SOCIO-CULTURAL CONTEXT OF SCHOOLS

	Very favourable socio-cultural context	Upper middle socio-cultural context	Lower middle socio-cultural context	Very unfavourable socio-cultural context	Nationwide total
Students with highly satisfactory performance (20-24 points)	21.0	8.4	3.4	2.0	6.8
Students with satisfactory performance (14-19 points)	45.6	35.3	23.2	15.7	27.8
Students with unsatisfactory performance (7-13 points)	30.6	49.7	60.7	64.4	54.5
Students with highly unsatisfactory performance (0-6 points)	2.8	6.7	12.7	17.9	10.9
Total	**100.0**	**100.0**	**100.0**	**100.0**	**100.0**

Source: "Evaluación nacional de aprendizajes en lengua materna y matemáticas. Sexto año de enseñanza primaria", Montevideo, Unidad de Medición de Resultados Educativos, Administración Nacional de Educación Pública, 1996.

Table VII.1.b
URUGUAY: RESULTS IN MOTHER TONGUE, BY SOCIO-CULTURAL CONTEXT OF SCHOOLS

	Very favourable socio-cultural context	Upper middle socio-cultural context	Lower middle socio-cultural context	Very unfavourable socio-cultural context	Nationwide total
Students with highly satisfactory performance (20-24 points)	41.9	19.5	9.8	5.0	15.8
Students with satisfactory performance (14-19 points)	43.3	48.1	40.9	32.8	41.3
Students with unsatisfactory performance (7-13 points)	14.0	29.7	43.2	52.7	37.7
Students with highly unsatisfactory performance (0-6 points)	0.8	2.8	6.1	9.5	5.2
Total	**100.0**	**100.0**	**100.0**	**100.0**	**100.0**

Source: "Evaluación nacional de aprendizajes en lengua materna y matemáticas. Sexto año de enseñanza primaria", Montevideo, Unidad de Medición de Resultados Educativos, Administración Nacional de Educación Pública, 1996.

organizations with strong community links, officials responsible for the planning and execution of social support programmes and, in general, all the bodies that can help to improve the forms of use (demand) of the available educational supply.

Since the quality of education is usually most deficient in schools catering to the lower-income sectors, this is where the community should act most energetically to help detect shortcomings, participate in efforts to improve management, and ask the appropriate bodies (the municipalities and the Ministry of Education) for the support needed to overcome the most urgent shortcomings. Without an informed and actively mobilized community, policies lose a vital element for promoting their effectiveness. The demand conditions of the poor should be strengthened through supplementary measures to keep the community informed.

Parents and the community can be strategic allies of the educational process, in so far as they are conscious of the value of education in the new-model working world, provided they have the necessary elements for supporting their children's learning process at home. Furthermore, if they obtain power and use it well ("empowerment"), this can help to form a stronger and more visible demand for education and a stimulus for more innovative approaches.

All this means that strategies for promoting greater equity in education go beyond the limits of the formal educational system. The close relationship between the social conditions in poor families, households and neighbourhoods and the educational performance of children and young people who live there should move various community actors to take steps to reverse the vicious circles of poor educational environments, depressed socio-cultural contexts and low educational performance and attainments. The mobilization of various actors in community life would make it possible to build up a support network for children and young people from low-income areas so as to increase the cultural capital available for raising their educational performance.

ii) Continuity of education: a viable and much-needed investment option

The unbroken continuation of education is a vital objective for increasing the benefits of education and improving the general options of the coming generation in terms of finding suitable employment and developing their potential. Unfortunately, the region displays a marked contrast between the high rates of enrolment and the poor record of continuation up to the end of the secondary educational cycle. The rates of repetition of grades and drop-out from school reflect faulty utilization of the resources invested in education and doom the drop-outs to a future of scanty opportunities.

In order to attain the goal of continuity of education, policies which take account of individual national features must be formulated (see table VII.2). Countries that have only reached rudimentary levels of achievement in this respect should concentrate on ensuring coverage and continuity at the basic level, whereas those which have more highly developed educational systems should seek to ensure continuity at the secondary level.

In order to improve the level of continuity, the education provided should be relevant in terms of curricula and of good quality, in order to obviate dropping-out. If the education is relevant to their needs, low-income students and their families will take a different view of the opportunity costs involved in staying in school, while if the education provided is of good quality it will promote greater achievements and generate a higher level of motivation among the students, thus encouraging them to stay in school and improve their performance.

Table VII.2
INDICATORS OF COVERAGE AND ACCESS TO SCHOOL SYSTEM

Subregion and country	Gross enrolment rates (percentage of age group corresponding to each level of school system)							Access to primary education	
	Pre-primary level	Primary level		Secondary level		Higher level		At corresponding age	At some point in time (minimum estimate)
	1991	1980	1991	1980	1993	1980	1991	1991	1991
South America	17.1	103	106	...	...	...	...	75.1	93.8
Argentina	21.6	106	107[c]	56	71[d]	22	43	92.4	98.3
Bolivia	9.8[e]	84	89	37	37[e]	18	23	61.4	95.7
Brazil	18.0	99	105	34	39[d]	12	12[c]	77.3	94.7
Chile	18.0	109	100	90	88	13	26[c]	37.6	100.0
Colombia	9.3[g]	113	111	41	62	10	14[f]	59.4	90.1
Ecuador	6.3[g]	117	113	53	55[e]	37	20[e]	81.5	100.0
Paraguay	4.7	104	107	26	37	8	10[c]	100.0	100.0
Peru	24.2	114	115	59	65	19	39	66.2	95.0
Uruguay	21.6	107	107	62	81	18	32	62.2	97.6
Venezuela	20.8	93	97	21	34[d]	21	30[e]	81.2	96.9
Central America and Panama	7.2	85	91	...	...	...	...	68.2	83.1
Costa Rica	12.2	105	103	48	47	23	28	47.6	100.0
El Salvador	8.9	75	80	24	29	4	16	67.5	80.9
Guatemala	5.0	71	78	18	24	8	9[h]	51.9	72.0
Honduras	5.9	98	108	30	32	8	9	100.0	100.0
Nicaragua	8.3	98	101	42	41	14	10	72.7	84.2
Panama	9.3	106	105	61	63[e]	22	24	76.3	97.9
Gulf of Mexico	19.6	118	108	...	...	...	...	93.5	97.1
Cuba	26.1	106	101	81	77	20	19	100.0	100.0
Haiti	3.1[h]	76	59	14	22[e]	1	1	1.3	44.1
Mexico	21.2	122	114	48	58	16	14	100.0	100.0
Dominican Republic	10.6[e]	118	90	42	37	...	19	57.1	63.9
English-speaking Caribbean	31.0	105	104	...	...	...	...	82.3	96.4
Antigua and Barbuda	...	...	...	...	...	...	...	...	...
Netherlands Antilles	...	...	...	...	...	...	...	...	...
Aruba	29.9	...	104	...	...	...	...	90.5	96.3
Bahamas	3.8[k]	98	105[k]	87	93[k]	19	...	84.4	87.7
Barbados	25.0	100	106	90	87[j]	16	18	87.3	100.0
Belize	15.0	...	109	...	...	...	...	79.9	100.0
Dominica	29.8	...	108	...	...	...	...	94.6	100.0
Grenada	35.5[e]	...	124	...	...	...	...	87.5	100.0
Guyana	17.5	101	99	57	57[g]	3	5[g]	73.0	100.0
British Virgin Islands	36.8	...	129	...	...	...	...	26.8	98.5
Jamaica	41.6[e]	103	99	67	62[e]	7	9	74.3	94.4
Montserrat	63.5	...	...	...	...	...	...	...	...
Saint Kitts and Nevis	35.1	...	87	...	...	...	...	78.8	98.6
St. Vincent and the Grenadines	14.7	...	132	...	...	...	...	85.4	97.9
Saint Lucia	12.2	...	128	...	...	...	...	81.3	100.0
Suriname	32.7	125	136	35	54[g]	7	9[e]	99.6	100.0
Trinidad and Tobago	4.7	99	100	70	79[d]	2	6	100.0	100.0
Latin America and the Caribbean	17.0	104	105.6[k]	45	53[k]	14	18[k]	79.2	93.4
Developed countries	...	101	101[k]	62	93[k]	30	42[k]	...	...
Developing countries	...	95	98	36	44	5	8	...	...
Lower-middle-income countries	...	...	...	...	...	...	...	...	...
Low-income countries	...	...	...	...	...	...	...	...	...

Source: Ernesto Schiefelbein (coord.), *Situación educativa de América Latina y el Caribe, 1980-1994*, Santiago, Chile, UNESCO Regional Education Office for Latin America and the Caribbean, 1996.
[a] Enrolment of population aged 0-5 years in pre-school education.
[b] Enrolment of population aged 20-24 years in higher education.
[c] 1993 data. d 1991 data.
[e] 1990 data.
[f] 1989 data.
[g] 1988 data.
[h] 1986 data.
[i] 1985 data.
[j] The 1991 rate is not comparable with that for 1980 because they refer to different age groups.
[k] 1992 data.

Complementary policies are required to support the educational continuity of poor children and young people, who display the highest drop-out and repetition rates. "Ensuring that children from poor families go to school and stay in it requires not only that they should be provided with good-quality education but also that there should be longer school hours in order to make up for the limitations on their learning capacity due to their family environment; nutritional programmes, and even a subsidy to cover the opportunity cost of forgoing possible job opportunities" (Franco and others, 1995).

Increasing the continuity of education is economically viable. In other words, the cost involved in increasing the proportion of the population who complete their secondary education is perfectly manageable for Governments, since it would mean increasing annual expenditure on secondary education by between half a percentage point of GDP and one point. Countries with lower rates of secondary school attendance would need more resources in order to achieve a major change in the same length of time, but even so this would be a perfectly attainable target.[54] The main effort should be concentrated on bringing back into secondary education the high percentage of drop-outs who are neither studying nor working and whose re-entry into the educational system would therefore involve a very low opportunity cost (see box VII.3).

Box VII.3

**CHILDREN AND YOUNG PEOPLE WHO NEITHER STUDY NOR WORK:
THE LOW OPPORTUNITY COST OF ACHIEVING CONTINUITY OF EDUCATION**

In the early 1990s, some 13% of children and young people between 13 and 17 (ages when they ought to be attending secondary school) in urban areas and nearly 23% in rural areas were neither studying nor working. For children and young people living in the lowest-income households (quartile 1), these percentages rise to some 20% and 30% in the respective geographical areas.

If this population group can be incorporated and retained in the secondary level, the proposed goals could probably be attained. Since this target population is practically idle —i.e., it does not have any social or personal opportunity costs— this makes it even more viable to reach the desired rate. In other words, the advantages of incorporating this group into regular secondary education are abundantly clear.

Nevertheless, the characteristics of this population group raise serious challenges for social and educational policy. By action or omission, the present policies have not been able to prevent or correct the existence of high proportions of children and young people who are not studying, yet who do not have any opportunity cost that justifies their abandonment of the school system, since they do not work.

Source: ECLAC, The strategic role of secondary education in achieving well-being and social equity (LC/G.1919), Santiago, Chile, 1996.

---

[54] See ECLAC (1996b), which gives a calculation of the cost/time ratio for increasing educational continuity in various countries of the region, grouped according to their rates of school attendance.

Improving continuity in the secondary educational cycle not only ensures better learning and symbolic integration for its beneficiaries but also has two additional benefits which make it more appropriate than any alternative investment.

Firstly, there are the benefits of making timely investments in secondary education, as compared with the cost of equivalent compensatory programmes (see table VII.3). These indicate that timely investment in education —that is to say, investment in the provision of education for young people while they are still of school age— is economically more appropriate and also produces greater positive externalities. With regard to the latter, it may be noted that such investment improves the cultural and social development of young people; complements activities in other fields such as health and sex education, etc.; helps to improve the educational climate of the students' homes and their capacity for socialization; and also provides more suitable intellectual preparation for those who hope to continue on to higher levels of education.[55]

Secondly, there are the significant inter-generational benefits offered by completion of secondary education, because of the strong influence of the educational level of the parents on the educational performance of their children. Improving in this way the educational climate of the homes which will be headed by those benefitting from this investment will have a favourable effect on the educational performance of children and young people of the next generation, will reduce drop-out and repetition rates, and will increase the number and relevance of the years of schooling completed. This fact is all the more significant because the available information reveals that the educational capital of children is more important than the economic status of their homes in determining their educational performance, even in the low-income strata.

b) Health policies

There is an urgent need to establish efficient and equitable health systems, which means that increases in health spending must be reflected in increases in the coverage and quality of the services provided, improvement of health conditions, and reduction of the current gaps and inequalities.

The results of the efforts made in the region provide a basis for some recommendations that should be taken into account in health sector reform processes (Sojo, 1996b; ECLAC/PAHO, 1994; Mesa-Lago, 1992).

i) Attempts to solve health problems must face up to the challenge of the multiple causes behind their conditioning factors. They should not, therefore, concentrate solely on sickness itself, but also on its prevention, health promotion, control measures, and the reduction and elimination of risks and harmful effects, at both the individual and the community level.

---

[55] Of course, this does not mean ruling out compensatory programmes, which are designed to serve populations with different ages and needs, because the training requirements of those who are already in the labour force are naturally not fulfilled through the improvement of formal education. The figures do suggest, however, that it is advisable to promote policies that stimulate and improve investment in education at the appropriate ages, because this will reduce the need for subsequent corrective measures which are more difficult and less effective.

Table VII.3

PRESENT COST OF COMPENSATORY PROGRAMMES FOR ADULTS (EQUIVALENT TO SECONDARY EDUCATION), COMPARED WITH THE COST OF FOUR YEARS OF CONVENTIONAL SECONDARY EDUCATION

(In US dollars)

	Compensatory programme (20 months) (A)	Four years of secondary education (B)	Country A ÷ B
Argentina	2 300	1 100	2.1
Brazil	1 200	790	1.5
Chile	1 700	770	2.2
Colombia	1 400	400	3.5
Ecuador	1 400	320	4.4
Guatemala	650	190	3.4
Honduras	900	320	2.8
Jamaica	1 100	750	1.5
Dominican Republic	1 000	190	5.3

Source: Guillermo Labarca, "Inversión en infancia: evidencias y argumentos para políticas efectivas" (LC/L.956), Santiago, Chile, Economic Commission for Latin America and the Caribbean (ECLAC), 1996.

Note: The present cost of the education has been estimated using a discount rate of 10% per year over the 1990 expenditure. The present cost of compensatory programmes has been estimated on the basis of 1994 minimum wages, using a discount rate of 0.8% per month.

ii) An intersectoral approach should be taken to health promotion which takes into account the variety of non-medical influences ranging from inherited genetic factors, through individual behaviour and social and family circumstances, to the conditions prevailing in the social and physical environment. Intersectoral coordination helps to improve decision-making processes because it makes it possible to adapt them to the complexity of the task at hand and to incorporate health problems in broader integrated schemes.

iii) It is necessary to promote the health activities that are most cost-effective, both in the area of infectious and contagious diseases and in that of chronic and degenerative ailments. Among the most fundamental intersectoral core elements are those connected with education, the mass media and the environment. Environmental health problems include those concerning the home, the workplace, and urban and rural spaces. Increasingly close links should be maintained between attention to women's health problems, general health education and population activities.

iv) In seeking more resources for health, due account must be taken of the need to increase equity and the positive impact that a healthier population will have in economies which form part of a globalized world. Furthermore, those countries whose health systems are less developed and lagging further behind in terms of reform will gain more opportunities if they take advantage of the experience built up inside and outside the region to increase the equity, efficiency and efficacy of their health systems and give due consideration to intersectoral policies.

v) Because of the structural features of health markets and the widespread poverty existing in the region, the State must continue to play an important role in the provision, financing and regulation of health services.

vi) The institutional framework must be suitably adapted to promote increased efficiency of health services, wider coverage, better quality and effectiveness of the services provided, clearer focusing of subsidies, and greater capacity for regulation and supervision.

vii) As regards the payment of suppliers of health services, new mechanisms must be incorporated based on prospective systems —such as payment on a capitation basis or by diagnostic-related groups and the use of the global budget of hospitals and health centres— so that payment is made before the service is actually provided.

viii) Clearer distinctions must be made between the functions of the various bodies making up the public health system: regulatory functions and those connected with the general institutional framework; functions relating to finance and the purchase of services; and functions involving the provision or production of services. In this way it will be possible to avoid overlapping of functions, to promote the establishment of an integrated and harmonious set of institutions, and to achieve a highly beneficial counterplay of interests which will ensure maximum efficiency.

ix) Differentiation of functions involves the challenge of coordinating the various components to facilitate their proper interaction and performance. For this purpose, it would be appropriate to establish "management agreements" stipulating the type of services to be provided, the level of resource allocation and transfer, and performance indicators for evaluating the fulfilment of the agreed goals. These contractual instruments make results and performance the basis for determining financing and allow the differences between the planned services and those actually carried out to be evaluated by means of predetermined indicators. In order to guarantee their viability and effectiveness it is essential that there should be prior agreement both with respect to the indicators and their interpretation and the missions and identities of the various bodies, their activities and the corresponding financial needs.

x) In order to increase the efficacy and quality of health policies it is not enough merely to evaluate the indicators of microeconomic performance, relating to inputs and products: the quality and impact of the service provided must be evaluated too.

xi) The best possible use must be made of human resources, and the staff must have a commitment to their work, which means that they must be given individual responsibilities. A measure which could help in this respect would be the adoption of new systems of remuneration, with flexible components and incentives that link wages to performance and the quality of the service provided: i.e., to productivity and results. The substantive elements in staff members' employment records should not only be seniority, but also the merit shown in their work, the quality of their performance, the nature of the tasks they perform, and their training record and experience. Hiring should also be made more flexible in order to facilitate the fulfilment of health services' and establishments' programmes of work.

This involves changing the criteria for entry into and continued employment in the health system, promoting recruitment for permanent staff positions by competition, and evaluating the staff's employment records for determining promotions and wage rises. The savings generated by increased efficiency and productivity can help to improve wage levels on the basis of the new criteria. Care should be taken to ensure that all geographical areas have a balanced supply of the necessary human resources, in order to promote equity.

xii) Management support facilities are required, such as cost centres which can increase the efficiency of resource use and promote savings, and information systems to provide the necessary timely information needed for good management.

xiii) The services provided by the various public sector bodies and the social security system must be reorganized. In most cases, this means making drastic reforms with regard to the current institutions, the level and quality of their services, and the cost of the benefits provided. In order to improve the latter, it is essential to make more efficient use of the infrastructure and to promote integration, or at least coordination, among the various suppliers of public services and between them and the private sector.

xiv) Financial reforms must seek to balance the allocation of resources among the various components and levels of care in the system, to promote equity in financing, and to strengthen the financial base of the social security system.

xv) The efficiency of the health sector can be improved by bringing in the private subsector, subject to certain regulatory conditions.

xvi) In order to keep costs under control, it is necessary to seek greater integration between health service providers and the insurance companies.

xvii) In order to avoid exclusion, especially of groups suffering from catastrophic illnesses and ailments typical of the elderly, altruistic components must be included in risk insurance.

xviii) Competition must be reconciled with solidarity: in other words, resources from contributions based on the principle of solidarity must be reconciled with income adjusted according to risk.

c) Housing policies

The statistics revealing the spread of poverty, now rooted mainly in the region's cities, make it urgent for human settlement policies to be geared decisively to improving the quality of life, particularly for lower-income households. In addition to the positive impact that increasing the productivity of cities can have on overcoming poverty in the future, urban development and housing plans and actions should help to ensure tangible benefits within shorter time-frames, especially for those who need them most. This was the conclusion reached by the Ministers of Housing and Urban Development of Latin America and the Caribbean in the regional preparatory process for the United Nations Conference on Human Settlements (Habitat II), held in Istanbul, Turkey, in June 1996.

Thus, at the Latin American and Caribbean Regional Meeting Preparatory to Habitat II (Santiago, Chile, November 1995), the Ministers adopted the Latin American and Caribbean Regional Plan of Action on Human Settlements (ECLAC, 1996c), which contains principles and proposals for overcoming the serious problems affecting the region as regards human settlements in general and housing in particular. This Plan reflects the proposals made by the ECLAC secretariat (ECLAC, 1996e), which may be summarized as follows insofar as they refer to the problem of housing:

Governments should:

i) Emphasize the goal of overcoming poverty and indigence in their territorial, urban and housing policies and link it to broader strategies and mechanisms for social development at the national and local levels. The Governments assume particular responsibility for prioritizing national urban, housing and environmental policy in order to increase social equity. All sectors will be included in the urban and housing management process, to ensure their access to education, preventive health care, safe drinking water, waste water disposal, green spaces, recreation, trade, transport, environmental protection and sources of employment.

ii) Increase housing solutions substantially in order to cope with the lack of shelter, especially for lower-income families. The number of units should at least equal the number of new households formed each year so as to prevent a continuing increase in the housing shortage.

iii) Expand programmes to provide sanitation, shelter, regularization of tenure and access to public infrastructure for marginal groups and settlements within cities. At the local level, these efforts will be coordinated with other social and employment programmes, so as to break the poverty cycles persisting in these settlements and prevent an increase in the spatial concentration of poverty that dominates the region's cities.

iv) Establish programmes to maintain and upgrade existing housing so as to prevent the shortage from increasing as a result of its functional and material obsolescence. Special attention will be paid to the management of existing urban housing in areas undergoing densification and renewal.

v) Implement clear mechanisms for transparent and effective subsidies that can provide the region's inhabitants with genuine access to urban goods and services and housing. Better targeting should reverse the declining trend in the region's public housing expenditure.

vi) Develop mechanisms aimed at improving the living conditions of the population by providing access to credit and allowing citizens to select the alternatives that best meet their needs: purchasing dwellings or lots, building, or improving or enlarging dwellings.

vii) Expand the resources available for financing housing and urban services by means of a combination of investments by the public and private sectors and the communities themselves. To achieve this goal, the countries will promote the use of efficient systems for financing both supply of and demand for urban and housing goods and services and encourage savings and co-financing arrangements to the extent that economic growth and improved employment levels make it feasible.

viii) Enable citizens' associations to play an active and effective social role in the drafting and monitoring of programmes and activities which aim to improve the quality of life of the population and, in particular, in providing support for self-help housing construction and the development of more structured, innovative and efficient systems of self-management, co-management and co-financing of housing, facilities and services.

ix) Encourage public investment, promote private investment and support social investment aimed at improving rural settlements and dwellings to ensure that the inhabitants of those areas have access to basic services, housing and employment similar in quality to those available to the urban population. It is thus essential to establish mechanisms to regulate private investment (particularly with respect to coverage of services and to charges), in order to ensure competitive and transparent incorporation of the private sector.

x) Integrate policies on housing, public infrastructure, basic services and preservation and restoration of the cultural, historical and architectural heritage into territorial and urban development and planning strategies, so as to stimulate new productive activities, enhance the accumulation of human capital and the strengthening of civic identity, and provide effective support for the development of regions and localities in a spirit of economy, by taking advantage of the cities that already exist.

xi) Set up coordinating mechanisms between the sectoral agencies and levels of government that deal with housing and urban development and the local governments, so that the responsibilities and, where applicable, the resources of the former in the field of human settlements can be effectively and gradually decentralized and transferred to the latter.

xii) Give special attention to easy access to jobs and urban services when deciding on the location of public housing, so as to integrate poor households into the life of the city and promote a reduction in the spatial segregation of poverty.

xiii) Incorporate the private sector into many activities traditionally carried out by the public sector in the field of housing and urban development and establish a clear and stable regulatory framework for the creation of markets and the regulation of competition in the field of the production and operation of urban services and housing, in order to make it possible to establish an effective partnership between the public and private sectors in this field.

d) Social insurance

i) Equity and dynamic efficiency: fiscal implications, saving and the spread of reforms in this field

Financing the altruistic components which are designed to supplement benefits for the retired population and provide benefits for those who did not make contributions can be a heavy social insurance burden for those of working age, especially in the transition from one social insurance system to another. Since such transfers finance pensions which are usually spent on consumption, it is argued that they have a negative effect on net saving between the two generations (those who are working and those who are retired).

It is held that private saving is higher when pensions are financed through a private insurance scheme rather than a social insurance system, especially if the latter is organized on a pay-as-you-go or unfunded basis: thus, insofar as the design of a pension system contributes to saving, investment and growth it can increase dynamic efficiency and promote the generation of employment and the demand for capital, which would help to increase the return on social security contributions.

This assessment has been questioned (Barr, 1993) on three grounds: first, that saving could be greater only during the period when the fund was being built up: subsequently, workers would save the same amount as the pensioners spent;[56] second, even when a fund is being built up, the compulsory saving may take the place of the voluntary saving that would have been generated in any case: an issue over which there is great controversy,[57] and third, there is no guarantee that the accumulation of a fund in the form of financial saving will be reflected in productive investment and, ultimately, in an increase in saving as measured in the national accounts (Held, 1994).

In the final analysis, the linkage between setting aside income for old age pensions and the accumulation of capital has at least two facets as regards the transition from one pension financing scheme to another (Diamond, 1995): one is the proportion of wealth that must be transferred to the generations already receiving pensions when the system is initiated, and the other is the way private saving and the government budget react to the specific design of the system.

The only case available for analysis is that of Chile, which has 15 years' experience of operating an individual capitalization system in the place of a pay-as-you-go system. Three lessons may be drawn from this experience:

a. The saving (and return on capital) of the mandatory capitalization pillar must be analysed in conjunction with the saving (and return on capital) of the redistributive component of the basic pillar. Both of these need to be considered together and compared with the effect on saving (and return on capital) of a single redistributive system. This phenomenon is particularly significant when there are pensions that have to be financed from the beginning of the new system: the burden of such financing has to be borne by the current contributors and must be taken into account in the calculations of saving (and return on capital).[58] In the Chilean case, it is considered that public saving must have been used to finance the costs of the transition.

b. The net effect of the change in system on family saving must be assessed. There is no sense in considering the transfer of contributions to savings accounts as a net contribution to workers' saving, without analysing the changes that have taken place in the saving of families, enterprises and the government itself as a result of such measures. In actual fact, a negative net effect on family saving has been observed in Chile (Arrau, 1996).

---

[56] Indeed, the Chilean case shows that, when passing from a mature pay-as-you-go system to an incipient capitalization system, the fiscal deficit due to the payment of pensions to retired persons and the payment of credit certificates for the past contributions of workers transferring to the new system is greater than the saving of the workers making contributions under the new arrangements (ECLAC, 1995b and Annex 2).

[57] Among the abundant literature published on this matter over the last 20 years, special mention may be made of Feldstein (1974 and 1979); Aarón (1982); Barro (1974 and 1978); Auerbach and Kotlikoff (1987 and 1990), and Leimer and Lesnoy (1982).

[58] Passing from defined benefits to defined contributions, there are two alternatives for financing the benefit commitments inherited from the system in force before the reform, and both have significant consequences for the transitional economic policy because they determine who must pay its cost. The first alternative is ordinary taxes, which means that the burden of payment of transfers to previous generations must be borne by the generations which are economically active during the transition, who are not necessarily the most suitable candidates for bearing this tax burden. The second alternative is to finance the transaction through indebtedness, thus converting implicit debt into explicit commitments. Such a conversion will be reflected in an increase in total indebtedness and may have indirect consequences, since it may affect those paying for the transfers which have been made, other taxes and government expenditure, or simply the prevailing perception in the bonds market (Diamond, 1995).

c. In so far as the reform promotes the acquisition of financial instruments with the funds built up, the contribution to increased saving will depend on the capacity of the capital market to channel the financial saving into real investment. In emerging markets, portfolios are usually made up mainly of State securities, secondary-market shares and bank deposits, which do not necessarily represent real investment. Only a small part is channelled into real investment through the purchase of freshly-issued shares, mortgage bills or company bonds.

In Chile, nearly 75% of the accumulated funds are concentrated in the first set of instruments: 40.4% in Central Bank securities (issued as a result of the monetary sterilization policy), 29% in secondary-market shares (which ensure capital gains but not the creation of new enterprises), and 5.1% in time deposits. Only 16.6% goes to housing construction, through the purchase of mortgage notes, and 4.8% to company bonds.[59] As may readily be seen, there is no direct link with real investment.

Figure VII.1 shows the effect on saving. The increase in saving in Chile is not due exclusively to the implementation of the new pension system but to the public saving effort, in order to cover the costs of the transition, and the increase in non-pension-related private saving as a result of fiscal incentives for companies to reinvest their profits (Arrau, 1996). In the absence of such efforts, the Chilean case would not register any increase in saving parallel to the implementation of the pension reform.

While the altruistic component has immediate distributive effects, increasing dynamic efficiency through the generation of saving and investment is not due solely to a given design of the system but depends on three factors:

a. *The economic rationality of the workers*. If the workers do not save voluntarily, neither the taxes paid nor the promise of future benefits could alter the level of saving: consumption would simply be transferred from the younger generations to the older ones. In contrast, if the workers are rational and voluntarily save for their old age, there will be a reduction in current saving in expectation of greater benefits, independently of any gain or loss of wealth throughout their lives. As both types of workers exist at the same time in the real world, the response of saving to the design of the pension system is difficult to predict.

b. *The way the State adjusts its budget to fit in with a given pension system design*. If the resources of the pension system help to finance and hence increase government consumption, it will not contribute to capital accumulation. If the transition makes it necessary to place the indebtedness of the pension system on an explicit basis and finance it, however, this may lead to changes in government saving and —depending on the form of financing— in private saving too.

c. *The degree of development of the capital market*. The portfolio's mix between public debt paper and private instruments will vary according to the size of the capital market. In big, fluid markets, the differences between the aggregates are due to small changes in the corresponding rates of return. A drop in the private rate and a rise in the public one will affect government investment and expenditure, but the aggregate long-term effect of an open-market operation which changes the portfolio's mix between public and private debt paper will not be very great. In small, segmented capital markets, in contrast, investments do not

---

[59] 5.1% is invested in bonds issued by financial establishments (1.24%), foreign securities (0.28%), shares in investment funds (2.65%) and bank shares (0.97%).

have much mobility, and this makes it more difficult to estimate the rate of return on workers' funds implicit in a retirement pension scheme.

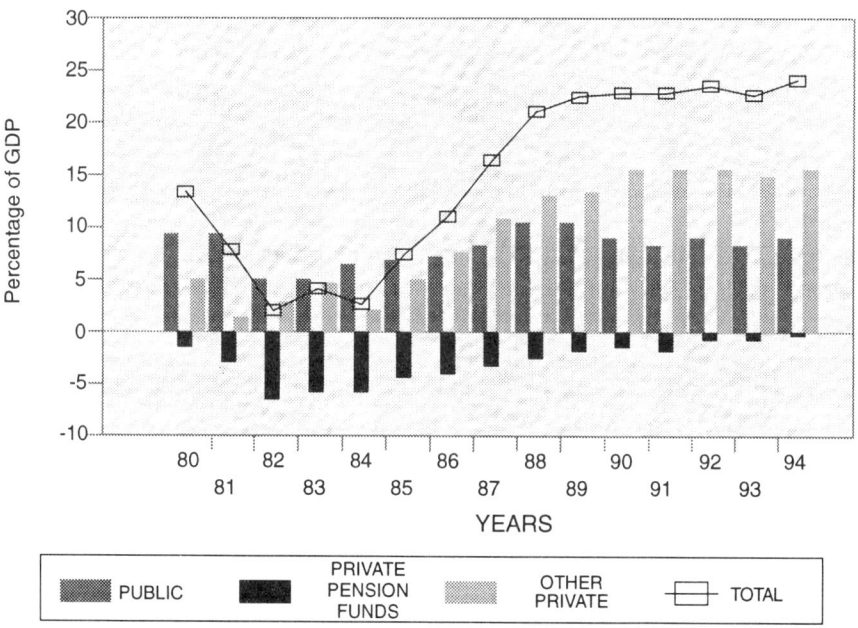

Figure VII.1
CHILE: COMPONENTS OF SAVING AS A PERCENTAGE OF GDP

SOURCE: P. Arrau, "Nota sobre el aumento del ahorro en Chile: 1980-1994", Financiamiento del desarrollo series, No. 39 (LC/L. 984), Santiago, Chile, ECLAC, 1996.

ii) Solidarity and dynamic efficiency: financing of fiscal costs, financial intermediation and coverage

The links between pension system design and equity are not easy to determine. In order to clarify them, we must look into the interrelations between the aim of establishing altruistic mechanisms and that of contributing to dynamic efficiency. The first of these aims involves a mechanism for targetting transfers and a progressive tax system; the second offers a source of finance for increasing the stock of physical capital, raising the per capita GDP and real wages and lowering interest rates.

In order to justify changing a pension system on the grounds of equity, two conditions must be fulfilled: first, the under-privileged sectors (the poor) must benefit from the change in the long run because the stock of capital will increase, thereby also increasing incomes, per capita GDP and real wages and bringing down real interest rates (dynamic efficiency), and second, these gains must be greater in sum than the loss of the net redistributive benefits of the former system (loss of solidarity).

Pension system reforms in Latin America, involving a change from pay-as-you-go systems to others with some element of personal pension accounting, will influence these results in three ways: i) the magnitude of the fiscal cost of the reform, and the way it is financed; ii) the use made of the pension funds through their financial intermediation, and iii) the prospects of broadening coverage to protect an increasingly large proportion of the population.

The amount and method of financing of the fiscal cost of the reform have important intergenerational redistributive implications. If it is sought to reduce the fiscal cost by reducing the benefits provided to pensioners, then they will be the losers in the transition. If a given proportion of the fiscal cost is financed with public saving, then this will adversely affect those who will no longer receive benefits due to public expenditure cuts, or those who will have to pay higher direct or indirect taxes. Finally, if the cost is financed with greater public indebtedness, then future generations will be affected because of the corresponding losses of capital.

With regard to this last point, it should be noted that the mere fact of accumulating resources in a fund does not guarantee an increase in the stock of physical capital, since the pension fund saving may take the place of other forms of family saving. The pension fund saving must be compared with the public sector outlays needed to carry out the distributive tasks required in order to ensure that there is a net positive effect on national saving. Moreover, pension fund saving is financial saving, and whether it is channelled into real investment or not depends on the pension fund management.

Finally, pension system reforms do not guarantee any contribution to equity in terms of expansion of the coverage of the population, which is very low in most of the systems operating in the region. The reasons for this lie in the very special structure of the labour markets of the region, which are marked mainly by informal-sector work and own-account activities (ECLAC, 1995b). The difficulty of monitoring the participation in pension schemes of those working in these segments of the labour market or of creating participation incentives for those with saving capacity has limited the expansion of coverage. The redistributive implications are considerable, because when they reach retirement age such workers can demand non-contributory benefits from the State, thus increasing the direct or indirect tax burden needed to finance pensions.

In the final analysis, the success of the system depends on guaranteeing paid employment to workers throughout their active life, and this depends on factors unrelated to pension system reforms, as well as to whether or not the dynamic efficiency obtained leads to the effective generation of productive employment.

BIBLIOGRAPHY

Aaron, H. J. (1982), *Economic Effects of Social Security*, Washington, D.C., The Brookings Institution.

"Acceso equitativo a los servicios básicos de salud: hacia una agenda regional para la reforma del sector salud" (1995), document presented at the Special Meeting on Health Sector Reform, organized by IDB, IBRD, ECLAC, OAS, PAHO/WHO, UNFPA, UNICEF and USAID, Washington, D.C., September.

Agosin, M. and others (1996), "Explicaciones del aumento del ahorro en Chile", Santiago, Chile, Red de Centros de Investigación Económica, Inter-American Development Bank (IDB), Department of Economics of the University of Chile, August, preliminary version.

Alburquerque, F. (1997), Desarrollo económico local y difusión del progreso técnico: una respuesta a las exigencias del ajuste estructural (LC/IP/R.174), Santiago, Chile, Latin American and Caribbean Institute for Economic and Social Planning (ILPES).

Arce, H.E. (1996), "Tendencias, escenarios y fenómenos emergentes en la configuración del sector salud en la Argentina", document presented at the Seminar "Reformas a la seguridad social en salud en Argentina, Chile y Colombia" by the ECLAC/GTZ project "Reformas del financiamiento de los sistemas de salud en América Latina y el Caribe", Santiago, Chile, November.

Argentina, Ministry of Health and Social Welfare (1995), "Informe de la República Argentina sobre la reforma del sector salud", document presented at the Special Meeting on Health Sector Reform, organized by IDB, IBRD, ECLAC, OAS, PAHO/WHO, UNFPA, UNICEF and USAID, Washington, D.C., September.

Arrau, P. (1996), "Nota sobre el aumento del ahorro en Chile: 1980-1994", Financiamiento del desarrollo series, No. 39 (LC/L.984), Santiago, Chile, ECLAC.

—— (1994), "Fondos de pensiones y desarrollo del mercado de capitales en Chile: 1980-1993", Financiamiento del desarrollo series, No. 19 (LC/L.839), Santiago, Chile, ECLAC.

Arrow, K. (1963), "Uncertainty and the welfare economics of the medical care", *The American Economic Review*, vol. 53, No. 5, December.

Ashby, J. and L. Sperling (1992), "Institutionalizing participatory, client-driven research and development", document presented at the Reunión de Cientistas Sociales of the Consultative Group on International Agricultural Research (CGIAR), The Hague, 17-20 August, unpublished.

Auerbach, A.J. and L.J. Kotlikoff (1990), "Demographic, fiscal policy and US saving in the 1980s and beyond", *Tax Policy and the Economy*, Lawrence H. Summers (ed.), vol. 4, Cambridge, Massachusetts, MIT Press.

────── (1987), *Dynamic Fiscal Policy*, Cambridge, Cambridge University Press.

Ayala, U. (1992), "Un sistema pensional de capitalización individual para Colombia", *Sistemas de pensiones en América Latina: diagnóstico y alternativas de reforma. Volumen 2: Bolivia, Brasil, Colombia, Guatemala, México*, A. Uthoff and R.Szalachmann (eds.), Santiago, Chile, S.R.V. Impresos.

Bajraj, R.F. and J. Chackiel (1996), "La población en América Latina y el Caribe: tendencias y percepciones", *Población y desarrollo: tendencias y nuevos desafíos*, Pensamiento Iberoamericano, No. 28 and Notas de Población, No. 62, Madrid, June.

Bamberger, M. and others (1993), "La focalización de programas de salud y nutrición para madres y niños de bajos ingresos en América Latina: principales cuestiones", presented at the PAHO/Economic Development Institute of the World Bank Seminar on "Focalización de programas de salud y nutrición para madres y niños de bajos ingresos en América Latina", Quito, June, unpublished.

Banuri, T. and others (1996), *Desarrollo humano sostenible: de la teoría a la práctica*, New York, United Nations Development Programme (UNDP).

Barbados, Ministry of Health and the Environment (1995), "Health sector reform, Barbados perspective", document presented at the Special Meeting on Health Sector Reform, organized by IDB, IBRD, ECLAC, OAS, PAHO/WHO, UNFPA, UNICEF and USAID, Washington, D.C., September.

Barr, N. (1993), *The Economics of the Welfare State*, second edition, Stanford, Stanford University Press.

Barro, R.J. (1978), *The Impact of Social Security on Private Saving: Evidence from the US Time Series*, Washington, D.C., The American Enterprise Institute.

────── (1974), "Are government bonds net wealth?", *Journal of Political Economy*, vol. 84.

Becattini, G. and Rullani, E. (1996), "Sistemas productivos locales y mercado global", *Información comercial española*, No. 754, Madrid, June.

Belize, Ministry of Health and Sports (1995), "Report on the reform of the health sector in Belize", document presented to the Special Meeting on Health Sector Reform, organized by IDB, IBRD, ECLAC, OAS, PAHO/WHO, UNFPA, UNICEF and USAID, Washington, D.C., September.

Bobadilla, J.L., Julio Frenk and Rafael Lozano (1990), "The Epidemiologic Transition and Health Priorities", Washington, D.C., World Bank/Health Sector Priorities Review, July, unpublished.

Bolivia, Ministry of Human Development (1995), "Bases para el proceso de reforma del sector salud en Bolivia", document presented to the Special Meeting on Health Sector

Reform, organized by IDB, IBRD, ECLAC, OAS, PAHO/WHO, UNFPA, UNICEF and USAID, Washington, D.C., September.

Brazil, Health Ministry (1995), "Informe sobre a reforma do setor Saúde no Brasil", document presented to the Special Meeting on Health Sector Reform, organized by IDB, IBRD, ECLAC, OAS, PAHO/WHO, UNFPA, UNICEF and USAID, Washington, D.C., September.

Canada, Health Canada (1995), "Canadian report to the Special Meeting on Health Sector Reform", document presented to the Special Meeting on Health Sector Reform, organized by IDB, IBRD, ECLAC, OAS, PAHO/WHO, UNFPA, UNICEF and USAID, Washington, D.C., September.

Carrión, Fernando (1995), "Violencia urbana y juventud", document presented at the Seminar "Los desafíos de la juventud urbana en América Latina", Caracas, Latin American Economic System /Inter-American Development Bank (SELA/IDB), 12-13 June.

Chile, Ministry of Public Health (1995), "Reforma del sector salud, reunión especial sobre reforma sectorial OMS/OPS", document presented at the Special Meeting on Health Sector Reform, organized by IDB, IBRD, ECLAC, OAS, PAHO/WHO, UNFPA, UNICEF and USAID, Washington, D.C., September.

──── , Superintendencia de Administradoras de Fondos de Pensiones (1994), "El sistema chileno de pensiones", Santiago, Chile.

Cohen, E. and R. Franco (1992), *Evaluación de proyectos sociales*, Mexico City, Siglo Veintiuno.

Colombia, Ministerio de Salud (1995), "El sector salud en Colombia, pasado, presente y futuro", document presented at the Special Meeting on Health Sector Reform, organized by IDB, IBRD, ECLAC, OAS, PAHO/WHO, UNFPA, UNICEF and USAID, Washington, D.C., September.

Commonwealth of Dominica (1995), "Report on Health Sector Reform", document presented at the Special Meeting on Health Sector Reform, organized by IDB, IBRD, ECLAC, OAS, PAHO/WHO, UNFPA, UNICEF and USAID, Washington, D.C., September.

Corbo, V. and K. Schmidt-Hebbel (1991), "Public policies and saving in developing countries", *Journal of Development Economics*, vol. 36, No. 1, July.

Costa Rica, Ministry of Planning and Economic Policy (1996), *Panorama social 1995. Balance anual social, económico y ambiental*, San José, August.

──── , Health Ministry (1995), "Informe sobre la reforma del sector salud", document presented at the Special Meeting on Health Sector Reform, organized by IDB, IBRD, ECLAC, OAS, PAHO/WHO, UNFPA, UNICEF and USAID, Washington, D.C., September.

Diamond, P. (1995), "Economic support in old age", *Proceedings of the World Bank Annual Conference on Development Economics*, Washington, D.C., May.

Dirven, Martine (1996), Agroindustry and small-scale agriculture: A comparative synthesis of different experiences (LC/R.1663), Santiago, Chile, ECLAC.

ECLAC (Economic Commission for Latin America and the Caribbean) (1997), *Social Panorama of Latin America. 1996 Edition* (LC/G.1946-P), Santiago, Chile. United Nations publication, Sales No. E.97.II.G.4.

―――― (1996a), *Strenghthening Development: the Interplay of Macro and Microeconomics* (LC/G.1898/Rev.1-P), Santiago, Chile. United Nations publication, Sales No. E.96.II.G.2.

―――― (1996b), The Strategic Role of Secondary Education in Achieving Well-being and Social Equity (LC/G.1919), Santiago, Chile.

―――― (1996c), Latin American and Caribbean Regional Plan of Action on Human Settlements (LC/G.1912), Santiago, Chile, February.

―――― (1996d), Producción de vivienda en América Latina y el Caribe: áreas de interés para una política habitacional innovativa (LC/L.972), Santiago, Chile, August.

―――― (1996e), Human settlements: The shelter of development (LC/L.906(Conf.85/3 /Rev.1)), Santiago, Chile, January.

―――― (1995a), *Social Panorama of Latin America. 1995 Edition* (LC/G.1886-P), Santiago, Chile. United Nations publication, Sales No. E.95.II.G.17.

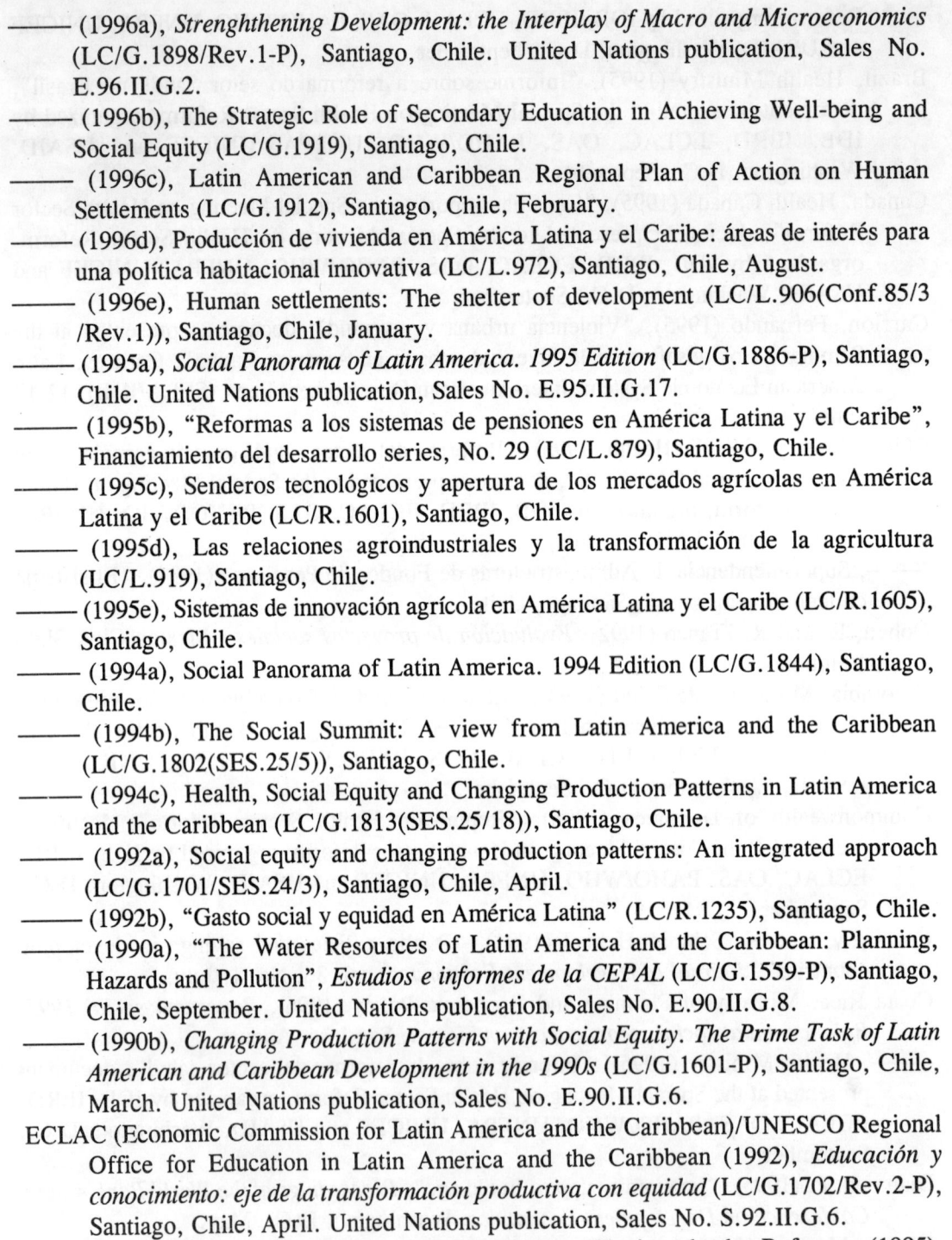

―――― (1995b), "Reformas a los sistemas de pensiones en América Latina y el Caribe", Financiamiento del desarrollo series, No. 29 (LC/L.879), Santiago, Chile.

―――― (1995c), Senderos tecnológicos y apertura de los mercados agrícolas en América Latina y el Caribe (LC/R.1601), Santiago, Chile.

―――― (1995d), Las relaciones agroindustriales y la transformación de la agricultura (LC/L.919), Santiago, Chile.

―――― (1995e), Sistemas de innovación agrícola en América Latina y el Caribe (LC/R.1605), Santiago, Chile.

―――― (1994a), Social Panorama of Latin America. 1994 Edition (LC/G.1844), Santiago, Chile.

―――― (1994b), The Social Summit: A view from Latin America and the Caribbean (LC/G.1802(SES.25/5)), Santiago, Chile.

―――― (1994c), Health, Social Equity and Changing Production Patterns in Latin America and the Caribbean (LC/G.1813(SES.25/18)), Santiago, Chile.

―――― (1992a), Social equity and changing production patterns: An integrated approach (LC/G.1701/SES.24/3), Santiago, Chile, April.

―――― (1992b), "Gasto social y equidad en América Latina" (LC/R.1235), Santiago, Chile.

―――― (1990a), "The Water Resources of Latin America and the Caribbean: Planning, Hazards and Pollution", *Estudios e informes de la CEPAL* (LC/G.1559-P), Santiago, Chile, September. United Nations publication, Sales No. E.90.II.G.8.

―――― (1990b), *Changing Production Patterns with Social Equity. The Prime Task of Latin American and Caribbean Development in the 1990s* (LC/G.1601-P), Santiago, Chile, March. United Nations publication, Sales No. E.90.II.G.6.

ECLAC (Economic Commission for Latin America and the Caribbean)/UNESCO Regional Office for Education in Latin America and the Caribbean (1992), *Educación y conocimiento: eje de la transformación productiva con equidad* (LC/G.1702/Rev.2-P), Santiago, Chile, April. United Nations publication, Sales No. S.92.II.G.6.

Ecuador, Consejo Nacional de Salud, Comisión Técnica de la Reforma (1995), "Lineamientos para la reforma del sector salud", document presented at the Special Meeting on Health Sector Reform, organized by IDB, IBRD, ECLAC, OAS, PAHO/WHO, UNFPA, UNICEF and USAID, Washington, D.C., September.

Fajnzylber, F. (1989), Industrialization in Latin America: From the "black box" to the "empty box": A comparison of contemporary industrialization patterns, *Cuadernos de la CEPAL* series, No. 60 (LC/G.1534-P), Santiago, Chile. United Nations publication, Sales No. E.89.II.G.5.

Feldstein, M.S. (1974), "Social security, induced retirement and aggregate capital accumulation", *Journal of Political Economy*, vol. 82.

Flood, M.C. de (1996), "Gasto y financiamiento en salud en Argentina", document presented at the Seminar "Reformas a la seguridad social en salud en Argentina, Chile y Colombia" by the ECLAC/GTZ project "Reformas del financiamiento de los sistemas de salud en América Latina y el Caribe", Santiago, Chile, November.

Franco, Rolando (1996), "Cuarenta y una proposiciones para diseñar e implementar una política social moderna que contribuya al desarrollo social", *Políticas sociales y pobreza*, Quito, Corporation for Development Studies (CORDES).

—— (1995), "Social policy paradigms in Latin America", *CEPAL Review*, No. 58 (LC/G.1916-P), Santiago, Chile, April.

Franco, Rolando and others (1995), "Viabilidad económica e institucional de la reforma educativa en Chile", Políticas sociales series, No. 11 (LC/L926), Santiago, Chile, ECLAC, December.

Frenk, J. and others (1993), "The health of the public: A public responsability?", *Proceedings of the World Bank Annual Conference on Development Economics, 1992*, Washington, D.C., World Bank (IBRD).

Gerstenfeld, P. and others (1995), "Variables extrapedagógicas y equidad en la educación media: hogar, subjetividad y cultura escolar", Políticas sociales series, No. 9 (LC/L.924), Santiago, Chile.

Government of Cuba (1995), "Informe sobre reformas del sector salud y seguimiento de los procesos de reforma en los países", document presented at the Special Meeting on Health Sector Reform, organized by IDB, IBRD, ECLAC, OAS, PAHO/WHO, UNFPA, UNICEF and USAID, Washington, D.C., September.

Government of the Dominican Republic (1995), "Reforma del sector salud en República Dominicana", document presented at the Special Meeting on Health Sector Reform, organized by IDB, IBRD, ECLAC, OAS, PAHO/WHO, UNFPA, UNICEF and USAID, Washington, D.C., September.

Government of El Salvador (1995), "Informe sobre reforma del sector salud y seguimiento de los procesos de reforma sectorial en el Salvador", document presented at the Special Meeting on Health Sector Reform, organized by IDB, IBRD, ECLAC, OAS, PAHO/WHO, UNFPA, UNICEF and USAID, Washington, D.C., September.

Government of Guyana, "Report on reform of the health sector and monitoring of the sectoral reform processes in Guyana", document presented at the Special Meeting on Health Sector Reform, organized by IDB, IBRD, ECLAC, OAS, PAHO/WHO, UNFPA, UNICEF and USAID, Washington, D.C., September.

Government of Honduras (1995), "Informe sobre reforma del sector salud y seguimiento de los procesos de reforma sectorial en los países", document presented at the Special Meeting on Health Sector Reform, organized by IDB, IBRD, ECLAC, OAS, PAHO/WHO, UNFPA, UNICEF and USAID, Washington, D.C., September.

Government of Puerto Rico (1995), "Situación actual del sector salud en Puerto Rico", document presented at the Special Meeting on Health Sector Reform, organized by IDB, IBRD, ECLAC, OAS, PAHO/WHO, UNFPA, UNICEF and USAID, Washington, D.C., September.

Government of Saint Kitts and Nevis (1995), "Health sector reform", document presented at the Special Meeting on Health Sector Reform, organized by IDB, IBRD, ECLAC, OAS, PAHO/WHO, UNFPA, UNICEF and USAID, Washington, D.C., September.

Government of Saint Vincent and the Grenadines (1995), "Report on health sector reform", document presented at the Special Meeting on Health Sector Reform, organized by IDB, IBRD, ECLAC, OAS, PAHO/WHO, UNFPA, UNICEF and USAID, Washington, D.C., September.

Government of Suriname (1995), "Report on health sector reform in Suriname", document presented at the Special Meeting on Health Sector Reform, organized by IDB, IBRD, ECLAC, OAS, PAHO/WHO, UNFPA, UNICEF and USAID, Washington, D.C., September.

Government of Trinidad and Tobago (1995), "Reform of the health sector, Trinidad and Tobago", document presented at the Special Meeting on Health Sector Reform, organized by IDB, IBRD, ECLAC, OAS, PAHO/WHO, UNFPA, UNICEF and USAID, Washington, D.C., September.

Government of Venezuela (1995), "El proceso de reforma del sector salud en Venezuela", document presented at the Special Meeting on Health Sector Reform, organized by IDB, IBRD, ECLAC, OAS, PAHO/WHO, UNFPA, UNICEF and USAID, Washington, D.C., September.

Grenada, Ministry of Health (1995), "Report on health sector reform", document presented at the Special Meeting on Health Sector Reform, organized by IDB, IBRD, ECLAC, OAS, PAHO/WHO, UNFPA, UNICEF and USAID, Washington, D.C., September.

Guatemala, Ministerio de Salud Pública y Asistencia Social (1995), "Informe sobre el proceso de la reforma del sector salud en Guatemala", document presented at the Special Meeting on Health Sector Reform, organized by IDB, IBRD, ECLAC, OAS, PAHO/WHO, UNFPA, UNICEF and USAID, Washington, D.C., September.

Held, G. (1994), "Liberalization of financial development?", *CEPAL Review*, No. 54 (LC/G.1845-P), Santiago, Chile, ECLAC, December.

Huneeus, Carlos (1996), *Latinobarómetro 1995: opiniones y actitudes de los ciudadanos sobre la realidad económica y social*, Santiago, Chile, ECLAC.

IDB (Inter-American Development Bank) (1996), *Economic and Social Progress in Latin America. 1996 Report. Making Social Services Work*, Washington, D.C.

Iglesias, A. and R. Acuña (1991), "Sistemas de pensiones en América Latina. Chile: experiencia con un régimen de capitalización 1981-1991", Santiago, Chile, S.R.V. Impresos.

ILO (International Labour Oorganization) (1996), *Panorama laboral, '96*, Lima, Regional Office for Latin America and the Caribbean.

————— (1995), *Panorama laboral, '95*, Lima, Regional Office for Latin America and the Caribbean.

————— (1994), *Panorama laboral, '94*, Lima, Regional Office for Latin America and the Caribbean.

Jamaica, Ministry of Health (1995), "Report on the major problems in the health sector the reforms adopted and/or could be adopted", document presented at the Special Meeting on Health Sector Reform, organized by IDB, IBRD, ECLAC, OAS, PAHO/WHO, UNFPA, UNICEF and USAID, Washington, D.C., September.

Kaztman, R. and A. Fuentes (1996), Marginalidad e integración social en Uruguay (LC/MVD/R.140/Rev.1), Montevideo, ECLAC Office in Montevideo.

Leimer, D.R. and S.D. Lesnoy (1982), "Social security and private saving: New time series evidence", *Journal of Political Economy*, vol. 90.

Marfán, M. (1984), "Una evaluación de la nueva reforma tributaria", *Colección estudios CIEPLAN*, No. 13, Santiago, Chile, Economic Research Corporation for Latin America (CIEPLAN), June.

Medici, A.C. (1994), "A dinâmica do setor saúde no Brasil: transformações e tendências nas décadas de 80 e 90", São Paulo, November.

Mesa-Lago, C. (1996), "Las reformas de las pensiones en América Latina y la posición de los organismos internacionales", *Revista de la CEPAL*, No. 60 (LC/G.1943-P), December.

————— (1992), *Health care for the poor in Latin America and the Caribbean*, Publicación científica, No. 539, Washington, D.C., Pan American Health Organization (PAHO)/Interamerican Foundation.

————— (1978), *Social Security in Latin America: Pressure Groups, Stratification and Inequality*, Pittsburgh, Pennsylvania, University of Pittsburgh Press.

Mexico, Ministry of Health (1995), "Reforma sectoral en salud", document presented at the Special Meeting on Health Sector Reform, organized by IDB, IBRD, ECLAC, OAS, PAHO/WHO, UNFPA, UNICEF and USAID, Washington, D.C., September.

Montoya, S. (1996), "Reformas al financiamiento del sistema de salud, Argentina", document presented at the Seminar "Reformas a la seguridad social en salud en Argentina, Chile y Colombia" by the ECLAC/GTZ project "Reformas del financiamiento de los sistemas de salud en América Latina y el Caribe", Santiago, Chile, November.

Morales, L.G. (1996), "El financiamiento del sistema de seguridad social en salud en Colombia", document presented at the Seminar "Reformas a la seguridad social en salud en Argentina, Chile y Colombia" by the ECLAC/GTZ project "Reformas del financiamiento de los sistemas de salud en América Latina y el Caribe", Santiago, Chile, November.

Morandé, F.G. (1996), "Savings in Chile: What went right?", Investigación series, No. 92, Santiago, Chile, Graduate Program in Economics, ILADES/Georgetown University.

Nicaragua, Ministry of Health (1995), "Informe avances reformas del sector salud", document presented at the Special Meeting on Health Sector Reform, organized by IDB, IBRD, ECLAC, OAS, PAHO/WHO, UNFPA, UNICEF and USAID, Washington, D.C., September.

Panama, Ministry of Health (1995), "Informe sobre la propuesta de reforma del sector salud de Panamá", document presented at the Special Meeting on Health Sector Reform, organized by IDB, IBRD, ECLAC, OAS, PAHO/WHO, UNFPA, UNICEF and USAID, Washington, D.C., September.

Paraguay, Ministry of Public Health and Social Welfare (1995), "Hacia un sistema nacional de salud", document presented at the Special Meeting on Health Sector Reform, organized by IDB, IBRD, ECLAC, OAS, PAHO/WHO, UNFPA, UNICEF and USAID, Washington, D.C., September.

Perú, Ministry of Health (1995), "La reforma del sector salud en el Perú: viabilidad y factibilidad", document presented at the Special Meeting on Health Sector Reform, organized by IDB, IBRD, ECLAC, OAS, PAHO/WHO, UNFPA, UNICEF and USAID, Washington, D.C., September.

Plaza, B. (1996), "Mecanismos de pago/Contratación del régimen contributivo dentro del marco de seguridad social en Colombia", document presented at the Seminar "Reformas a la seguridad social en salud en Argentina, Chile y Colombia" by the ECLAC/GTZ project "Reformas del financiamiento de los sistemas de salud en América Latina y el Caribe", Santiago, Chile, November.

Pollak, M. (1994), "Evaluación de los fondos de inversión social en el contexto de las economías latinoamericanas", document presented at the First Conference on FISE/OAS Social Network, Quito, October.

Puryear, Jeffrey M. and José Joaquín Brunner (1994), "An agenda for educational reform in Latin America and the Caribbean", Policy Brief, Inter-American Dialogue, August.

Ramos, J. (1994), "Síntesis del planteamiento de la CEPAL sobre la equidad y transformación productiva", Desarrollo productivo series, No. 17 (LC/G.1841), Santiago, Chile, ECLAC.

Rivero, José (1995), "Las propuestas del cambio educativo en América Latina", *Educación peruana: hacia un nuevo rumbo*, Lima.

Rosales, O. (1996a), "Economic policy, institutions and productive development in Latin America", *CEPAL Review*, No. 59 (LC/G.1931-P), Santiago, Chile, August.

—— (1996b), "Brecha externa y competitividad en América Latina", *Situación*, No. 1, Banco Bilbao Vizcaya.

—— (1994), "Industrial policy and promotion of competitiveness", *CEPAL Review*, No. 53 (LC/G.1832-P), Santiago, Chile, August.

Saint Lucia, Ministry of Health (1995), "Report on health sector reform", document presented at the Special Meeting on Health Sector Reform, organized by IDB, IBRD, ECLAC, OAS, PAHO/WHO, UNFPA, UNICEF and USAID, Washington, D.C., September.

Salas, A. (1996), "Costa Rica: una reforma dentro del sistema de salud vigente", Las reformas sociales en acción: salud, Políticas sociales series, No. 15, Santiago, Chile, ECLAC.

Schejtman, A. (1989), "Gestión local y seguridad alimentaria", *Cómo enfrentar la pobreza. Estrategias y experiencias organizacionales innovadoras*, B. Kliksberg (ed.), Buenos Aires, Grupo Editor Latinoamericano.

Schulthess, W. and G. Demarco (1993), *Sistema de pensiones en América Latina. Argentina: evolución del Sistema Nacional de Previsión Social y propuesta de reforma*, Santiago, Chile, S.R.V. Impresos.

Siri, G. (1996), "Social investment funds in Latin America", *CEPAL Review*, No. 59 (LC/G.1931-P), Santiago, Chile, August.

Sojo, A. (1996a), "Potential limits of health management reform in Chile", *CEPAL Review*, No. 59 (LC/G.1931-P), Santiago, Chile, August.

—— (1996b), "La política social frente al ajuste y al incremento de la productividad en América Latina y el Caribe", *Situación*, No. 1, Bilbao, Banco Bilbao Vizcaya.

Stumpo, G. (1996), "Encadenamientos, articulaciones y procesos de desarrollo industrial", Desarrollo productivo series, No. 36 (LC/G.1934), Santiago, Chile, ECLAC, November.

SUR (Centre for Social Studies and Education) (1996), "Campesinado y Mercosur", *Temas Sociales*, No. 62, Madrid, June.

Tafani, R. (1996), "Informe sobre reformas al sector salud", document presented at the Seminar "Reformas a la seguridad social en salud en Argentina, Chile y Colombia" by the ECLAC/GTZ project "Reformas del financiamiento de los sistemas de salud en América Latina y el Caribe", Santiago, Chile, November.

Tapia, L. and L. Van Hemelryck (1996), "Planes y políticas de fomento a la microempresa en América Latina", Documento de trabajo, No. 154, Santiago, Chile, June.

UNICEF (United Nations Children's Fund) (1996), *State of the World's Children, 1996*, Oxford, Oxford University Press.

UNDP (United Nations Development Programme) (1996), *Human Development Report, 1996*, New York, Oxford University Press.

—— (1991), *Human Development Report, 1991*, New York, Oxford University Press.

—— (1990), *Human Development Report, 1990*, Bogotá, Tercer Mundo Editores.

Uthoff, A. (1995), Promoción del ahorro y los sistemas de pensiones (LC/R.1608), Santiago, Chile, ECLAC, November.

Uthoff, A. and R. Szalachmann (eds.) (1991), *Sistemas de pensiones en América Latina: diagnóstico y alternativas de reforma. Costa Rica, Ecuador, Uruguay y Venezuela*, Santiago, Chile, S.R.V. Impresos.

—— (1992), *Sistemas de pensiones en América Latina: diagnóstico y alternativas de reforma. Volumen 2: Bolivia, Brasil, Colombia, Guatemala, México*, Santiago, Chile, S.R.V. Impresos.

Valdés-Prieto, S. (1994), "Distributive Concerns when Replacing a Pay-as-you-Go System with a Fully Funded System", Policy Research Working Paper, No. 1366, Washington, D.C., World Bank (IBRD), October.

Vázquez, A. and Garofoli, G. (eds.) (1995), *Desarrollo económico local en Europa*, Madrid, Colegio de Economistas de Madrid.

Vial, J. and M. Marfán (1995), "Políticas para el crecimiento económico en los 90: el caso de Chile", *Notas técnicas*, No. 157, Santiago, Chile, Economic Research Corporation for Latin America (CIEPLAN), March.

Whitehead, M. (1990), *Conceptos y principios de igualdad y salud*, Madrid, Ministerio de Sanidad y Consumo.

WHO (World Health Organization) (1996), *The World Health Report, 1996. Fighting Disease, Fostering Development*, Geneva.

World Bank (1996), "From Vision to Action in the Rural Sector", Washington, D.C., World Bank (IBRD).

—— (1995), *Priorities and Strategies for Education*, Washington, D.C.

——— (1993), *Investing in health. World Development Report, 1993*, Washington, D.C., January.
——— (1991), "Feeding Latin America's children: An analytical survey of food programs", Report No. 9526-LAC, Washington, D.C., November.
——— (1990), *Poverty. World Development Report, 1990*, Washington, D.C.
Zahler, R. (1995), Discurso preparado con ocasión del 70° aniversario del Banco Central de Chile, Santiago, Chile.

ECLAC publications

ECONOMIC COMMISSION FOR LATIN AMERICA AND THE CARIBBEAN
Casilla 179-D Santiago, Chile

PERIODIC PUBLICATIONS

CEPAL Review

CEPAL Review first appeared in 1976 as part of the Publications Programme of the Economic Commission for Latin America and the Caribbean, its aim being to make a contribution to the study of the economic and social development problems of the region. The views expressed in signed articles, including those by Secretariat staff members, are those of the authors and therefore do not necessarily reflect the point of view of the Organization.

CEPAL Review is published in Spanish and English versions three times a year.

Annual subscription costs for 1997 are US$20 for the Spanish version and US$22 for the English version. The price of single issues is US$10 in both cases.

The cost of a two-year subscription (1997-1998) is US$35 for Spanish-language version and US$40 for English.

Estudio Económico de América Latina y el Caribe			Economic Survey of Latin America and the Caribbean		
1980,		664 pp.	1980,		629 pp.
1981,		863 pp.	1981,		837 pp.
1982,	vol. I	693 pp.	1982,	vol. I	658 pp.
1982,	vol. II	199 pp.	1982,	vol. II	186 pp.
1983,	vol. I	694 pp.	1983,	vol. I	686 pp.
1983,	vol. II	179 pp.	1983,	vol. II	166 pp.
1984,	vol. I	702 pp.	1984,	vol. I	685 pp.
1984,	vol. II	233 pp.	1984,	vol. II	216 pp.
1985,		672 pp.	1985,		660 pp.
1986,		734 pp.	1986,		729 pp.
1987,		692 pp.	1987,		685 pp.
1988,		741 pp.	1988,		637 pp.
1989,		821 pp.	1989,		678 pp.
1990,	vol. I	260 pp.	1990,	vol. I	248 pp.
1990,	vol. II	590 pp.	1990,	vol. II	472 pp.
1991,	vol. I	299 pp.	1991,	vol. I	281 pp.
1991,	vol. II	602 pp.	1991,	vol. II	455 pp.
1992,	vol. I	297 pp.	1992,	vol. I	286 pp.
1992,	vol. II	579 pp.	1992,	vol. II	467 pp.
1993,	vol. I	289 pp.	1993,	vol. I	272 pp.
1993,	vol. II	532 pp.	1993,	vol. II	520 pp.
1994-1995,		348 pp.	1994-1995,		332 pp.
1995-1996,		349 pp.	1995-1996,		335 pp.
1996-1997,		354 pp.	1996-1997,		335 pp.

(Issues for previous years also available)

Anuario Estadístico de América Latina y el Caribe / Statistical Yearbook for Latin America and the Caribbean (bilingual)

1980,	617 pp.		1989,	770 pp.
1981,	727 pp.		1990,	782 pp.
1982/1983,	749 pp.		1991,	856 pp.
1984,	761 pp.		1992,	868 pp.
1985,	792 pp.		1993,	860 pp.
1986,	782 pp.		1994,	863 pp.
1987,	714 pp.		1995,	865 pp.
1988,	782 pp.		1996,	866 pp.

(Issues for previous years also available)

Libros de la CEPAL

1 *Manual de proyectos de desarrollo económico*, 1958, 5th. ed. 1980, 264 pp.
1 **Manual on economic development projects,** 1958, 2nd. ed. 1972, 242 pp.
2 *América Latina en el umbral de los años ochenta*, 1979, 2nd. ed. 1980, 203 pp.
3 *Agua, desarrollo y medio ambiente en América Latina*, 1980, 443 pp.
4 *Los bancos transnacionales y el financiamiento externo de América Latina. La experiencia del Perú*, 1980, 265 pp.
4 **Transnational banks and the external finance of Latin America: the experience of Peru,** 1985, 342 pp.
5 *La dimensión ambiental en los estilos de desarrollo de América Latina*, Osvaldo Sunkel, 1981, 2nd. ed. 1984, 136 pp.
6 *La mujer y el desarrollo: guía para la planificación de programas y proyectos*, 1984, 115 pp.

6   Women and development: guidelines for programme and project planning, 1982, 3rd. ed. 1984, 123 pp.
7   África y América Latina: perspectivas de la cooperación interregional, 1983, 286 pp.
8   Sobrevivencia campesina en ecosistemas de altura, vols. I y II, 1983, 720 pp.
9   La mujer en el sector popular urbano. América Latina y el Caribe, 1984, 349 pp.
10 Avances en la interpretación ambiental del desarrollo agrícola de América Latina, 1985, 236 pp.
11 El decenio de la mujer en el escenario latinoamericano, 1986, 216 pp.
11 **The decade for women in Latin America and the Caribbean: background and prospects,** 1988, 215 pp.
12 América Latina: sistema monetario internacional y financiamiento externo, 1986, 416 pp.
12 **Latin America: international monetary system and external financing,** 1986, 405 pp.
13 Raúl Prebisch: Un aporte al estudio de su pensamiento, 1987, 146 pp.
14 Cooperativismo latinoamericano: antecedentes y perspectivas, 1989, 371 pp.
15 CEPAL, 40 años (1948-1988), 1988, 85 pp.
15 **ECLAC 40 Years (1948-1988),** 1989, 83 pp.
16 América Latina en la economía mundial, 1988, 321 pp.
17 Gestión para el desarrollo de cuencas de alta montaña en la zona andina, 1988, 187 pp.
18 Políticas macroeconómicas y brecha externa: América Latina en los años ochenta, 1989, 201 pp.
19 CEPAL, Bibliografía, 1948-1988, 1989, 648 pp.
20 Desarrollo agrícola y participación campesina, 1989, 404 pp.
21 Planificación y gestión del desarrollo en áreas de expansión de la frontera agropecuaria en América Latina, 1989, 113 pp.
22 Transformación ocupacional y crisis social en América Latina, 1989, 243 pp.
23 La crisis urbana en América Latina y el Caribe: reflexiones sobre alternativas de solución, 1990, 197 pp.
24 **The environmental dimension in development planning I,** 1991, 302 pp.
25 Transformación productiva con equidad, 1990, 3rd. ed. 1991, 185 pp.
25 **Changing production patterns with social equity,** 1990, 3rd. ed. 1991, 177 pp.
26 América Latina y el Caribe: opciones para reducir el peso de la deuda, 1990, 118 pp.
26 **Latin America and the Caribbean: options to reduce the debt burden,** 1990, 110 pp.
27 Los grandes cambios y la crisis. Impacto sobre la mujer en América Latina y el Caribe, 1991, 271 pp.
27 **Major changes and crisis. The impact on women in Latin America and the Caribbean,** 1992, 279 pp.
28 **A collection of documents on economic relations between the United States and Central America, 1906-1956,** 1991, 398 pp.
29 Inventarios y cuentas del patrimonio natural en América Latina y el Caribe, 1991, 335 pp.
30 Evaluaciones del impacto ambiental en América Latina y el Caribe, 1991, 232 pp.
31 El desarrollo sustentable: transformación productiva, equidad y medio ambiente, 1991, 146 pp.
31 **Sustainable development: changing production patterns, social equity and the environment,** 1991, 146 pp.
32 Equidad y transformación productiva: un enfoque integrado, 1993, 254 pp.
33 Educación y conocimiento: eje de la transformación productiva con equidad, 1992, 269 pp.
33 **Education and knowledge: basic pillars of changing production patterns with social equity,** 1993, 257 pp.
34 Ensayos sobre coordinación de políticas macroeconómicas, 1992, 249 pp.
35 Población, equidad y transformación productiva, 1993, 2nd. ed. 1995, 158 pp.
35 **Population, social equity and changing production patterns,** 1993, 153 pp.
36 Cambios en el perfil de las familias. La experiencia regional, 1993, 434 pp.
37 Familia y futuro: un programa regional en América Latina y el Caribe, 1994, 137 pp.
37 **Family and future. A regional programme in Latin America and the Caribbean,** 1995, 123 pp.
38 Imágenes sociales de la modernización y la transformación tecnológica, 1995, 198 pp.
39 El regionalismo abierto en América Latina y el Caribe, 1994, 109 pp.
39 **Open regionalism in Latin America and the Caribbean,** 1994, 103 pp.
40 Políticas para mejorar la inserción en la economía mundial, 1995, 314 pp.
40 **Policies to improve linkages with the global economy,** 1995, 308 pp.
41 Las relaciones económicas entre América Latina y la Unión Europea: el papel de los servicios exteriores, 1996, 300 pp.
42 Fortalecer el desarrollo. Interacciones entre macro y microeconomía, 1996, 116 pp.
42 **Strengthening development. The interplay of macro- and microeconomics,** 1996, 116 pp.
43 Quince años de desempeño económico. América Latina y el Caribe, 1980-1995, 1996, 120 pp.
43 **The economic experience of the last fifteen years. Latin America and the Caribbean, 1980-1995,** 1996, 120 pp.
45 La grieta de las drogas, 1997, 218 pp.

MONOGRAPH SERIES

Cuadernos de la C E P A L

1 *América Latina: el nuevo escenario regional y mundial / **Latin America: the new regional and world setting,*** (bilingual), 1975, 2nd. ed. 1985, 103 pp.
2 *Las evoluciones regionales de la estrategia internacional del desarrollo,* 1975, 2nd. ed. 1984, 73 pp.
2 ***Regional appraisals of the international development strategy,*** 1975, 2nd. ed. 1985, 82 pp.
3 *Desarrollo humano, cambio social y crecimiento en América Latina,* 1975, 2nd. ed. 1984, 103 pp.
4 *Relaciones comerciales, crisis monetaria e integración económica en América Latina,* 1975, 85 pp.
5 *Síntesis de la segunda evaluación regional de la estrategia internacional del desarrollo,* 1975, 72 pp.
6 *Dinero de valor constante. Concepto, problemas y experiencias,* Jorge Rose, 1975, 2nd. ed. 1984, 43 pp.
7 *La coyuntura internacional y el sector externo,* 1975, 2nd. ed. 1983, 106 pp.
8 *La industrialización latinoamericana en los años setenta,* 1975, 2nd. ed. 1984, 116 pp.
9 *Dos estudios sobre inflación 1972-1974. La inflación en los países centrales. América Latina y la inflación importada,* 1975, 2nd. ed. 1984, 57 pp.
s/n ***Canada and the foreign firm,*** D. Pollock, 1976, 43 pp.
10 *Reactivación del mercado común centroamericano,* 1976, 2nd. ed. 1984, 149 pp.
11 *Integración y cooperación entre países en desarrollo en el ámbito agrícola,* Germánico Salgado, 1976, 2nd. ed. 1985, 62 pp.
12 *Temas del nuevo orden económico internacional,* 1976, 2nd. ed. 1984, 85 pp.
13 *En torno a las ideas de la CEPAL: desarrollo, industrialización y comercio exterior,* 1977, 2nd. ed. 1985, 57 pp.
14 *En torno a las ideas de la CEPAL: problemas de la industrialización en América Latina,* 1977, 2nd. ed. 1984, 46 pp.
15 *Los recursos hidráulicos de América Latina. Informe regional,* 1977, 2nd. ed. 1984, 75 pp.
15 ***The water resources of Latin America. Regional report,*** 1977, 2nd. ed. 1985, 79 pp.
16 *Desarrollo y cambio social en América Latina,* 1977, 2nd. ed. 1984, 59 pp.
17 *Estrategia internacional de desarrollo y establecimiento de un nuevo orden económico internacional,* 1977, 3rd. ed. 1984, 61 pp.
17 ***International development strategy and establishment of a new international economic order,*** 1977, 3rd. ed. 1985, 59 pp.
18 *Raíces históricas de las estructuras distributivas de América Latina,* A. di Filippo, 1977, 2nd. ed. 1983, 64 pp.
19 *Dos estudios sobre endeudamiento externo,* C. Massad and R. Zahler, 1977, 2nd. ed. 1986, 66 pp.
s/n ***United States – Latin American trade and financial relations: some policy recommendations,*** S. Weintraub, 1977, 44 pp.
20 *Tendencias y proyecciones a largo plazo del desarrollo económico de América Latina,* 1978, 3rd. ed. 1985, 134 pp.
21 *25 años en la agricultura de América Latina: rasgos principales 1950-1975,* 1978, 2nd. ed. 1983, 124 pp.
22 *Notas sobre la familia como unidad socioeconómica,* Carlos A. Borsotti, 1978, 2nd. ed. 1984, 60 pp.
23 *La organización de la información para la evaluación del desarrollo,* Juan Sourrouille, 1978, 2nd. ed. 1984, 61 pp.
24 *Contabilidad nacional a precios constantes en América Latina,* 1978, 2nd. ed. 1983, 60 pp.
s/n ***Energy in Latin America: The Historical Record,*** J. Mullen, 1978, 66 pp.
25 *Ecuador: desafíos y logros de la política económica en la fase de expansión petrolera,* 1979, 2nd. ed. 1984, 153 pp.
26 *Las transformaciones rurales en América Latina: ¿desarrollo social o marginación?,* 1979, 2nd. ed. 1984, 160 pp.
27 *La dimensión de la pobreza en América Latina,* Oscar Altimir, 1979, 2nd. ed. 1983, 89 pp.
28 *Organización institucional para el control y manejo de la deuda externa. El caso chileno,* Rodolfo Hoffman, 1979, 35 pp.
29 *La política monetaria y el ajuste de la balanza de pagos: tres estudios,* 1979, 2nd. ed. 1984, 61 pp.
29 ***Monetary policy and balance of payments adjustment: three studies,*** 1979, 60 pp.
30 *América Latina: las evaluaciones regionales de la estrategia internacional del desarrollo en los años setenta,* 1979, 2nd. ed. 1982, 237 pp.
31 *Educación, imágenes y estilos de desarrollo,* G. Rama, 1979, 2nd. ed. 1982, 72 pp.
32 *Movimientos internacionales de capitales,* R. H. Arriazu, 1979, 2nd. ed. 1984, 90 pp.
33 *Informe sobre las inversiones directas extranjeras en América Latina,* A. E. Calcagno, 1980, 2nd. ed. 1982, 114 pp.
34 *Las fluctuaciones de la industria manufacturera argentina, 1950-1978,* D. Heymann, 1980, 2nd. ed. 1984, 234 pp.
35 *Perspectivas de reajuste industrial: la Comunidad Económica Europea y los países en desarrollo,* B. Evers, G. de Groot and W. Wagenmans, 1980, 2nd. ed. 1984, 69 pp.
36 *Un análisis sobre la posibilidad de evaluar la solvencia crediticia de los países en desarrollo,* A. Saieh, 1980, 2nd. ed. 1984, 82 pp.
37 *Hacia los censos latinoamericanos de los años ochenta,* 1981, 146 pp.

s/n *The economic relations of Latin America with Europe*, 1980, 2nd. ed. 1983, 156 pp.

38 *Desarrollo regional argentino: la agricultura*, J. Martin, 1981, 2nd. ed. 1984, 111 pp.

39 *Estratificación y movilidad ocupacional en América Latina*, C. Filgueira and C. Geneletti, 1981, 2nd. ed. 1985, 162 pp.

40 *Programa de acción regional para América Latina en los años ochenta*, 1981, 2nd. ed. 1984, 62 pp.

40 ***Regional programme of action for Latin America in the 1980s***, 1981, 2nd. ed. 1984, 57 pp.

41 *El desarrollo de América Latina y sus repercusiones en la educación. Alfabetismo y escolaridad básica*, 1982, 246 pp.

42 *América Latina y la economía mundial del café*, 1982, 95 pp.

43 *El ciclo ganadero y la economía argentina*, 1983, 160 pp.

44 *Las encuestas de hogares en América Latina*, 1983, 122 pp.

45 *Las cuentas nacionales en América Latina y el Caribe*, 1983, 100 pp.

45 ***National accounts in Latin America and the Caribbean***, 1983, 97 pp.

46 *Demanda de equipos para generación, transmisión y transformación eléctrica en América Latina*, 1983, 193 pp.

47 *La economía de América Latina en 1982: evolución general, política cambiaria y renegociación de la deuda externa*, 1984, 104 pp.

48 *Políticas de ajuste y renegociación de la deuda externa en América Latina*, 1984, 102 pp.

49 *La economía de América Latina y el Caribe en 1983: evolución general, crisis y procesos de ajuste*, 1985, 95 pp.

49 ***The economy of Latin America and the Caribbean in 1983: main trends, the impact of the crisis and the adjustment processes***, 1985, 93 pp.

50 *La CEPAL, encarnación de una esperanza de América Latina*, Hernán Santa Cruz, 1985, 77 pp.

51 *Hacia nuevas modalidades de cooperación económica entre América Latina y el Japón*, 1986, 233 pp.

51 ***Towards new forms of economic co-operation between Latin America and Japan***, 1987, 245 pp.

52 *Los conceptos básicos del transporte marítimo y la situación de la actividad en América Latina*, 1986, 112 pp.

52 ***Basic concepts of maritime transport and its present status in Latin America and the Caribbean***, 1987, 114 pp.

53 *Encuestas de ingresos y gastos. Conceptos y métodos en la experiencia latinoamericana.* 1986, 128 pp.

54 *Crisis económica y políticas de ajuste, estabilización y crecimiento*, 1986, 123 pp.

54 ***The economic crisis: policies for adjustment, stabilization and growth***, 1986, 125 pp.

55 *El desarrollo de América Latina y el Caribe: escollos, requisitos y opciones*, 1987, 184 pp.

55 ***Latin American and Caribbean development: obstacles, requirements and options***, 1987, 184 pp.

56 *Los bancos transnacionales y el endeudamiento externo en la Argentina*, 1987, 112 pp.

57 *El proceso de desarrollo de la pequeña y mediana empresa y su papel en el sistema industrial: el caso de Italia*, 1988, 112 pp.

58 *La evolución de la economía de América Latina en 1986*, 1988, 99 pp.

58 ***The evolution of the Latin American Economy in 1986***, 1988, 95 pp.

59 ***Protectionism: regional negotiation and defence strategies***, 1988, 261 pp.

60 *Industrialización en América Latina: de la "caja negra" al "casillero vacío"*, F. Fajnzylber, 1989, 2nd. ed. 1990, 176 pp.

60 ***Industrialization in Latin America: from the "Black Box" to the "Empty Box"***, F. Fajnzylber, 1990, 172 pp.

61 *Hacia un desarrollo sostenido en América Latina y el Caribe: restricciones y requisitos*, 1989, 94 pp.

61 ***Towards sustained development in Latin America and the Caribbean: restrictions and requisites***, 1989, 93 pp.

62 *La evolución de la economía de América Latina en 1987*, 1989, 87 pp.

62 ***The evolution of the Latin American economy in 1987***, 1989, 84 pp.

63 *Elementos para el diseño de políticas industriales y tecnológicas en América Latina*, 1990, 2nd. ed. 1991, 172 pp.

64 *La industria de transporte regular internacional y la competitividad del comercio exterior de los países de América Latina y el Caribe*, 1989, 132 pp.

64 ***The international common-carrier transportation industry and the competitiveness of the foreign trade of the countries of Latin America and the Caribbean***, 1989, 116 pp.

65 *Cambios estructurales en los puertos y la competitividad del comercio exterior de América Latina y el Caribe*, 1991, 141 pp.

65 ***Structural Changes in Ports and the Competitiveness of Latin American and Caribbean Foreign Trade***, 1990, 126 pp.

66 ***The Caribbean: one and divisible***, 1993, 207 pp.

67 *La transferencia de recursos externos de América Latina en la posguerra*, 1991, 92 pp.

67 ***Postwar transfer of resources abroad by Latin America***, 1992, 90 pp.

68 *La reestructuración de empresas públicas: el caso de los puertos de América Latina y el Caribe,* 1992, 148 pp.
68 The restructuring of public-sector enterprises: the case of Latin American and Caribbean ports, 1992, 129 pp.
69 *Las finanzas públicas de América Latina en la década de 1980,* 1993, 100 pp.
69 Public Finances in Latin America in the 1980s, 1993, 96 pp.
70 *Canales, cadenas, corredores y competitividad: un enfoque sistémico y su aplicación a seis productos latinoamericanos de exportación,* 1993, 183 pp.
71 *Focalización y pobreza,* 1995, 249 pp.
72 *Productividad de los pobres rurales y urbanos,* 1995, 318 pp.
73 *El gasto social en América Latina: un examen cuantitativo y cualitativo,* 1995, 167 pp.
74 *América Latina y el Caribe: dinámica de la población y desarrollo,* 1995, 151 pp.
75 *Crecimiento de la población y desarrollo,* 1995, 95 pp.
76 *Dinámica de la población y desarrollo económico,* 1995, (en prensa).
77 *La reforma laboral y la participación privada en los puertos del sector público,* 1996, (en prensa).
77 Labour reform and private participation in public-sector ports, 1996, 160 pp.
78 *Centroamérica y el TLC: efectos inmediatos e implicaciones futuras,* 1996, 164 pp.
79 *Ciudadanía y derechos humanos desde la perspectiva de las políticas públicas,* 1997, 124 pp.
82 *A dinámica do Setor Saúde no Brasil,* 1997, 220 pp.

Cuadernos Estadísticos de la CEPAL

1 *América Latina: relación de precios del intercambio,* 1976, 2nd. ed. 1984, 66 pp.
2 *Indicadores del desarrollo económico y social en América Latina,* 1976, 2nd. ed. 1984, 179 pp.
3 *Series históricas del crecimiento de América Latina,* 1978, 2nd. ed. 1984, 206 pp.
4 *Estadísticas sobre la estructura del gasto de consumo de los hogares según finalidad del gasto, por grupos de ingreso,* 1978, 110 pp. (Out of print; replaced by No. 8 below)
5 *El balance de pagos de América Latina, 1950-1977,* 1979, 2nd. ed. 1984, 164 pp.
6 *Distribución regional del producto interno bruto sectorial en los países de América Latina,* 1981, 2nd. ed. 1985, 68 pp.
7 *Tablas de insumo-producto en América Latina,* 1983, 383 pp.
8 *Estructura del gasto de consumo de los hogares según finalidad del gasto, por grupos de ingreso,* 1984, 146 pp.
9 *Origen y destino del comercio exterior de los países de la Asociación Latinoamericana de Integración y del Mercado Común Centroamericano,* 1985, 546 pp.
10 *América Latina: balance de pagos, 1950-1984,* 1986, 357 pp.
11 *El comercio exterior de bienes de capital en América Latina,* 1986, 288 pp.
12 *América Latina: índices del comercio exterior, 1970-1984,* 1987, 355 pp.
13 *América Latina: comercio exterior según la clasificación industrial internacional uniforme de todas las actividades económicas,* 1987, Vol. I, 675 pp; Vol. II, 675 pp.
14 *La distribución del ingreso en Colombia. Antecedentes estadísticos y características socioeconómicas de los receptores,* 1988, 156 pp.
15 *América Latina y el Caribe: series regionales de cuentas nacionales a precios constantes de 1980,* 1991, 245 pp.
16 *Origen y destino del comercio exterior de los países de la Asociación Latinoamericana de Integración,* 1991, 190 pp.
17 *Comercio intrazonal de los países de la Asociación de Integración, según capítulos de la clasificación uniforme para el comercio internacional, revisión 2,* 1992, 299 pp.
18 *Clasificaciones estadísticas internacionales incorporadas en el Banco de Datos del Comercio Exterior de América Latina y el Caribe de la CEPAL,* 1993, 313 pp.
19 *América Latina: comercio exterior según la clasificación industrial internacional uniforme de todas las actividades económicas (CIIU) - Volumen I - Exportaciones,* 1993, 285 pp.
19 *América Latina: comercio exterior según la clasificación industrial internacional uniforme de todas las actividades económicas (CIIU) - Volumen II - Importaciones,* 1993, 291 pp.
20 *Dirección del comercio exterior de América Latina y el Caribe según principales productos y grupos de productos, 1970-1992,* 1994, 483 pp.
21 *Estructura del gasto de consumo de los hogares en América Latina,* 1995, 274 pp.
22 *América Latina y el Caribe: dirección del comercio exterior de los principales productos alimenticios y agrícolas según países de destino y procedencia, 1979-1993,* 224 pp.
23 *América Latina y el Caribe: series regionales y oficiales de cuentas nacionales, 1950-1994,* 1996, 130 pp.
24 *Chile: comercio exterior según grupos de la Clasificación Uniforme para el Comercio Internacional, Rev. 3, y países de destino y procedencia, 1990-1995,* 1996, 480 pp.

Estudios e Informes de la C E P A L

1. *Nicaragua: el impacto de la mutación política*, 1981, 2nd. ed. 1982, 126 pp.
2. *Perú 1968-1977: la política económica en un proceso de cambio global*, 1981, 2nd. ed. 1982, 166 pp.
3. *La industrialización de América Latina y la cooperación internacional*, 1981, 170 pp. (Out of print, will not be reprinted.)
4. *Estilos de desarrollo, modernización y medio ambiente en la agricultura latinoamericana*, 1981, 4th. ed. 1984, 130 pp.
5. *El desarrollo de América Latina en los años ochenta*, 1981, 2nd. ed. 1982, 153 pp.
5. **Latin American development in the 1980s**, 1981, 2nd. ed. 1982, 134 pp.
6. *Proyecciones del desarrollo latinoamericano en los años ochenta*, 1981, 3rd. ed. 1985, 96 pp.
6. **Latin American development projections for the 1980s**, 1982, 2nd. ed. 1983, 89 pp.
7. *Las relaciones económicas externas de América Latina en los años ochenta*, 1981, 2nd. ed. 1982, 180 pp.
8. *Integración y cooperación regionales en los años ochenta*, 1982, 2nd. ed. 1982, 174 pp.
9. *Estrategias de desarrollo sectorial para los años ochenta: industria y agricultura*, 1981, 2nd. ed. 1985, 100 pp.
10. *Dinámica del subempleo en América Latina. PREALC*, 1981, 2nd. ed. 1985, 101 pp.
11. *Estilos de desarrollo de la industria manufacturera y medio ambiente en América Latina*, 1982, 2nd. ed. 1984, 178 pp.
12. *Relaciones económicas de América Latina con los países miembros del "Consejo de Asistencia Mutua Económica"*, 1982, 154 pp.
13. *Campesinado y desarrollo agrícola en Bolivia*, 1982, 175 pp.
14. *El sector externo: indicadores y análisis de sus fluctuaciones. El caso argentino*, 1982, 2nd. ed. 1985, 216 pp.
15. *Ingeniería y consultoría en Brasil y el Grupo Andino*, 1982, 320 pp.
16. *Cinco estudios sobre la situación de la mujer en América Latina*, 1982, 2nd. ed. 1985, 178 pp.
16. **Five studies on the situation of women in Latin America**, 1983, 2nd. ed. 1984, 188 pp.
17. *Cuentas nacionales y producto material en América Latina*, 1982, 129 pp.
18. *El financiamiento de las exportaciones en América Latina*, 1983, 212 pp.
19. *Medición del empleo y de los ingresos rurales*, 1982, 2nd. ed. 1983, 173 pp.
19. **Measurement of employment and income in rural areas**, 1983, 184 pp.
20. *Efectos macroeconómicos de cambios en las barreras al comercio y al movimiento de capitales: un modelo de simulación*, 1982, 68 pp.
21. *La empresa pública en la economía: la experiencia argentina*, 1982, 2nd. ed. 1985, 134 pp.
22. *Las empresas transnacionales en la economía de Chile, 1974-1980*, 1983, 178 pp.
23. *La gestión y la informática en las empresas ferroviarias de América Latina y España*, 1983, 195 pp.
24. *Establecimiento de empresas de reparación y mantenimiento de contenedores en América Latina y el Caribe*, 1983, 314 pp.
24. **Establishing container repair and maintenance enterprises in Latin America and the Caribbean**, 1983, 236 pp.
25. *Agua potable y saneamiento ambiental en América Latina, 1981-1990 / Drinking water supply and sanitation in Latin America, 1981-1990* (bilingual), 1983, 140 pp.
26. *Los bancos transnacionales, el estado y el endeudamiento externo en Bolivia*, 1983, 282 pp.
27. *Política económica y procesos de desarrollo. La experiencia argentina entre 1976 y 1981*, 1983, 157 pp.
28. *Estilos de desarrollo, energía y medio ambiente: un estudio de caso exploratorio*, 1983, 129 pp.
29. *Empresas transnacionales en la industria de alimentos. El caso argentino: cereales y carne*, 1983, 93 pp.
30. *Industrialización en Centroamérica, 1960-1980*, 1983, 168 pp.
31. *Dos estudios sobre empresas transnacionales en Brasil*, 1983, 141 pp.
32. *La crisis económica internacional y su repercusión en América Latina*, 1983, 81 pp.
33. *La agricultura campesina en sus relaciones con la industria*, 1984, 120 pp.
34. *Cooperación económica entre Brasil y el Grupo Andino: el caso de los minerales y metales no ferrosos*, 1983, 148 pp.
35. *La agricultura campesina y el mercado de alimentos: la dependencia externa y sus efectos en una economía abierta*, 1984, 201 pp.
36. *El capital extranjero en la economía peruana*, 1984, 178 pp.
37. *Dos estudios sobre política arancelaria*, 1984, 96 pp.
38. *Estabilización y liberalización económica en el Cono Sur*, 1984, 193 pp.
39. *La agricultura campesina y el mercado de alimentos: el caso de Haití y el de la República Dominicana*, 1984, 255 pp.
40. *La industria siderúrgica latinoamericana: tendencias y potencial*, 1984, 280 pp.
41. *La presencia de las empresas transnacionales en la economía ecuatoriana*, 1984, 77 pp.

42 Precios, salarios y empleo en la Argentina: estadísticas económicas de corto plazo, 1984, 378 pp.
43 El desarrollo de la seguridad social en América Latina, 1985, 348 pp.
44 Market structure, firm size and Brazilian exports, 1985, 104 pp.
45 La planificación del transporte en países de América Latina, 1985, 247 pp.
46 La crisis en América Latina: su evaluación y perspectivas, 1985, 119 pp.
47 La juventud en América Latina y el Caribe, 1985, 181 pp.
48 Desarrollo de los recursos mineros de América Latina, 1985, 145 pp.
48 Development of the mining resources of Latin America, 1989, 160 pp.
49 Las relaciones económicas internacionales de América Latina y la cooperación regional, 1985, 224 pp.
50 América Latina y la economía mundial del algodón, 1985, 122 pp.
51 Comercio y cooperación entre países de América Latina y países miembros del CAME, 1985, 90 pp.
52 Trade relations between Brazil and the United States, 1985, 148 pp.
53 Los recursos hídricos de América Latina y el Caribe y su aprovechamiento, 1985, 138 pp.
53 The water resources of Latin America and the Caribbean and their utilization, 1985, 135 pp.
54 La pobreza en América Latina: dimensiones y políticas, 1985, 155 pp.
55 Políticas de promoción de exportaciones en algunos países de América Latina, 1985, 207 pp.
56 Las empresas transnacionales en la Argentina, 1986, 222 pp.
57 El desarrollo frutícola y forestal en Chile y sus derivaciones sociales, 1986, 227 pp.
58 El cultivo del algodón y la soya en el Paraguay y sus derivaciones sociales, 1986, 141 pp.
59 Expansión del cultivo de la caña de azúcar y de la ganadería en el nordeste del Brasil: un examen del papel de la política pública y de sus derivaciones económicas y sociales, 1986, 164 pp.
60 Las empresas transnacionales en el desarrollo colombiano, 1986, 212 pp.
61 Las empresas transnacionales en la economía del Paraguay, 1987, 115 pp.
62 Problemas de la industria latinoamericana en la fase crítica, 1986, 113 pp.
63 Relaciones económicas internacionales y cooperación regional de América Latina y el Caribe, 1987, 272 pp.
63 International economic relations and regional co-operation in Latin America and the Caribbean, 1987, 267 pp.
64 Tres ensayos sobre inflación y políticas de estabilización, 1986, 201 pp.
65 La industria farmacéutica y farmoquímica: desarrollo histórico y posibilidades futuras. Argentina, Brasil y México, 1987, 177 pp.
66 Dos estudios sobre América Latina y el Caribe y la economía internacional, 1987, 125 pp.
67 Reestructuración de la industria automotriz mundial y perspectivas para América Latina, 1987, 232 pp.
68 Cooperación latinoamericana en servicios: antecedentes y perspectivas, 1988, 155 pp.
69 Desarrollo y transformación: estrategia para superar la pobreza, 1988, 114 pp.
69 Development and change: strategies for vanquishing poverty, 1988, 114 pp.
70 La evolución económica del Japón y su impacto en América Latina, 1988, 88 pp.
70 The economic evolution of Japan and its impact on Latin America, 1990, 79 pp.
71 La gestión de los recursos hídricos en América Latina y el Caribe, 1989, 256 pp.
72 La evolución del problema de la deuda externa en América Latina y el Caribe, 1988, 77 pp.
72 The evolution of the external debt problem in Latin America and the Caribbean, 1988, 69 pp.
73 Agricultura, comercio exterior y cooperación internacional, 1988, 83 pp.
73 Agriculture, external trade and international co-operation, 1989, 79 pp.
74 Reestructuración industrial y cambio tecnológico: consecuencias para América Latina, 1989, 105 pp.
75 El medio ambiente como factor de desarrollo, 1989, 2nd. ed. 1991, 123 pp.
76 El comportamiento de los bancos transnacionales y la crisis internacional de endeudamiento, 1989, 214 pp.
76 Transnational bank behaviour and the international debt crisis, 1989, 198 pp.
77 Los recursos hídricos de América Latina y del Caribe: planificación, desastres naturales y contaminación, 1990, 266 pp.
77 The water resources of Latin America and the Caribbean - Planning hazards and pollution, 1990, 252 pp.
78 La apertura financiera en Chile y el comportamiento de los bancos transnacionales, 1990, 132 pp.
79 La industria de bienes de capital en América Latina y el Caribe: su desarrollo en un marco de cooperación regional, 1991, 235 pp.
80 Impacto ambiental de la contaminación hídrica producida por la Refinería Estatal Esmeraldas: análisis técnico-económico, 1991, 189 pp.

81 *Magnitud de la pobreza en América Latina en los años ochenta*, 1991, 177 pp.
82 *América Latina y el Caribe: el manejo de la escasez de agua*, 1991, 148 pp.
83 *Reestructuración y desarrollo de la industria automotriz mexicana en los años ochenta: evolución y perspectivas*, 1992, 191 pp.
84 *La transformación de la producción en Chile: cuatro ensayos de interpretación*, 1993, 372 pp.
85 *Inversión extranjera y empresas transnacionales en la economía de Chile (1974-1989). Proyectos de inversión y estrategias de las empresas transnacionales*, 1992, 257 pp.
86 *Inversión extranjera y empresas transnacionales en la economía de Chile (1974-1989). El papel del capital extranjero y la estrategia nacional de desarrollo*, 1992, 163 pp.
87 *Análisis de cadenas agroindustriales en Ecuador y Perú*, 1993, 294 pp.
88 *El comercio de manufacturas de América Latina. Evolución y estructura 1962-1989*, 1993, 150, pp.
89 *El impacto económico y social de las migraciones en Centroamérica*, 1993, 78 pp.
90 *El papel de las empresas transnacionales en la reestructuración industrial de Colombia: una síntesis*, 1993, 131 pp.
91 *Las empresas transnacionales de una economía en transición: La experiencia argentina en los años ochenta*, 1995, 193 pp.
92 *Reestructuración y desarrollo productivo: desafío y potencial para los años noventa*, 1994, 108 pp.
93 *Comercio internacional y medio ambiente. La discusión actual*, 1995, 112 pp.
94 *Innovación en tecnologías y sistemas de gestión ambientales en empresas líderes latinoamericanas*, 1995, 206 pp.
95 *México: la industria maquiladora*, 1996, 237 pp.

Serie INFOPLAN: Temas Especiales del Desarrollo

1 *Resúmenes de documentos sobre deuda externa*, 1986, 324 pp.
2 *Resúmenes de documentos sobre cooperación entre países en desarrollo*, 1986, 189 pp.
3 *Resúmenes de documentos sobre recursos hídricos*, 1987, 290 pp.
4 *Resúmenes de documentos sobre planificación y medio ambiente*, 1987, 111 pp.
5 *Resúmenes de documentos sobre integración económica en América Latina y el Caribe*, 1987, 273 pp.
6 *Resúmenes de documentos sobre cooperación entre países en desarrollo, II parte*, 1988, 146 pp.
7 *Documentos sobre privatización con énfasis en América Latina*, 1991, 82 pp.
8 *Reseñas de documentos sobre desarrollo ambientalmente sustentable*, 1992, 217 pp.
9 *MERCOSUR: resúmenes de documentos*, 1993, 119 pp.
10 *Políticas sociales: resúmenes de documentos*, 1995, 95 pp.
11 *Modernización del Estado: resúmenes de documentos*, 1995, 73 pp.
12 *Gestión de la información: reseñas de documentos*, 1996, 152 pp.
13 *Políticas sociales: resúmenes de documentos II*, 1997, 80 pp.

كيفية الحصول على منشورات الأمم المتحدة
يمكن الحصول على منشورات الأمم المتحدة من المكتبات ودور التوزيع في جميع أنحاء العالم . استعلم عنها من المكتبة التي تتعامل معها
أو اكتب إلى : الأمم المتحدة ،قسم البيع في نيويورك او في جنيف .

如何购取联合国出版物

联合国出版物在全世界各地的书店和经售处均有发售。请向书店询问或写信到纽约或日内瓦的联合国销售组。

HOW TO OBTAIN UNITED NATIONS PUBLICATIONS

United Nations publications may be obtained from bookstores and distributors throughout the world. Consult your bookstore or write to: United Nations, Sales Section, New York or Geneva.

COMMENT SE PROCURER LES PUBLICATIONS DES NATIONS UNIES

Les publications des Nations Unies sont en vente dans les librairies et les agences dépositaires du monde entier. Informez-vous auprès de votre libraire ou adressez-vous à: Nations Unies, Section des ventes, New York ou Genève.

КАК ПОЛУЧИТЬ ИЗДАНИЯ ОРГАНИЗАЦИИ ОБЪЕДИНЕННЫХ НАЦИЙ

Издания Организации Объединенных Наций можно купить в книжных магазинах и агентствах во всех районах мира. Наводите справки об изданиях в вашем книжном магазине или пишите по адресу: Организация Объединенных Наций. Секция по продаже изданий. Нью-Йорк или Женева.

COMO CONSEGUIR PUBLICACIONES DE LAS NACIONES UNIDAS

Las publicaciones de las Naciones Unidas están a la venta en librerías y casas distribuidoras en todas partes del mundo. Consulte a su librero o diríjase a: Naciones Unidas, Sección de Ventas, Nueva York o Ginebra.

Las publicaciones de la Comisión Económica para América Latina y el Caribe (CEPAL) y las del Instituto Latinoamericano y del Caribe de Planificación Económica y Social (ILPES) se pueden adquirir a los distribuidores locales o directamente a través de:

Publicaciones de las Naciones Unidas
Sección de Ventas – DC-2-0853
Fax (212)963-3489
E-mail: publications@un.org
Nueva York, NY, 10017
Estados Unidos de América

Publicaciones de las Naciones Unidas
Sección de Ventas, Fax (22)917-0027
Palais des Nations
1211 Ginebra 10, Suiza

Unidad de Distribución
CEPAL – Casilla 179-D
Fax (562)208-1946
E-mail: publications@eclac.cl
Santiago de Chile

Publications of the Economic Commission for Latin America and the Caribbean (ECLAC) and those of the Latin American and the Caribbean Institute for Economic and Social Planning (ILPES) can be ordered from your local distributor or directly through:

United Nations Publications
Sales Sections, DC-2-0853
Fax (212)963-3489
E-mail: publications@un.org
New York, NY, 10017
USA

United Nations Publications
Sales Sections, Fax (22)917-0027
Palais des Nations
1211 Geneve 10, Switzerland

Distribution Unit
CEPAL – Casilla 179-D
Fax (562)208-1946
E-mail: publications@eclac.cl
Santiago, Chile